THE COYOTÉ OAK:

BURGEONING WISDOM

BY

CARLISLE BERGQUIST

Reality Press
An imprint of Reality Entertainment, Inc.

For information contact:

REALITY ENTERTAINMENT
P.O. Box 91
Foresthill, CA 95631

ph: 530-367-5389, fx: 530-367-3024

www.reality-entertainment.com

ISBN: 0-9791750-6-2

VANTAGE QUEST:

Stimulating Personal Growth, Transformation, and Higher Creativity.

901 W. South Street
Salina, KS 67401
(785) 827-1835
www.vantagequest.org

Book cover artwork created by:

Carlisle Bergquist
Vantage Quest Design

Author's portrait taken by:

Duane Billings

Dedicated to the memory of:
James Armstrong & Andrew Levine
Who were created to dream,
and with whom,
I lived the dream of creating.

Acknowledgements

"You're a songwriter," James said, entering my small cabin in the California mountains, "and I want to have a recording studio. We should get together and record sometime." That began a friendship that would last a lifetime. A few years later, when his dream joined with others, he invited me to be a part of a uniquely creative outpost, The Silvery Moon Studios in LA. Like its namesake, the studio waxed and waned but what we experienced there changed our lives forever. In the years after closing the studio, I went to graduate school and became a transpersonal psychotherapist. James began writing screenplays with Andrew. Then one day I got a call informing me that James had died. At his funeral, I asked Andrew to show me some of the work that meant so much to James. One five-page story idea captured my imagination and, along with Andrew, we planned to finish the screenplay in honor of James. Then another phone call; Andrew was dead and so was the screenplay. I tucked the orphaned story away for several years until I noticed that it blended with another tale I had written and this story was born.

I cannot give enough credit to my wife Geralyn for her contribution of ideas, encouragement and patience. She let her head float the creative ethers with me, and dedicatedly weeded my wordiness while uplifting my imagination. Diane Luboff, also made critical suggestions and extra effort that helped me clarify the story.

Then there is the river of souls in which I often recognize others who, like me, have served a common purpose for who knows how long, brothers and sisters in the oldest of families. My very deep gratitude goes to John Jay Harper, one such being in the river, with whom I am pleased to create.

Special thanks to Stanley Krippner for teaching me more about the phenomena beyond the horizon of rational explanation and for helping me learn to write about it.

Others who assisted with proofreading, suggestions, and cheerleading are Paul Krumm, Judy Edmunds, Bev Cole, Chris Booth, Rose Booth, Paul Bondy, Doris Beddinger, Nolene Davis, Karen Hauser, and Carrie Tatro.

Finally, I would like to acknowledge my cousin Bob Anderson in whose barn great childhood adventures seeded my imagination.

As I share the adventure written on the coming pages with you, I want to acknowledge the contributions made to my experience and imagination by James Armstrong, Andrew Levine, and all those mentioned above. In my gratitude, I have named the main character in James' honor. Thank you always my brothers and sisters.

CONTENTS

To flourish in the light,
put your roots down deep
and grow away from them.
Lay down your dogma
and pickup your faith.

CHAPTER 1
THE LEGEND OF COYOTÉ OAK

A blue-silver ribbon drapes across the prairie horizon marking the boundary between yesterday and tomorrow. The thin luminous band reminds that we gather spiritual insight oftentimes, only in present darkness. All around me, the dome of night masks the colors of life but from the distant ceiling, stars singe the blackness and the wisdom of their ancient rays merges into the promise of morning. By their light, the stars testify that well-aged truth crosses time's boundary bridging the knowledge of deeds remembered with the challenges to come. I watch as the ribbon widens and the once clear edge of daybreak, no longer poignant, diffuses upon a waking world.

The tall woods stand high on an eastern slope where the growing dawn silhouettes the trees' knurled branches and their swollen buds are waking from winter slumber. With primeval presence they stand, as they have for tens of thousands of mornings awaiting the warm wash of sunlight. I wait with them. Etched in silent revere, their branches stretch the four directions against the sky and Owl perches far out upon a north-reaching bough.

Darkness is fading quickly as Owl posts watch over the remnants of his nocturnal kingdom. The night eagle's swift flight is over for a time and he must surrender the sky to creatures of daylight. Drawing a great breath and with all his being, Owl leaned forward, giving a great hoot toward the coming sun. Repeatedly, Owl thrust his body forward, propelling his salute skyward and ruffling his breast feathers with each declaration as if to punctuate its importance. Then with nonchalance befitting his wisdom, his large golden eyes directed at me, he proclaimed, "You have come on a special morning. Watch this day, learn, and remember." Without another word, Owl raised one last commanding cry then swooped from his roost and glided into a nearby hollow.

I thought myself only an observer of this scene, peering for a moment into the depths of a vivid imagination but the piercing glance of Owl made it clear that I am also the observed. I am a full participant. Encircling me, the daily shift change of nature's workers scurried to and from burrow and nest to the accompaniment of the twilight songbirds that announce this transition twice daily. Never have I witnessed earth's circadian exchange so vividly where unconcerned by my presence, animals of all kinds passed, adapting their routine from night into day. Owl's greeting had jerked me from silent contemplation and pushed me into the thick of life.

Sparkling in the first rays of light, Spider finished the last stitches of her night's weaving and settled for a moment's rest at the center of her remodeled web. She knew soaring insects would soon take flight in the warm sunlight and bring nourishment for her night's labor. Coming up the trail just beyond Spider's web, Coyoté, her head down, approached with a weary gate. "You look sad," I thought to myself, upon which Coyoté raised her muzzle and said, "It was a hard night. Rabbit was very clever, slipping into that bramble thicket. My pups will be hungry today." I was astonished she had heard my thoughts but Coyoté picked up the cue and immediately continued my education.

"Do you know where you are?" Coyoté asked, causing me to realize that I didn't. I last remembered being atop the hill above my vineyard waiting for the sunrise and had no recollection of how I got to this curious place. Coyoté gave a cunning smile and said, "You are in the 'Tall Wood,' before time. Things here are probably very different from the world you know. All beings are more connected here and haven't suffered the separation. That is why you knew Spider's thoughts and I understood your kindness to me. Everything here communicates with everything else and we are all grateful for the gift of each other. The same way the Tall Wood appreciates the rocks and rain that bring it nourishment, I thank Rabbit whose sacrifice feeds my family." I interjected, "But you were so discouraged because you didn't catch Rabbit last night." Coyoté answered, "If I caught Rabbit every night there would be no Rabbit at all. This forest would overgrow with trees and I would have no food. It's all a balance. Rabbit's victory is ultimately my own for it keeps our dance going."

"How did I get here?" I asked, intrigued by Coyoté's willingness to teach me. "You are not the first to visit," Coyoté remarked, "but visitors are few and find their way here for good reason. You slipped across the border between the past and future, the ribbon of light preceding the sunrise. You could have gone many places but Spirit brought you here. 'Watch this day, learn, and remember,' as Owl advised for he speaks truth and you should pay attention to his counsel. He does get a bit pompous though with all that ruffling and hooting but I suppose he thinks me a bit mad howling happily at the Moon. I guess we appreciate each other's antics. Well, I am tired and need to get back to my den so if you have no further questions, I'll be on my way." Overwhelmed that I had had this conversation at all, I could think of nothing further to ask and wished her, and her pups, a good rest. As Coyoté lopped off, she turned to say, "Oh, while you are here, time will be different, a few hours or many seasons may pass. Don't be concerned; merely follow Owl's advice. Good Day to you, my friend," and with that, she dashed around a bend in the trail.

The encounters with Owl and Coyoté all happened so naturally. It wasn't the least bit strange to communicate and I suspected they knew much more than they revealed. Now I was starting to question if I had gone quite crazy or if I would ever return to "normal," whatever that had been. I couldn't remember that, either. I found a rock outcropping over the hollow and thought it a good idea to rest while I coped with this new world. With joking courtesy, I asked Rock if it would be OK for me to rest on it. Of course, it answered me with a welcoming, "Yes." At least my delusion is consistent, I thought, to which Rock replied, "It's no delusion. You are really welcome to rest here." I gave up and sat down thinking it better not to argue with something as hardheaded as a boulder.

The sun was only a thin crescent on the horizon. It felt as though my exploits had taken hours, not the few minutes the crescent confirmed. Vivid colors gilded the sky, gold and orange overlaid splashes of magenta all in contrast to the azure blue of space. It was as beautiful a sunrise as I have ever seen. Rock whispered up at me, "The view is resplendent from here, isn't it?" I agreed, impressed by Rock's sentient acuity. The sunlight streamed down on the trees below making the buds swell up and open to reveal the fresh green leaves of spring. Each leaf was perfect, unblemished by wind and weather. Each tree embodied both the stalwart wisdom of antiquity and the lithe exuberance of youth. My eyes wandered down to the rich soil beside me where the earth slowly pressed upward. In a few moments a small green shoot pushed its way through like a tiny bulldozer, stood itself upright and unfurled two primary leaves that promptly turned sunward. Beside the seedling lay the two weathered halves of the acorn shell. I bent forward and said, "Welcome to the world Little Oak. May your roots be deep, your heart grow strong, and your limbs carry the blessing of life." I was pleased to be part of this birth and act as if I was a veteran in my newfound world. The Little Oak excitedly asked, "Is it always this beautiful?" Rock, sensing that I didn't know, quickly responded, "Yes. The earth is good but life comes with struggles. Let the beauty fill your heart, young one, and you'll be fine." With that, the seedling stretched with joy toward the dappled sky.

With the sun fully up and its warm light flowing down the hillside, I decided to explore the trail where Coyoté had departed earlier. Perhaps I would see her but in daylight, the night creatures safely nested out of sight. A short way around the bend, the trail descended into the hollow and I could see a stream flowing. Carefully, I moved downward over the sandstone ruff when I noticed the outcropping above where I had watched the sunrise. To my amazement, the Tall Wood had already grown dense with foliage, and the seedling was now a young sapling standing a few feet tall. Just as Coyoté foretold, time was different here.

I accepted the shift in time for after all, in this world all the rules are extraordinary. I looked back up at Little Oak who seemed another few inches taller as Squirrel rippled along the slope and scrambled up beside him. At least Squirrels still move the same in this world with their hurry-scurry impertinence, I mused. Squirrel sat up on his hind legs furiously expounding. "No! No! No!" He chattered. "I buried your acorn here myself last fall as part of my winter supply. I chose this spot because it was high and would remain dry. You were never supposed to grow here, NEVER! NEVER!" he repeated stamping his foot. "Furthermore," he prattled, "There is not enough moisture for you on a hill. You had just better move along. This is my winter storage cellar."

Little Oak looked wilted with his small limbs hanging low. Squirrel's scolding had clearly hurt his feelings and the incessant rebuke continued until I felt compelled to hurl something at his tormentor. The little verbose piece of fur had to know his place. I took aim on the contentious rodent but then, Little Oak stood erect and with great determination pronounced, "Enough. I'll move." That is impossible, I reasoned, until wriggling root after root out of the ground, I saw Little Oak, fully twice his height atop them, ambling downhill towards me. Moving with centipede-like precision, the roots flagellated in synchronous waves as the little tree approached. "How did you do that? Don't you have to grow where you're planted?" I asked and was stunned when Little Oak replied, "I don't think so. Can't you move on your legs and toes?" I shook my head thinking, "Maybe if you don't know what you can't do, you can do anything." Little Oak just gave me a perplexed look and continued his synchronized saunter until he found a perfect spot beside the stream.

The young sapling, reversing the earlier process, wriggled his roots back into the soil near a grove of large oak trees. The only thing still amazing was that each event I saw seemed more amazing then the last. Certainly, there had been much to watch this day and I couldn't help but remember such phenomenal encounters. Nevertheless, what was I to learn? That remained unclear and nothing I had seen applied to the world I lived in. It was beyond description and only further questioned my sanity.

I walked down the trail occasionally engaging an insect, field mouse, plant, or bird in conversation and stopping to smell the roses, they informed me, as they smelled me back, that my after-shave wasn't so pleasing. This was a world without guile or pretense and all things being equal, ALL things seemed particularly equal here. Some time must have passed when I became aware that the sun was very warm and headed for the grove of oaks at the bottom of the hollow for a little shade.

The cool shadows were a welcome change as I entered the woods. Filtered beams of light streamed through a delicate brume, giving a feeling of high magic. The densely grouped oaks grew in deep soil, giving them massive erect trunks. Column after column they evoked reverence. Their towering carriage humbled me yet, I felt a penetrating peace as I advanced into their community. High above, their canopy guarded the space and its verdant light illumined the arched branches like trusses of a great cathedral. There, resting quietly, slept Owl. In the hush of this sacred place, I walked in silence.

With solemn strides, I moved into the center of the grove, where concentric circles of stones surrounded a fire pit with seven stones each bearing a petroglyph on the innermost row. I didn't recognize the marks yet they seemed hauntingly familiar. Some reminded me of Aramaic letters while others resembled cave paintings and every carving evoked a primal response. In this undisturbed surrounding, my footsteps alone entered uninvited on holy ground and I quietly made my exit. As I left, the intensely spiritual ambiance wafted though my being as if the meaning of one of these cryptic symbols had engraved itself upon my heart.

The stream flowed down from the grove and drawn to follow its course, I found the Oak trees interspersed with marshes and grassy banks. The water widened into a small pond and I saw Little Oak standing just across from me. A natural dam stretched across the waterway where Beaver and her young were swimming with a good-sized branch in tow. I watched while she carefully wove the branch into her lodge as if she were following an architect's blueprint; completing her work with exact precision, she promptly dived back into the water and headed for the opposite bank. With pointed determination, she swam directly to the bank beneath Little Oak, crawled up and began gnawing away at his four inch trunk. In minutes, Little Oak tumbled over succumbing to her sharp teeth and builder's determination. Dragging him to the shoreline, she towed and inserted him in her lodge wall. Responding to my alarm, her thoughts rang urgent in my mind. "Winter is coming. Winter is coming; the lodge must be finished before it becomes too cold."

Mirroring my mood, the skies begin to cloud over. A thick gray overcast brought a chill to the air, the wind shifted to the north and the day changed as quickly as my feelings had. Looking across the pond at the stump remaining where Little Oak stood, I saw a new shoot had already grown a few inches tall. It started snowing heavily by the time I excitedly returned to the tree and above the white blanketed landscape Little Oak's heart-wood gleamed a bright golden orange. Unlike the venerating silence near the hearth, the trees on the outskirts of the grove murmured and stirred amongst themselves. The ruckus seemed focused and charged with emotion. Finally, a nearby tree bent towards the exposed stump and dogmatically announced, "You are not one of us. You have to go!" "But I am an oak." Little Oak protested. "I grew from an acorn, just like you! Squirrel planted me on top of that ridge." Another tree replied mockingly, "Look at your heartwood. That is not the color of our wood. You are not an oak like us. Go!" With that pious censure, all the trees turned away shunning him and the distress showed in his sagging stance. He squirmed from the soil beneath him, exposing large radiant golden yellow roots, and ambulated towards a barren knoll.

Attracted by the bright orange wood, Rabbit bounded from the underbrush and nibbled the tender shoot right down to the ground. Surely, this disheartened little sprout will not survive this time and I sadly knelt down over the masticated stub of remains, my tears dripping onto the colorful heartwood beneath me. As if replying to my anguish, a shoot burst upward from the besieged trunk which, quite different from the last, was stronger and covered with rigid thorns. Little Oak then quietly told me he must now rest for the winter. Would I be in this world when spring returned? I questioned, rising to walk away when a humanoid form startled me from behind. The being appeared to be a primitive human though his arms and legs attached strangely in that his legs came more from the front of his torso while his arms fastened slightly towards his back. He wore pelts of various animals and a helmet-like feather sheath with two long curved antelope antlers protruding from his head. Curiously, there were no footsteps in the snow other than my own.

"You need not be concerned; the young tree's transformation is complete," the frightening man-beast extolled. "He is not prisoner to his form. From his first glimpse of the sunrise, he learned to change drawing dawn's beauty into his heart. Its colors live in his heartwood and golden roots; even when rejected, that beauty did not fade. He sacrificed himself to sustain others and with each gesture, he grew stronger learning to alter his form for protection while avoiding harm to others. He is the first of a long lineage that will spread across the plains and serve for lifetimes. They will call him by many names, but I call him *The Coyoté Oak*, for his wisdom burgeons and he shape shifts like Coyoté and me. Now, you must seek warm shelter." As if to emphasize his message he jumped into the air, became Raven and with a penetrating squawk, flew away before my eyes.

My body shivered as the cold wind cut through me jogging towards the grove. My questions raced as quickly as my feet. Had I met a Shaman, a Medicine Man, if so, where was his tribe? Whom did he serve here? In the cloistered hollow of the grove, the temperature was comfortable; the winds quieted and my pace slowed reverently to a walk in the sacred emanation of the place. A fire glowed from the pit within the stone circles and, as I gratefully moved to its warmth, one intriguingly large feather awaited right outside the fire's reach. I imagined the feathered Shaman might reveal himself but in sacrosanct seclusion, I was alone.

Larger than an Eagle's or Hawk's it was a tightly knit wing feather made to endure the winds of flight. Most striking, it displayed an array of colors with unusual iridescence in shades I have never seen. Absorbed, as I lifted the precious plume, I abruptly hurtled upward with dreadful speed and in an instant was well out in space falling quickly back towards the earth. Terror struck; my heart pounded wildly like a drummer in a seventh grade garage band and understanding a completely new meaning for shooting star, I saw my burnout looming. Almost instinctively, I stretched out my arms trying to control my trajectory and remarkably, I was flying. Glid-ing a pathway along the edge of sunlight and shadow, I cruised downward towards the Earth, the rising slopes of the Andes before me. Approaching above the equatorial Amazon, I followed the great river inland.

The flight brought me from the early daylight back into the pre-dawn shadows as I sailed above a hunting party of Orinoco Indians along the river's edge who pointed skyward at my passing. Looking back, I saw a multihued wake tracing my flight across the sky. I had traversed the span of space with no comprehension of flight, my path somehow guided to land in the dark rain forest where a trail beckoned me to a destination glimmering in the trees.

Forward I progressed towards the light, until I was amidst a crowd filling concentric stone circles around a fire pit. The group included every race, deeply carved lines of hoary sagacity etched the faces of these men, and women gathered in their diverse dress. Common to all was a single unknown purpose and such a wise counsel I approached modestly, questioning my place. Flamboyantly garbed in a feathered cape and headdress, a Shaman stood at the center motioning me to come forward. Standing in the shadows, beyond clear vision, was another being that appeared as if it was a bird arrayed in a human form. Cautiously, I approached as summoned hearing the Shaman announce to the group, "This is James." When all eyes fell upon me, I was instantly atop my familiar hillside above the farm.

A blue-silver ribbon of light draped across the horizon marking the boundary between yesterday and tomorrow. The sun still hung like a sliver on the border of earth and sky so this must have been a delusion transpiring in an instant. Yet alone in the tall grass, my hand still clutched the feather. My feet sodden by the wet spring kiss of morning dew around me I saw only the small grove of hedge trees beside my vineyard, the Amazon rain forest and the Tall Wood were gone from view. I will remember this day; the feather trophy from a far off vision insures that, but it doesn't belong in this world nor can I explain how I ventured into its domain. How can I recount such magical events and mysterious transport from that realm to this? How could I clarify it to Andrea, let alone to myself?

CHAPTER 2
BETWEEN THE DREAMTIME

Memories of yesterday and dreams of tomorrow shape the course we plod here and now, between the dreamtime. Crossing through a gateway from one world into another seemed more dreamlike and never a course I had imagined. The world of Owl, Coyoté, and Little Oak still felt palpable, as if it were around me, but temporarily hidden from view. I expected the animals and rocks to greet me but where there had been dialogue and repartee, there were nature's usual sounds. The journey back to normal life seemed difficult; I needed an explanation but didn't have one. Walking back to the house, replaying the images and events I decided, it must have been a dream, but I held this odd feather like a trophy that proved otherwise. If I weren't crazy, I was in for more questions than answers, an alien abduction would be easier to believe. Still there was the feather evincing the veracity of something, but what?

The buds were breaking in the vineyard and the fresh green leaves glistened in the early morning light. I needed to feel my feet firmly on the ground, so I sauntered slowly back to the house, taking the long way with a new appreciation for ordinary existence. I love morning in the vines and the walk brought my thoughts to home and family. "OK, I guess I'm ready," I said to myself. I turned through the orchard toward the house taking time to inhale the sweet perfume of the apple blossoms. This time the trees returned no comments; I was both relieved and disappointed.

I climbed three steps to the back porch, walked through the door and was surprised to see Andrea awake and standing naked in the middle of the kitchen with her back to me lecturing our cat Lorenzo. Trash covered the floor, successfully distributed around the room from the overturned waste-basket. Well scattered amid the trash were the contents of a cereal box and countless shards of glass, the remnants of a stack of dishes that normally sat on the upper shelf where Lorenzo now rested with devilish pride. Andrea could not move from her spot in her bare feet. All she could do was vociferously vent her anger at the tabby gray feline. Lorenzo, who had clearly won this battle and taken her hostage, wagged his tail with little concern.

"You're expendable! You're nothing but a coddled drifter!" Andrea threatened.

This would be a great time to hear what Lorenzo had to say for himself, I thought. Across the porch and through one doorway, I had completed the transition from the magical to the mundane where Andrea stood like a maiden in distress, beautifully vulnerable, waiting for her deliverer.

"Greetings Madam, may I be of service," I said, as I bowed and swooped in glibly to lighten her predicament.

"Remove that beast, Good Sir! Save me from this desolation and I am forever in your debt," Andrea replied playfully relieved that her ordeal was about to end.

Crossing the room was noisy business. I crunched, crackled and popped with each step, finally reaching Lorenzo who was now willing to surrender his preeminent post. I plucked him from the shelf, crunched to the door, and deposited him on the back porch.

"I can accept your gratitude now, Fair Maiden." I posited, returning to Andrea and with one easy motion, I scooped her up, carried her down the hall into the bedroom, and placed her gently down on the bed; my mind and body had already embarked on another flight of fantasy.

"I'm already late thanks to Lorenzo's rubbishing," she continued, dropping her playful character. Her feet back on the ground, Andrea headed for the shower giving me an enticing backward glance just as the phone rang. Assured that she would return my affections later, I went to the kitchen to answer it.

"Hey Chief," the voice said which I recognized as my friend and employee Mace. "There's a farm auction Friday out at the old Flycht place on Wyman Road," he continued. "There's supposed to be a couple of small tractors for sale that are 'butter sweet.' Think we can schedule it?"

"Maybe, but I'm not sure about buying a tractor this week, we'll see on Friday," I said, knowing he thought me a well-intentioned, slightly obsessive, planner. Mason always knew the auction score and if he said they were worth a look, he was probably right.

Hanging up the phone, I turned to see the phenomenal plume standing upright in a vase on the table. The source of that feather preoccupied my mind, not tractor shopping. Bidding against plowshare pragmatists at a farm auction might bring me back to a normal routine but kitchen restoration required immediate attention, stopping occasionally to reassure myself the feather was actually there, I began the cleanup.

"You couldn't have orchestrated it better," Andrea announced as she came into the room. "The wastebasket falling over woke me up, but when I tried to get Lorenzo away, he scrambled across the floor and up onto the counter hitting the cereal box. He finally made a desperate leap to the shelf, knocking everything to the floor. I watched the stack of dishes tip and slide off one by one like a deck of cards. Shattered glass surrounded me in seconds and I couldn't do a damn..."

Andrea stopped cold. Her eyes widened as she stared towards the table with the sizeable feather jutting upward from the vase.

"It's a feather," I replied before she could ask, continuing to collect the slivers of glass from the floor and not quite ready to explain it.

"It's not like any feather I've ever seen. Where did...?" she inquired hesitantly.

"It's a long story. I'll tell you later." I said stopping the reclamation knowing I had no ready answer.

"Well, I want to hear ALL about it this evening," she replied, staring at the feather and then at me with bewilderment. "I had... well... a really weird dream last night. Maybe we can talk about that, too." She concluded with a kiss good-bye, and then able to cross the shard free floor, she zipped out the door. I picked up the feather feeling its hefty spine, watched its colors stream in the incandescent light and placed it on the desk in my office.

My wife Andrea had a holistic fitness center in town called "Perfect Form." The name came from her days as an athlete; her coaches said she had perfect form when she ran. The name not only described the mission of the gym, it still described her. Inside and out, Andrea had remarkable strength, forged in the hard work and steely determination she learned on the track. She taught several classes each day, along with other instructors and worked fervently to make the unorthodox business a small town success. "Perfect Form" was a personal victory in her life that had taken years to achieve though her private struggle had gone on even longer.

Andrea's path to wellness was a resurrection. The passion to run captured her before she held her first Teddy Bear's tea party and as she grew, she spent hours training and striving to improve. Her exacting skill drew more attention than she expected but gaining confidence, she achieved speed, execution and grace. She had perfect form in hurdles and high jump, always pushing beyond the ideal towards her ardent ambition, to be an Olympian. In her first year in college, she was the first alternate on the Olympic team and in the following four years, she won national and international competitions entering the trials as a contender for Olympic gold. She almost tasted the fruit of her labors when tragedy struck.

Running a back road she'd trained on hundreds of times, a car lost control rounding a curve and hit her head-on. It was no small accident. Though she tried to leap to safety, she ricocheted from the windshield into a guardrail breaking her collarbone, left tibia, and seriously injured her spleen, liver and kidneys. In a fraction of a second, the goal she felt born to achieve became a shelf of tarnished mementos banished to the memories

of those who almost ran. After a long hospitalization with physical rehabilitation and years of recovery ahead, Andrea shuddered that her Olympic
glory could never come true.

Over the next couple of years, Andrea slipped into a deep depression.
While her bones mended, her spirit did not. With purpose torn from her
soul, doctors could not restore her will and her liver functions continued to
fail. Sheer desperation finally led her to a hospital in Beijing specializing
in Qigong where the Chinese approach refreshed her spirit and brought
health to her organs. She learned Tai Chi to complement her healing then,
her body revitalized, she studied meditation and yoga with exiled Tibetan
monks in India. Through exposure to these ancient arts, she found a new
perspective, a purpose in her prefect form, and her pilgrimage was complete. The injury that devastated her dreams, in the end, was the gateway
to her new awareness.

Andrea always caught my attention and my attraction to her was immediate; I first saw her sprinting like a gazelle through *DeGall International
Airport* in Paris. As graceful off the track as on, when this beautiful blond
woman sat next to me on the flight, I felt like a lucky man whose life was
about to change. For the first several minutes, I tried nervously to think
of anything to start a conversation beyond the usual courtesies needed
to endure a long flight together. Finally, she blurted, "Well, someone
as thoughtful as you ought to be good boyfriend material." Andrea was
unedited but still turned beet red realizing how forward that sounded. She
didn't realize how attractive she was, or how she affected me, but with
the levity, I relaxed. In the remaining hours of that connecting flight, we
soared in conversation. If parallel lines never meet, how fortunate it was
that parallel hearts often do.

A few minutes and several crunching steps later, I had cleaned up the mess
from Lorenzo's fiasco. I went back into my office determined to recollect and record my morning vision. I typed *The Legend of Coyoté Oak*
at the top of the page. Should that be the title? Yes. The words flowed
onto the page easily with a passion for detail, feeling as natural as the
events when I had experienced them. It felt like visiting old friends as I
wrote about Coyoté, Owl and Little Oak. Describing the Shaman though,

felt disjointed, even a bit preposterous saying that he turned into a Raven and vanished. Dream or delusion, rational or absurd, I held nothing back anxious that eventually it would make sense. No matter how well I told the tale, the feather beside me begged for a sensible explanation so I also turned my attention to researching its origin.

Hoping to identify the feather's source, I logged on the Internet exploring the ornithology departments at major universities but produced no results. Several zoos have large Aviaries, I thought; maybe one of their birds has this kind of feathering. I looked at hundreds of pictures examining various species. Some had similar coloring but not the right shape. Others had the correct shape, but the wrong color. Most of all, nothing came close to the right size. I checked from ostrich to osprey, eagle to egret, heron to hawk; nothing met all the criteria.

Finally, I searched for a classification key for the biological "Class" *Aves*. Following through the key's decision tree, the feather seemed to have come from a member of the "Order" *Falconiformes*, in either the "Family" group *Accipitridae*, the hawks and eagles, or *Falconidae*, the falcons but the feather was much bigger than those of the California Condor (Family *Cathartidae*). I even compared the ratio of the Condor's size to the size of their feathers. By that formula, the creature that bore this feather must weigh hundreds of pounds and stand more than seven feet tall with a wingspan exceeding twenty feet. A bird like that on the wing couldn't hide; why couldn't I find anything?

If no information existed about a living species, perhaps it's thought extinct. Maybe I have found the feathered version of Sasquatch or the Loch Ness monster. I turned to paleornithology journal studies hoping some record existed and found two fossils. Said to be about 10,000 years old, they showed a bird's footprint and a feather the shape and size of the one on the desk. The journal listed the specimen as unidentified but someone else's evidence of this bird partially validated my find, yet one huge question remained, "This feather is from a live bird, so where have they been for 10,000 years?"

I leaned back in my chair staring at the quill in question atop the desk.

Like the feather, the old roll-top was a relic out of its time. The nooks and crannies once useful, and its roll-top that granted privacy, now prevented the desk from moving into the digital age. Computers relegated it to a thing of collected beauty. The feather likewise failed to fit the surroundings. A bird this big could hardly survive in a world of airplanes, automobiles, and shrinking habitats. I heard Andrea's car turn in the drive by the time I had run out of ideas and was surprised that the day had gone by so quickly; I anxiously went out to the yard to meet her.

Andrea parked, slumped out of the car and walked hesitantly towards me looking exhausted, which was unusual. Generally, her work invigorated her and she was the healthiest person I knew. We retreated to our cloister on the porch, and I asked what was wrong as Lorenzo emerged from the steps waggling with privileged pomp to join us.

"The dream last night was so vivid, like it was almost real; it kept creeping into my thoughts," Andrea explained. "I couldn't get the dark images out of my head. Then the phone rang all day long; real-estate agents, lawyers, and bankers all trying to buy my property. Saying NO didn't matter to them; they kept offering more money and made some not so subtle threats."

"If they threatened you, shouldn't you talk to the police?" I asked.
"No, not yet, it's just a feeling; there's nothing concrete to tell them," she replied.

When it came to problem solving, Andrea was determined and very capable. She liked being the answer-person every bit as much as I did and I knew from experience that she wanted to solve this alone. Still, I felt her frustration and could help by letting her vent.

"You've mentioned the dream twice. What was it that bothered you?" I asked, noting the dark coincidence of the dream and the calls.

"I just want it off my mind," Andrea answered emphatically. "Talking about it will only stir it up again." I could see it coming: When she didn't want to talk about something, she changed the subject.

"Tell me what happened to you this morning," she said. Her ploy worked, and before I knew it, I had retrieved the feather and was handing her my written encounter.

"*The Legend of Coyoté Oak*, a title and everything ay, this ought to be interesting," she began with a tease.

I acknowledged her remark and sat quietly in the porch swing to let her read with the feather in my hand deliberating over our meeting in the Paris airport, curious how another life event connected to flight. What was beginning here? The sun was setting as color splashed across the sky; it seemed fitting to end the day as it began, enjoying the sky, the earth, and open space. Coyotés begin their wake-up yelps out in the hills and I thought how it almost seemed scripted, a sound effect to enhance the story. The whole day had been magical for me but apparently very different for her.

"Great story, it's very imaginative; now where did you really find this?" Andrea asked while leaning over beside me to get a better look at the feather.

"That story IS what happened and this feather is no figment. Also, it doesn't come from any known living bird." I said telling her about my methodical research.

"Maybe it's an apport. You know, when a yogi, or someone with psychic ability, produces a physical object out of nowhere. It's physical medium-ship," she explained.

"I don't think I have that ability," I replied.

"It sounds like you had a vision," she continued. "Perhaps you were in an unusually deep state of consciousness and produced the feather."

Neither of us had a better explanation, so for now, we decided that I had produced an apport of a 10,000-year-old feather while in my vision state. I wouldn't try to convince anyone else of that, but the explanation put the subject to rest and ended a day of extremes. While Andrea took a relaxing bath, I brought the feather to its new home, a large vase in my office, where it would stand in the corner with a few sprigs of Pampas Grass as if it were a designer's touch.

An hour or so had passed at my computer when I looked up to find Andrea standing in the doorway to my office. Wearing a delicate flowing negligee, she held a bottle of wine and two glasses in her hands. She enjoyed playing dress-up and still a perfectionist, even as a seductress, she looked good. With a come-hither glint in her eye, Andrea disappeared gracefully down the hall to the bedroom without a word -- I followed. We talked together in loving repose to the flicker of candles and the flavor of our first vintage wine. The fruits of our labor, in this unlikely setting, rewarded our pocketbooks, as well as our palates. As it does with fine wine, time enriches love, and the embers of our desire fanned into a deeper encounter when we touched.

"... to sleep: perchance to dream: ay. there's the rub;
For in that sleep of death what dreams may come..." Hamlet.

The air was moist with a heavy fog and I could but vaguely see the rust and chipped paint beneath my prone pose. I found myself crawling on my hands and knees. The texture of dilapidated steel abraded my palms as I inched my way along some unknown terrain. The clangor and groan of trepid metal deluged my senses as I realized that wherever I was, it was no place to be. I scrambled in horror looking for some change in my environment, some avenue of escape or refuge that felt the least bit safe. Everywhere I turned, I collided with corroded bulwarks barricading me from safety. Finally, I found an open pathway and clambered frantically towards freedom. Within a few feet, my hand slipped into nothingness and I nearly fell forward into some unknown abyss. Sprawled fearfully half over the edge, I clung to any incrustation I could sense upon the sullen surface of my seeming stockade. Lying there, I could hear water far below me in the darkness. I could hear the sound of waves breaking against a surface beneath my view. It sounded as if I were on a ship. I turned away from the edge feeling slightly more at ease to know my surroundings, still unable to reconcile my presence there. If this was a dream, it was far too real.

I was lucid, aware of all my senses. The sound of the engines caught my attention as if I were hearing them for the first time. The odor of diesel fumes and spilled oil filled my nose mixed with the smell of the ocean. I could see a little farther now through the dense fog, so I slowly stood up and began to explore what appeared to be a ship's deck. Whatever this vessel was, it was in a critical state of disrepair and I knew why the deck was shaking. I cautiously worked my way down the bulkhead toward what seemed to be an open cargo bay until I peered over the edge of the ship's hold. The stench of rotting fish, human feces and diesel fumes wafting up from the hold knocked me back gagging for air. Coming from the depths of the hold, I heard the mummer of voices. Surely, no one could be in there. I drew a breath of air away from the open hold and leaned down over the edge staring into the murky chasm. Sixty feet down in the hold, I saw a small kerosene lamp and in its dim radiance, the faces of several dozen people gazing up at me in despair. How could anyone survive in these conditions? These poor beings were soaking wet and heaped together atop a shipping container for protection. Bilge water sloshed about the hold splashing up on them each time the bow swayed in the heavy seas. Wretched squalor surrounded this island of discarded humanity.

"You come food?" One old man asked in broken English as he motioned to me. Answering that I had none caused the group to clamor amongst themselves in what sounded like Chinese, their body language clearly showing disappointment.

"How long have you been here," I asked, inquiring about their plight.

"Leave port seven days ago," a teenage looking girl replied. "Give us no food, no help."

"We pay go San Francisco," one said. Another answered, "They promise job, better life."

Most of them I imagined had spent everything they had and would still be in debt to their patrons when they arrived in the States. It sounded as if their transporter had sold them into the underground lives that face many illegal immigrants who unwittingly sell their souls for a chance at freedom. My heart broke knowing the hard fate likely to befall them. The rank fumes coming up from the hold mixed with the diesel exhaust searing my nose and filling my eyes with tears. However, the gravity of their situation had overtaken me; I no longer noticed or cared, I felt helpless and hopelessly inadequate. The sound of another ship approached, I stood up hoping help may arrive only to see the bow of a massive ship lunging out of the dark mist and heading directly into the middle of this decrepit vessel.

Towering many stories above the small freighter, the supertanker rode up over the side splitting the freighter apart and driving pieces of the broken hull beneath the rolling seas. The suction of the sinking hull dragged me down and then swept me outward into the powerful currents of the passing tanker. I was breathless, meters below the water's surface and I swam frantically upward towards air and life. Debris began floating to the surface along with a few survivors who were screaming in terror amid the devastation. I could see the ship's name, *HITAM EMAS* showing in large white letters through the gloomy fog as it powered away into the darkness. It cruised away without even noticing the wreckage left in its wake; how could they just leave and could any of us survive in the chilly waters? Another wave swept over me and gasping for air, choking unmercifully, I sank beneath the turbulence down into the dark cold tomb of the sea.

The black depths enveloped me. I was drowning. My body limp and useless, I used my last mental faculties to make peace with my maker. Visions of my life flashed through my last beams of consciousness as the blackness crawled inside. I was sinking endlessly as my awareness faded to one last opening of light. This must be death, I thought. Here is the tunnel leading to the light, my last prayers uttered; I surrendered to my fate. Then something landed on my chest as I jerked with a start to discover familiar surroundings and Lorenzo standing on top of me. I felt like kissing him as if he had saved my life. Awakened, my celestial beacon turned out to be the yard light shimmering through the bedroom blinds. Hamlet's soliloquy came to my mind "For in that sleep of death what dreams may come." What a dream I thought; what dreams indeed. Happily awake, I quietly got out of bed, thankful to be between the dreamtime.

The Coyoté Oak: Burgeoning Wisdom

CHAPTER 3
DAYLIGHT DELIBERATIONS

It was 4:00 A.M. I often awakened early but not this early, and never this bewildered. The past 24 hours had been relentless. I knew enough about dreams to know that this one wasn't ordinary; it felt psychotic, like the dream of someone depressed. I sometimes wrote my dreams down but a dream like this I didn't even want to remember even though, like the vision, I knew I would deliberate about it all day. Walking softly to the kitchen, I started my morning coffee as Lorenzo dashed to the door, reaching up and swatting at the knob. His conduct confirmed that his waking me was not altruistic; he only wanted out. He couldn't open the door, but he certainly knew how it worked and if he had an opposing thumb on his paws, he would meander as he pleased. For now, I was the designated doorman.

Upon fulfilling my doorkeeper obligation, I went to my office to I enjoy the first cup of my morning elixir organizing my thoughts and planning for the day. I looked forward to its flavor but this morning, it was more an effort to find normality amidst the past hours of abnormal experience. The dream haunted my senses completely like a posttraumatic flashback. It was a dream, I told myself; nightmares go away. This one lingered. The stink of the hold, the cold bite of the water, and the cries of those disheartened souls assaulted my reason. I still embodied the disenfranchisement of watching the tanker indifferently slip into the night, acting too important to bother with the imperiled lives strewn in its maelstrom. This dream was too real, it wasn't going away and despite my desire to forget, I'd have to reckon with it.

I quickly re-read a magazine article called, *Dreaming in Real Time: Surviving the Morning after Lucidity*, which explained the aftereffects of having a lucid dream, one where you are conscious that you are dreaming and interact with its images. It discussed the difficulty I was having of separating the dream from reality upon waking. Unfortunately, it didn't explain enough, my dream was so vivid that I felt I really had been there. The article mentioned a website called *Dream Working* where people did exactly that. Reluctantly I went to the Internet, hesitant to post the nightmare knowing the effect it had had on me. Silly or not, it was worth a shot and if they think I'm cracking up, at least I'll have a second opinion. Unlike most of my dreams, I had no trouble recounting every detail. Once I finished posting, I logged off not knowing what to expect but from my window, the early colors of dawn were showing; this morning, I'd skip my sunrise ritual and try to have a bit more inconsequential day.

Longing for the return of normality, I decided to surprise Andrea with Eggs Benedict and Crepes. Incongruous with her commitment to health, it was our treat when we wanted an exception to the rules. Within minutes, the kitchen filled with the aroma of Hollandaise and the sizzle of crepes on the griddle. The fragrant invitation drew a quick response.

"I must have been good last night," Andrea said in a flirty tone, poking her head through the doorway with a sleepy smile.

I answered by pulling her chair out for her to be seated. Somewhere between the crepes and eggs, our discussion turned to my lack of sleep and I mentioned the nightmarish episode.

"That sounds like me yesterday," she replied. "If you want to talk about it I can listen." I didn't really, but began a vague description of the fog and the rusty metal deck, when Andrea's eyes dilated and her face turned an ashen white.

"Were you on a ship, a broken-down old freighter with Chinese immigrants on board?" she interrupted, clearly anxious.

"Yes, but how did you know?" I said with an astonished gulp when

Andrea began telling my dream back to me scene-by-scene, sensation by sensation.

"What's going on here?" she probed with exasperation.

"My dream was exactly as you recounted." I replied, a tingle creeping up my spine and wondering how she had held the intense feelings inside. Stunned silence was the only response either of us could raise. The breakfast I had intended to lighten things up had taken a sadly unexpected turn. The next minutes passed in a solemn hush. In our quandary, the food seemed to lose its savor; eating became just a feeble attempt to undo our shock. The reality that we both experienced the same dream, amplified the scare we each felt having it. Having the identical dream, and on successive nights, was unknown to either of us. Whatever it meant, the dream was foreboding as if we had tread too far into some anomalous paradox. The dream wasn't paranormal; our synchronous experience of it was, and its inconceivable dark realism spawned disquiet uncommon to our lives starting the day with a pall.

"I posted the dream on an Internet discussion board. Maybe someone, somewhere, will make sense of it," I said when she returned ready for work.

"I hope you're right, so this dream dies today. I never want another day like yesterday; I wanted to crawl right out of my skin so I hope your day goes better," she said, changing the topic of conversation to my plans for the day.

The morning was as bright blue as the dream had been dismal. Springtime in Kansas is a fresh burst as the wheat fields awaken to green and early wildflowers bloom. As Andrea drove away, I walked across the yard to the work shed, my place to tinker with a variety of things, enjoying the warm sun. Like me, grapes need lots of sun and we had lots of it with clear fresh air, which made it an excellent, though unexpected, place for a vineyard. No doubt, we got plenty of stares from people who were more accustomed to seeing cows and cornfields, but as the vines covered the trellises, others planted too. Mace calls me a "dreamer with calluses" who still dreams big and works harder than most, even for the ones that don't come true. I certainly have the calluses.

My two-room shed is a bit of a catchall place, generally disorganized, and covered with whatever the project at hand requires, but the back room, is my sanctuary from the world, my space to create. In the corner stood an old, round woodstove from another nearby farm auction. It was at least 100 years old and still had its original chrome and nickel adornments. The stove gave off good heat and connected me to the past. Homesteaders settled around here in the mid-1800s and this was undoubtedly a symbol of someone's hard won success on the land. The early cabins, dugouts, and sod houses offered little comfort and even less separation from the elements but a stove like this would provide climate control and its ornamentation brightened up the drab environment. I always enjoyed imagining the stories of Conestoga wagon trains, buffalo stampedes, and cold, cold winters it may have had heard in its time.

A large window in the room looked out over our pond that allowed me to watch the wildlife as I worked. One computer inside, was for writing and design. The other, interfaced with a previous life – recording music. Now these musical instruments sat like littered leftovers of a lost lifestyle; but once, they were the tools of my trade. I had been a songwriter, and likely still would be had the trends in music not shifted. The music business was more mercurial then it was apollonian, shifting in a constant search for the next big thing, the next muse. You didn't know you were in until you were on your way out, and once you were out, you were a dinosaur; I was a dinosaur. I have more memories than money, but luckier than most, we were able to move out of the city, well out, and pursue a different life. Now, this room is my only stage.

I am a vintner besides being a writer, or maybe it's the other way around. Either way it takes a dreamer, it is hard work and sure rubs calluses inside and out. Honing an idea down to a simple phrase or the poetic lyric of a song brings me clarity and often times healing; but writing about this dream would be daunting. I chose instead, to work out the last details of trellises, today's project in the vineyard, until I heard the garbled grate of crushed rock brattling a car's wheel well in the driveway. That would be

Mason, I thought, he'll know where to find me.

"Chief, you out here? What's our mission for today?" Mason boomed, strolling in and plopping down on the couch by the window.

"You found me, Mace, come on in and I'll show you. When Jake comes, we'll go take a look at those tractors," I answered, hurrying to make the last measurement.

Mason wears his dents on the outside like an old rattletrap pick-up truck that should have died a hundred times but keeps running anyway. In his early fifties, he grew up on a farm nearby and had been fixing farm equipment since he was big enough to hold a wrench. On the other hand, I can work the soil, build and create in a dozen ways, but inevitably, if it has grease and moving parts, I muck it up. Mason is a much needed, and appreciated, reservoir of skill and knowledge.

After several years in the Army, Mason returned to the area. Enlisting out of high school, he hoped to train in engineering but ended up as a helicopter mechanic instead. Bored that he was still working at the sweat end of a wrench, Mace entered Special Forces training just in time to go to Vietnam. Some months later, deployed deep in the jungle near the supply routes from the North, an enemy division of more than 5,000 soldiers, overran his platoon and killed everyone in a hopeless, blood-spattered mêlée, everyone that is, but Mason. Left for dead in his foxhole, it was several weeks later when a Marine helicopter pilot spotted him wandering near the Laotian border delirious, and near death. After a long rehabilitation, he was discharged, returning home with scars on his body, trauma in his mind, and survivor's guilt scorched through his heart for his lost comrades.

Mason married Maria, a girl he had dated in high school, and worked in an aircraft manufacturing plant but never quite fit in. Angry and defensive much of the time, he frequently got into arguments and started drinking heavily. He told me that every morning he got up early, sat in his truck with pistol loaded, and had a beer for breakfast. He had to "stand watch," to be sure that the neighborhood was safe before going to work. Mason always carried a weapon when he went out and kept guns loaded in the house that he demanded Maria know how to use. She hated the guns but hated his tormented worry more. Eventually Maria was unable to take it any more and left with their son Jake; she couldn't watch his slow self-destruction, growing paranoia and depression, or allow Jake to grow up watching his father sink into alcoholism.

The loss of his marriage pushed Mason over the edge. He drank every-thing away, hitting bottom on the streets with a bottle of Bourbon as his only friend. The hard reality of sleeping on cold cement finally brought him to the VA Hospital for treatment. In recovery, he learned how many Vietnam Vets suffered similarly, living isolated lives and never feeling they had returned home. He finally stopped feeling like the sole survivor imprisoned by the past and though no longer a family, his isolation from Maria and Jake turned into a supportive relationship. Working outdoors in the vineyard, helps dispel the demons that vex Mason's soul.

"Jake's here to help," Mason said, brought to his feet by the beep of a car horn and bounding out.

In contrast to Mason, Jake wears his feelings privately, perhaps a result of the turmoil growing up. He's a keen observer who weighs people, and every side of a situation, with a unique perspective that gives his small landscape business design flare and an uncanny ability to create environ-ments exactly suited for his clients.

Following Mace out to the drive, I proposed that we go to the Flycht auction as he had suggested. Two hours later, I was making the twelve-mile drive back home on a small John Deere with them following slowly behind. Once home, we headed out in to the vineyard with tools filling the pickup bed and enough wire to fence off a small city. Not being a native Kansan, I broached the subject of any large birds that might live in the area as we made the slow quarter mile drive out to the new plant-ing. Without going into the full story, I only revealed the unusually large feather I couldn't identify. Neither of them knew of any native birds larger than a wild turkey but said there was a person a few miles away who raised Ostriches and Emus.

"It's more like a giant hawk feather," I said, responding to their suggestions. "I'll just have to show you when we take a break. It's very peculiar..." I said, stopping to notice Jake smirking as Mace prepared to offer another suggestion.

"I think you found a Jayhawk feather Chief. They're rare these days, but that's the biggest bird ever was around here." He cajoled, with a perfectly straight face.

"Nice try, Mace, but even a "Left Coaster" like me knows a Jayhawk is blue and red, and dribbles a basketball better than it flies. If you had told me it came from a buffalo's wing I might have believed it," I responded, trying to match Mason's sardonic wit. "Besides stringing yarns today, we need to string wire and get these trellises done." I said, dropping the subject.

Over the last several weeks, we had planted 5,000 grapevines, bringing our vineyard up to about 25 acres and we would need more help when these began to grow. It felt good to see the young grapes leafing out; but it was great for all of us to know we were nearing the end of what had been long, hard labor. With three of us, the job of stretching wire went quickly; by mid-afternoon, we had finished the section and the three-man crew was ready for rest. Over the course of several trips, I brought some sodas and whatever snacks I could find back to my office where they had already discovered the feather.

"What the hell, that's gotta be fake," Mason blurted out while inspecting it closer and passing it to Jake who showed equal amazement.

"I don't know what bird it's from but I found it on the hill yesterday. It's the one I told you about," I said, satisfied that they were baffled and somewhat proud of my discovery.

For several minutes, we speculated about its origin but produced no new conclusions. I didn't mention anything mystical, figuring why bring it up if I couldn't explain it, and they would want an explanation. There was plenty to conjecture about but I would see them again on Monday, it was

Friday, and everyone was ready for the weekend.

A member of the generation between Mason and Jake, I was at ease with both of them and often served as the "universal translator" between two very different mindsets, especially about weekend plans. In this three-horse town, entertainment choices consisted of a movie at the Bijou, bowling, buffets, or trolling the local bars. Mason delighted in bowling and buffets. Unlike his father, Jake was young enough to still enjoy the nightlife and handsome enough always to have his dance card filled by hopeful young women eager to win his attention. He was like a eucalyptus tree growing in a forest of cottonwoods, and no matter that he was big enough to hold his ground, Jake's character stood out from the surroundings. A lot like me, he had an artist's temperament struggling to survive in a worker's wilderness. Jake's talent gleamed through canvass, sculpture, and stained glass. His landscaping focused on design, giving him some outlet for his abilities, still, his genius deserved recognition in the finer arts.

Working outdoors all day kept my mind occupied but how could it not return to the dream. *HITAM EMAS*, the ship's name stuck in my mind so I searched the Internet and surprisingly found several websites that contained the name ranging from local propane dealers to a pizza parlor called "Hit'em N'Mass." Then one site for a company called Oil Resources and Transportation Incorporated, (ORTI), showed a picture of their flagship, *HITAM EMAS*. Right down to the lettering, it looked exactly like the tanker in the dream. The supertanker had a Liberian registry and operated between Southeast Asia and their refineries on the West Coast of the United States but why would I dream of a real ship about which I knew nothing?

I was anxious to see if Andrea recognized this vessel but she wouldn't be home for another hour so I continued my research. There was no record of an accidents or spills for the ship in any maritime database; by all accounts, the ship operated safely within international law. ORTI was a publicly traded U.S. corporation that from Asia to Arizona, Canada to the Caspian Sea owned oil and mining operations from wellhead to gas pump, mine to manufacturing and every stage in between. Their holdings were massive. They also owned three large chemical facilities that produced compounds used in production, and a host of other products. The corporate energy giant was a supplier focused on international trade and was a model of capitalist acquisition.

The C.E.O. and Chairman of the Board of ORTI was R. Harry Nash. His Vitae contained little personal information but stated that he had served in various positions with energy companies located in the Middle East and South America, interspersed with terms in government foreign service and intelligence. I thought the notable absence of detail in his job history sounded like the chronicle of a former CIA or NSA operative whose activities and whereabouts remain shrouded from public view. Luther Mallory Inc., listed as the "Principal Stockholder," had no officers on the ORTI board, which seemed noteworthy, as I would think anyone with the controlling interest of a company would have an active hand directing it. Luther Mallory's website was bare with only one-page about the company which seemed odder still for such a powerful company. The information stated that LMI was a financial holding company, a private investment brokerage, and a member of the New York Stock Exchanges. There was no contact information, no location, nor any information about, investors, holdings, or clientele, only this mission statement:

Luther Mallory Inc. engages global economic development through the implementation of long-term maintenance.

A rather enigmatic summary for a major corporation I thought, which intensified my curiosity about Luther Mallory and its meaning. I checked with the Securities Exchange Commission to verify that Mallory was a current broker discovering that he was also a member of the Tokyo, London, Hong Kong, Sao Paulo and Johannesburg exchanges. He must wield tremendous wealth diversifying since his first 1906 stock trades in New York.

Since I had a date and a place, I continued my search in the archives of *The Wall Street Journal* and the *New York Times* hoping to find more references about his activities. The Journal had a few short articles referring to him as an "Eccentric Youth" or as "Washington's Wunderkind," but all mention of Mallory stopped after 1910. Likewise, the *Times* society pages had a few brief references to him attending the opera and the symphony around that time, one even listing him as New York's most eligible bachelor. Many disgruntled reporters commented about his idiosyncratic aversion to any interviews or that any pictures taken of him were always candid shots from far away. After 1910, occasional articles speculated on the whereabouts of Mallory. Howard Hughes' disappearing act, even with a corporate spokesperson to stand the limelight, didn't match the sudden and absolute invisibility of Mallory. He was a mystery who somehow remained out of sight and equally confounding, was why our dream conjured the doings of this turn-of-the-century Wall Street wizard.

Three short beeps and one long one sounded from a car horn in the driveway. Andrea often used this signal to bring me in from wherever I was "out on the 80."

"You'll never guess what I found out today," I said noticing she was looking towards the vineyard and surprised that I greeted her from the porch.

"OK, I'll bite; what?" she replied, looking back with a mulish glance as if she had enough surprises lately.

I didn't want to lead her to any conclusions so I sat her in my office chair, pulled up the ORTI web page with the picture of the super tanker and said, "Here, take a look."

"Well, it just gets weirder and weirder, that's the ship! She said in a befuddled sigh.

Pleased that my search had found something, even though it enlarged our surrealistic dilemma instead of resolving it, I pulled up the additional sites asking if she had any knowledge of ORTI or Luther Mallory Inc. She did not. With no more satisfying solutions, Andrea suggested we needed a fresh air walk in the vines to get this dream-think out of our heads and see some real world progress, something that made sense.

We walked out to a beautifully colored sky with sunlight pouring through holes in the bulging clouds. Looking skyward, we could see thunderheads gleaming like golden towers above us while in the distance, light created magical vistas where the rays danced between shadow and mist. The moment felt safe and secure as we peered upward at the power and beauty above us. It felt good to let go of the confounding events of the past days. The clouds were building and a thunderstorm was likely brewing for this evening. The air felt energized before the storm. Lightning, thunder, and nature's drama were some of the reasons we loved country life and we enjoyed watching the tempests form. Our walk continued towards the barn where Lorenzo shot past us and pounced on a leaf waving in the breeze. The feline tagalong's playfulness was often entertaining; that is, when he wasn't breaking every dish in the kitchen.

Having thoroughly vanquished the leaf, Lorenzo looked around for his next adversary. That twig a few feet away, or perhaps the butterfly flaunting itself slightly above his reach; to which conquest would he commit? The fluttering butterfly turned out to be irresistible. Lorenzo hunkered down, wiggling with anticipation, and drew aim on the colorful creature. Then with a great spring, he lunged upward towards his prey grasping wildly with his front paws. The butterfly glided peacefully upward as Lorenzo plummeted back to earth. He wouldn't foil that easily though; he continued his chase leaping every few feet at its erratic trajectory. The pursuit continued around the corner of the barn and out of sight when suddenly we heard a loud hiss followed by intense growling.

"Sounds like the butterfly might be winning. I better see if he needs backup," I told Andrea, hastening my step to his aid.

I saw a turgid tail protrude from the corner as Lorenzo cautiously backed up. His back arched; every hair stood on end. Clearly, the hunter had become the prey. Perhaps the danger was a displaced raccoon or Coyoté so I hurried ahead to his rescue. Lorenzo, realizing he had the chance to escape, shot back to the house and most certainly underneath the porch, as I darted to the barn's corner ready to defend. Then I stopped dead. The hair on the back of my neck stood on end and if I had a tail, it would have puffed up too. Ten feet in front of me, standing about eight feet tall was the largest winged animal I'd ever seen and it could easily carry me off or bite a sizable chunk out of me.

"What is it? Are you alright?" Andrea called out, seeing me freeze at the corner.

"It's a bird... at least I think it's a bird. You better wait there!" I warned. A magnificent, but frightening, creature stood before me. Its head was that of a raptor with a large beak and eyes that faced straight forward. Dark purple crowned the head and blended to lavender farther down its neck. Like a rainbow, one hue merged into the next down its breast and wings until it stood on two stocky crimson talons. This was a formidable fowl. I didn't know if I should run, or study it, but this must be the source of my feather. Then the bird's head turned towards me and fixed its gaze in mine. I surged with adrenaline and felt it was time to run when I heard a gentle voice.

"Sorry I scared your cat." I looked around to see who spoke; there was only the bird and me. I looked back at the bird, whose gaze had not wavered.

"I'm Sorrano. There's nothing to fear." Sorrano said, "Watch this day, Learn, and Remember!"

My stomach sank. How could he know those words? This daylight deliberation must be a hallucination. What about Lorenzo? He saw something I assured myself. I heard Andrea running up the side of the barn, certain I'm sure of my danger. Sorrano made a slight hop, took one flap with his wings and disappeared completely.

"Honey, what is it?" Andrea said, rounding the corner.

"It was just here," I said, pointing to where the great bird had been. Andrea seeing nothing gave me a worried look and walked in that direction. "I don't see any..." she started to say and then, after kneeling to the ground, she stood up and turned around holding another large feather in her hand.

CHAPTER 4
THE QUICKENING

"I am a feather for each wind that blows," wrote Shakespeare in *The Winter's Tale*. The past few days circumstances had blown me about as easily as the feather to which Shakespeare referred; but thank God for feathers. Only moments ago, Andrea looked at me as if I was crazy as a loon. The plume she held in her hand, and Lorenzo's retreat, I thought were evidence enough to keep me out of the asylum. Still, it's odd that this feather is the plausible proof that my reason remained intact.

"It's like the other one you found isn't it?" Andrea said approaching me.

"Yes, I guess we found the missing link," I quipped, "but where the hell did the bird go? It was standing right there until you came; it hopped as if it was going to fly and vanished. Nothing can fly away that fast, can it?" I queried as I slid open the rear barn door and stepped inside looking in each stall to see if the great bird had slipped inside.

"Weren't you afraid? Lorenzo sure was but I thought I heard another voice. Who were you talking to?" Andrea inquired, following me into the barn.

The barn was dark except for a few beams of sunlight streaming in between the cracks in the siding. Two old steel wagon wheels that had hung on the wall for probably the last 80 years glowed in the dim illumination. Above them, there was a swallow's nest made from mud carried in from the edges of the pond. A springtime pairing that called the nest home darted out with our intrusion but there was no giant bird in the barn.

35

"That's more of the mystery," I replied to Andrea. "The bird was talking to me; it apologized for scaring Lorenzo and told me not to be afraid. I was afraid; it stood as high as the barn roof. It was huge… huge!" I repeated stretching my arms upward to demonstrate its size.

"Shouldn't we call someone?" Andrea asked as if she thought we really should.

"What would we tell them," I responded taking the ornate prize from Andrea, "who would believe something this big?" I extended my arms as if they were a pair of wings holding the feather downward as part of them, "Look, it's enormous. Could we tell them the bird talked and introduced itself as Sorrano? Let's finish our walk, it all sounds too crazy and I want to know more before I convince the world I'm nuts."

The clouds continued their celestial ascent and swelled like giant mushrooms a short distance away. Lightning flashed across the sky followed by rumbles of thunder. Within the clouds, we could see the greenish light that always accompanied severe storms. Beneath the thunderheads, dark blue bands of rain fell and looked as if they were heading our way. The grapes hadn't produced yet so hail wasn't a worry, we needed a heavy rain and the ponds needed filling before the heat of summer came. We hurriedly walked through the trellises wired today imagining the vines covering the new acreage. With this planting, the vineyard had taken the leap from an oversized hobby, to a viable business but despite my desire to put the bird back in its cage, the encounter remained foremost in our minds. We tried to have a regular conversation but our abnormal bird watch kept interrupting.

The sky overhead had become very dark and the clouds were lowering as the storm moved in quickly. We needed to be out of the weather and soon. Our walk became a jog as the first raindrops fell then a sprint down the hill but by the bottom, we were soaking wet. As we came to the farmyard, a bolt of lightning struck the top of an old cedar tree about fifteen feet away with a blast that knocked both of us back. The jolt tossed us a few feet in the air flopping us down to the earth like a couple of rag dolls who looked up, stupefied at the smoldering evergreen. Scrambling to our feet as the shock of our near miss wore off, we dashed for the safety of the porch. At first, we stood in silence as the danger started to sink in. The adrenaline was pumping, our hearts still racing and after the bewildered hush, Andrea started to laugh nervously, talking about my silly expression upon landing on my butt. It all happened too fast and was a potent reminder that we were small beings living in a very powerful natural system. The system had served us notice that its purpose, and power, was greater than our own.

The squall line upon us, it was raining heavily and the chilly wind gusts against our wet clothes made it time to get inside. Andrea peeled off her soggy attire leaving it on the porch and headed for the shower. Feeling the chill myself, I undressed and started towards the warm shower when I realized that we hadn't carried the feather into the house so I franticly sorted through the wet pile. The feather was not there! I darted out through the puddled yard towards the charred cedar tree; we must have dropped it there I assured myself. The rain was cold against my skin and the fresh mud squirmed between my toes. All I could think about was finding the missing feather.

Several inches of water had quickly covered the area around the cedar; streaming out of the farmyard, it swirled towards the pond. The brightly colored treasure wasn't anywhere. Down on my hands and knees, I felt around the ground beneath the water's course hoping that it had lodged somehow and not carried further. I searched in vain. The current must have swept it into the pond, I thought so I hastily followed the spontaneous flow until I collided with a soft wall of fluff.

"Are you looking for this?" A voice said as quickly as I jumped back. The great bird stood before me with the mislaid treasure in its beak. He bent down lightly releasing the feather, which glided through the wind directly into my hand. Standing upright, the bird flapped its wings, ruffled its feathers, and shook from head to tail in the rain the way other birds do in a lawn sprinkler. Like smaller fowl, it seemed joyous in this bathing ritual. It's one thing to watch a tiny sparrow in a birdbath, but standing only a few feet away from this shaking celebration with a bird bigger than me, felt alarmingly chaotic and the constant flicker of lightning made the scene all that much more surreal.

"How is it that you can speak?" I asked, overcoming my shock and realizing I had many questions for the creature called Sorrano.

"Well, how else could I communicate with you? You speak don't you?" Sorrano replied. At that moment however, I was speechless. Realizing my predicament he continued calmly, "I know you have questions James and I will answer them, but right now you must go, Andrea is worried about you. Meet me by the barn in the morning."

I accepted Sorrano's direction, and turned towards the house; in the misty glow of the porch light, I saw Andrea standing wrapped in a towel, peering out into the night.

"James, where are you?" She called with a worried tone.

"Coming" I yelled through the strapping squall and ran for sanctuary on the dry porch.

"Hurry up; I was concerned when you didn't come into…." She bellowed and immediately started laughing as I approached the light. "What on earth have you been doing? Look at…you look like a mud wrestler waiting for the hose down after a brawl."

"I went out to find this," I said holding up the mired spoils worthy of my efforts.

"Oh good" she replied, "I forgot that when the lightning struck." Andrea took it from me saying, "Now off to the shower, you're a mess. I'll put this with the other one." She darted towards my office before I had the chance to tell her I had seen the bird again.

The warm shower felt good after sloshing about in the wind and rain. I stood with my head under the warm gush and let all the tumult of the past hour drain away. I breathed deeply, bringing in the steamy mist to clear my lungs and fend off the cold I had endured. For me, the gentle gurgle of water spurting on my head and down my body is my moment of solace when my mind, body, and soul can rest from daily affairs. After several minutes, I heard the door of my anchorite asylum open.

"James, you better come look at this!" Andrea said handing me a towel and then scooting into the hall. What could be so important? I questioned to myself.

"All replies to your posting," Andrea said, pointing to the full computer screen as I entered the office. "Read this one," she concluded bringing it up on the screen.

I had a dream two nights ago, exactly like yours. Ever since, I've been too afraid to sleep well. I don't know what the dream means but it feels creepy, as if something awful is happening and I can't do anything about it. Can you help? I sent you an email that describes more.

Janell in Florida

"There are a lot more to read," Andrea said, her hands on my shoulders urging me into the chair.

My inquiry elicited the predictable responses with symbolic interpretations for the ship, the ocean, the fog and even the name *Hitam Emas.* Their theories were insightful but didn't fit; this dream was not internal conflict resolution or wish fulfillment. Many found it unusual that we shared the dream but on separate nights with no dialogue between us. Towards the bottom of the board was another post like Janell's, then another and another. All experienced the same events within the last two days and all had the same untoward feelings. Andrea's comment that "it just gets weirder," became too true.

Messages inundated me like a river flooding its banks once I clicked the button to look for Janell's email. An electronic stream of message upon message poured in from people who had read my dream account and wanted to affirm their conflict with the same images. Dozens of emails had arrived, in the last hour; this was way too much energy. So many people from around the world exceeded any probability of chance occurrence. It was too intense, too many inexplicable details to digest. Maybe this was all a dream I couldn't awaken from but I feared imagining where answering these messages might lead. I would wait at least until tomorrow to reply. Tonight I only hoped for a good rest.

The storm was over and a rain freshened breeze blew in the office window cooling the air; you could almost hear the gratitude of every living creature. It had been several weeks since we had received even a modest rain. Plants, animals, and we humans, all needed a respite. Long dry spells are part of the natural cycles, some seasonal, some lasting several years, but living close to the land; one can't help but notice the change in climate. The cold of winter isn't as harsh, spring rains come less frequently, even the summer heat oscillates between a hazy malaise and scalding clarity at an irregular pace. The cycles seem out of cadence as if the planet itself is under duress. This rain would help but I hoped it signaled the end of the two-year drought and a return to the rhythm of nature. Perhaps this quickening would enliven the parched land. As I pulled on a sweater, a spicy aroma blended with now rarefied evening zephyr.

"Tea's ready, are you? It's the spiced blend you like." Andrea called from the kitchen.

"On my way," I replied and followed the heady bouquet to where Andrea had poured us each a warm mug. "Lets sit out on the porch and watch the storm" I suggested.

The night sky divided; a sliver of moon and the stars filled the western sky, clouds veiled the east. The faint light of the moon revealed the towering thunderheads that had marched over us and had not diminished since their visit to our thankful ground. Lightning streaked across the east piercing sky and earth as if gallant warriors from the hoary heavens were hurling fiery lances back and forth between themselves. Zeus, Thor, Jehovah, Xango, Jupiter, Aditi, Ra, cultures across time have given so many names to the Creator who wields this astronomical force. We spend so much effort trying to befriend, understand, appease, or even evade a celestial power that eclipses our own.

Andrea and I sat humbled watching the awesome strength of nature, strength that had swayed our path this night, yet chosen to spare us. The jolt that knocked us about like a puff of down was only a small part of the energy released when each fiery lance flies. An article I remembered told about the energy released upward from each lightning bolt; NASA satellites had photographed these events calling these energy phenomenon elves and sprites. Contrary to the petite stature the names suggest, elves and sprites are massive energy exchanges traversing huge distances in the upper atmosphere but we didn't need names to be awestruck, or value our minute place within the living system.

The ground quavered beneath our feet in synchronous dance with the low rolls of distant thunder. I was terrified of that sound, of that power, as a child. It's interesting how the things that frighten us most, turn out not to be the source of the fear at all. Our resistance to the harbingers brings us terror. Sound has become a locus of my search for enlightenment as it has been for many through millennia. From the quiescent lilt of a mountain brook, to the rhythm of the heart, sound is a pathway that takes me to the deep reaches of my psyche. Resonance gives access to reverie states wherein I find insight, healing, growth, and my highest creativity. Sound -- vibration -- grants passage because it accesses the core of my being.

Music first led me along that passage. The pure sound of a note well played had the capacity to open the heart and touch the soul. As a songwriter, I followed that passage from one note to the next, learning to find the place where one soul communicated with another, the place where all hearts understood. First, it was communion with the muse, and sharing that union with another, that evoked my mystical experience. It spawned my exploration of the state from which it sprang, to master its sacred use. I wanted to discover the reverie that sound had drawn me to and through which it had effected change. In my search, I studied Eastern and Occidental texts; I looked at scientific studies and esoteric traditions to explain the doorway in consciousness through which I traveled. Eventually the vibration itself transported me and resonated with my experiences as if, along with so many before me, we had grown from the same roots.

Shamans, and other mystical traditions, had used drumming in every part of the world since the beginning of time. Now I too had begun to drum. Perhaps the thunder's rumbling pulsation, or maybe the porch swing's rhythmic sway triggered it, but vivid images flooded my mind and senses swiftly like a succession of flashbacks. Drum beats, the smell of incense, the noises of civilization packed too tightly on itself, and celebration. Not another vision; these were reemerging memories, delicious images of my pilgrimage projecting like flashing signposts along a passage inward.

Standing outside a small temple in Brazil, I watched a crowd of people move along the shabby narrow street and through its entrance. Stepping from darkness beneath a palm tree, I followed inside the unadorned temple to see the crowd gathered around a low balustered railing forming a u-shaped perimeter enclosing an open wooden floor. On a platform at the far end of the floor, stood several statues festooned with flowers and three great conga drums standing to the side of this altar. Through the din of excitement, I saw three men dressed in white take a solemn stance behind each drum while The Father of the Saints, the temple leader, welcomed us. Then all I heard was the unremitting pound of the player's hands on drum leather.

The sound was thunderous, shaking the hardwood floor and pale green concrete walls of the diminutive sanctuary. A dozen or so individuals walked onto the wooden floor and, capturing the rhythm of the drums, they danced to the resounding *Candomble*[1] cadence vibrating through the room, through my body, and entraining the crowd. Each dancer wore a costume emulating the *Caboclos*[2], or the Old Black Men[3]. These dancers embodied the pulse, each becoming more distinct as the ritual progressed, their movements more idiosyncratic until they made flesh the spirit conjured in the course of their journey. On the sound of the drums, they fell into a trance state.

---

1) An African-Brazilian religion widely practiced in Brazil that uses trance dancing.
2) Indian/white half-breeds who, rejected by both races, were the poorest of the poor whose spirits now help the living poor.
3) They are the slaves who first carried these traditions to Brazil.

I was in a *favilla*[4] of São Paulo, Brazil at an Umbanda[5] ceremony. This ritual invoked spirits that came to heal and guide those present through the dancing trance-mediums who had spread out lighting cigars and blowing smoke to enhance their spirit's presence. I joined the crowd forming into lines in front of the various personages, each person choosing the embodied spirit best suited to guide them. I watched healing passes[6] and overheard others giving helpful insight into life problems. Present were the poor fringes of humanity in a room filled with the tang of stale cigar smoke and abject poverty.

I stood before a gray-haired *Caboclo* shrouded in smoke with a feathered headdress and a beaded vest. He puffed his cigar smoke and looked directly in my eyes.

"You question why your talents in music were not rewarded," the *Caboclo* said. "The spirits tell me that music was your awakening, but not your path. Though your talent was sufficient, you were chosen for another task that will become clear to you. They will ask you to help repair the world." Without saying more, he turned his focus on my ring, blowing smoke on it and rubbing cigar ash onto it. "The ring is a potent talisman," he told said as he charged it, intensifying its effect and my capacity to do the work.

More than 6000 miles from home, this man carved the gem of truth from my sorrowed soul. He couldn't possibly have known about my career in music, or the grief I felt from its absence. A sharp clap of thunder brought my awareness back to the porch swing. Like a benevolent presence, it reminded me that I felt the power of sound and that on that night in Brazil, and this, the quickening that unfolds Spirit, like the storm passing, is rhythmic and comes at its chosen time. Perhaps, I'll learn his prophecy, I mused, looking at the ring remaining on my finger, but how could I help repair the world?

4) The very poor slums found in some Brazilian cities.
5) An African-Brazilian religion that combines much of Candomble with Catholic symbols.
6) The practice of moving the hands down the body to clear energy blocks and heal.

"I don't know who is behind it but they're trying to buy a large area around Elm Street and several people have already taken their offer." Andrea interrupted breaking the silence with talk of her business as the storm moved on. "Mason won't like that 'The Buffalo's Back Buffet' sold out; it's his favorite restaurant. The farm store you go to is also gone. Rumor has it that a big corporation will build a plant there, which makes people excited about jobs. I want to keep my great location."

"Didn't they make you a good enough offer?" I asked, stopping the swing's gentle roll.

"No, that's not it; it's how they pushed themselves on me." She answered. "No was not an acceptable response. They offered three times the property value and implied that if I didn't take the offer, I'd regret it. I don't think they meant only the money."

"Maybe you better call the police, or at least find an attorney yourself," I suggested. She agreed and with that, the subject dropped.

"I didn't tell you how I found the second feather," I said bluntly. "I ran strait into the bird. It asked, 'Are you looking for this?' then dropped the feather right in my hand."

"Why don't I ever see this bird?" Andrea asked, chagrined that she missed it again.

"I don't know," I emphasized. "I wish you actually would see what I have! Being branded a "West Coast Wacko" is one thing," I said half joking, "but talking with a giant bird makes me more of an odd duck than I care for. Maybe this bird is a fake, like someone is trying to make me think I'm crazy."

"That's paranoid," Andrea returned, looking me in the eye. "Why would anyone bother? You're no native Kansan, but you're sane as an owl."

"It could be connected to getting your property." I continued with my train of thought derailed by why she had used the word "owl." "Both events started about the same time. Isn't that a bit odd?" I persisted.

"Odd yes, but still too much of a stretch," Andrea concluded.

"Good or a bad idea, I'll find out more in the morning," I responded, explaining my agreement to meet Sorrano by the barn in the morning.

"I'm coming along!" Andrea interrupted emphatically. "I want to see this creature."

"No, I don't mean to leave you out, but sorry, I need to follow this through alone. If it's not there, then I'll know I've lost it, but if it shows up, my delusion is consistent which unfortunately," I said with a shrug of my shoulders, "well…it means I'm really nuts." Thankful for the distraction, I attended to Lorenzo who, skulking from his storm shelter under the porch stretched for the doorknob.

The storm had moved off to the east now leaving behind a freshened landscape on the dried up earth and restoring every farmer's hope. Like lightning launched by ancient gods, a quickening bolt knocks you off your feet, and as surely as thunder follows, it is a clarion, calling you back to attention, back to center. Visions and dreams, sinister threats and a sentient bird, all knocked us from our feet but augured very different paths. The quickening, like the growth it stimulates, comes in cycles as my memories remind but its arrival does not always reveal its purpose.

The Coyoté Oak: Burgeoning Wisdom

CHAPTER 5
THE GROVE

With one click of the mouse, I started a deluge. For ten minutes or more, email messages flooded into my computer; nearly all of them were about my dream posting. Morning had come quickly it seemed. Though I had awakened before my normal hour, shortly before sunrise, I felt extraordinarily refreshed. I headed out to start coffee as usual but this day was not likely to be usual, as the surge of emails demonstrated. The meeting with Sorrano was yet to come; we set no time to meet, but he would likely find me. The great bird seemed to be aware of all my thoughts and movements up to this point. The awareness he possessed suggested he was telepathic, or perhaps he was merely a well-crafted figment of my imagination. I wasn't sure which.

"When are you going to meet the bird?" Andrea asked; uncharacteristically awake for a Sunday morning.

I indicated that I wanted to wake up more before formulating questions for this feathered figment. For obvious reasons, I needed to come away from this meeting feeling I had a grip on reality. Andrea had a few questions too I imagined and interposed that she would read the letters while I met Sorrano. I clicked the mouse one more time only to watch the tide of tales pour in again.

"Look at all these," I said directing her to the emails. "I never expected this kind of response."

"I don't know how we can even read, let alone respond to them if all this keeps up." Andrea muttered, clearly stunned by the recurrent influx.

"Glance through them, we'll decide what to do later," I suggested. "Finding out about this bird will be strange enough for me this morning."

Noticing the sun was up now, I knew my encounter with Sorrano was at hand. Andrea said she would sort the flood and think about our response, but clearly, she would prefer to accompany me and I heard "I'll be waiting!" as I walked out the door.

The ground squished beneath my feet as I walked across the farmyard. Last night's rain had soaked deep into the soil and the once parched panorama was responding. Verdant, young, dew covered shoots of grass shimmered in the morning rays where dusty barrens lay yesterday. Puffballs, mushrooms, and toadstools came forth from their subterranean realm to kiss the moist spring morning. The air, laden with the scent of clover blossoms and horsemint, caressed my senses. The dawn was enchanted. Sounding its matin call, a Cardinal swooped down from flight onto the charred crest of the cedar. Lightning burned half of the cedar's trunk blackening it all the way down to the soil. The firebrand vividly reminded me how easily nature's force had tossed us aside as it impressed the earth. This was the morning after; even this sign of last night's fury bode of forging strength, portended creation of character and re-growth previously unimagined. Exactly as I saw its mark upon the cedar, I felt that something was recreating me, and that this day would reveal more than I expected.

Reaching the corner of the barn, I stopped to scrape the thick layer of mud from my shoes. The rain had helped bring the plants to health, but walking was a little difficult. I picked up a stick, pried a chunk of sticky goop off my shoe and flung it.

"Looks like you could use a pair of these" I heard coming from the horse pen. I looked up to see Sorrano perched on one leg on top of the fence while waving his other talon towards me with a taunting smile.

"Better yet," I said, as Sorrano bent forward and glided down from the fence to land right in front of me, "if I had your wings and I could sail over the bog…."

"Hop on then" he interrupted as if he had known my request all along. I had hesitantly situated myself when he leaned forward and with a few skillful flaps, we were airborne. Sorrano headed out over the vineyard and started to climb higher. Sensing that I was feeling a bit fearful he asked, "Have you ever seen your land from up here?"

"Not like this," I muttered in reply. "I mean…" swallowing my words, I didn't have much to say.

We flew over the pond, the farmyard, and hovered above the fresh green shoots of the vineyard until we landed amidst the profusion of peach blossoms in the orchard, well out of the mud but I was mired completely in the absurdity of believing the present experience.

"Maybe we better keep our feet on the ground. I don't want you to forget all your questions," Sorrano teased. "So James, ask away."

I was completely disarmed, surprised he knew my name, and struggled to recall any one of the myriad of questions that had filled my head since finding the feather.

"Are you real, or am I going nuts?" I finally blurted out like an idiot. "If I wasn't real, how could you have flown? Seeing that view wasn't nuts, was it?" Sorrano questioned in return.

"But, birds don't talk. At least they don't reason when they speak or have conversations with people," I countered, puzzled why he seemed to be testing me with his answers.

"Have you ever tried to communicate with them?" he questioned again. "What's really going on here?" I fired back. "Why do I keep meeting you? Who, or what, are you REALLY, and don't answer me with another question?"

"Wait a minute," Sorrano intervened as if he was satisfied that he had challenged me enough and I was ready for the information. "You and I both know that I'm not your ordinary bird." Sorrano said, starting to walk slowly towards the vineyard thinking quietly to himself as if he were drawing me in to his reasoning. "Let's start with the important issues. I have much to convey.

"First James, you are not crazy. This IS happening, and I am not a figment." As quickly as I noticed he had repeated my concerns precisely, he continued, "Yes, I can perceive some of your thoughts." He admitted but I felt completely exposed and cautiously agreed just to listen.

"While this is real, it's not what it seems. This is my first time on Earth, so there are some things I can't explain. I'm sort of the 'advance man,' well, 'advance bird' if you prefer, beginning an imperative charge." Sensing my question, Sorrano said, "Yes, I'll tell you about the work, but first...."

Sorrano quickened his pace as we walked through the vines shimmering with droplets until we were heading towards a grove of Osage Orange trees, or hedge trees, as the farmers call them, which stood to the north of the vineyard. I was still trying to grasp this meeting when Sorrano approached the edge of the grove and another bird like himself fluttered down out of the thicket.

"James, I'd like you to meet my mate, Bashira," Sorrano said turning back to me.

Bashira was smaller than Sorrano and not quite as brightly colored but with more delicate features. Sorrano's rich amber gold eyes were scrutinous when he looked at you. In contrast, Bashira's eyes were deep soothing emerald and her glance revealed unbounded empathy. Together they made a regal pair.

"Very nice to meet you James, I believe they have chosen wisely." Bashira said.

"It's nice, though quite puzzling, to meet you too." I replied curious about who had chosen wisely, if she was talking about me and for what purpose. Up until now, I had been trying to resolve an anomaly, a strange feather and a single bird from which it originated. Now there was a pair, which suggested I might have encountered a completely new species. That fact would bring an entirely new set of problems to solve, and then of course, they were speaking to me.

"Who and what will be clear to you," Sorrano joined in, responding to my inquiring thoughts. "I'm not avoiding your questions, but my answers may sound unbelievable. James I assure you it is true. Our Elders carefully selected you for this work; our task is to confirm their decision, once we contacted you."

"How am I … I mean what am I…?" I asked dissatisfied with his explanation.

"In a minute James," Sorrano reassured, "Andrea is about to join us." Fearing they were about to vanish again, and to my disbelief, I turned to see Andrea walking through the vineyard as Bashira flew out to meet her taking care not to frighten her.

"They'll catch up with us shortly. Let's walk on." Sorrano said, leading me into the clump of hedge from which Bashira had flown earlier.

I didn't question, assuming we were going to their nest, if that's what I should call it. This thicket was a very familiar place to me where I often rested in the shade when working at this end of the vineyard. A few steps into my accustomed grove, reality was in question again. With each step, it seemed the modest sized hedge trees grew taller, the limbs reached higher and the foliage became more luxuriant. At first, I said nothing. I was unsure if it was my eyes adjusting from bright sunshine to shade, but after a few more steps, the change in proportions was too great to ignore.

"Are these trees growing or am I getting smaller?" I asked waggishly, feeling like I had followed the white rabbit down the hole.

"Do you know where you are?" Sorrano smiled and asked.

"I thought I was in my hedge grove but now I...." I stopped mid-sentence as Sorrano stepped aside to reveal a fire pit surrounded by seven stones.

"Remember being here?" I heard him ask in my mind.

"Yes...but that wasn't...." I stuttered tentatively, "that was a vision, or delusion...or something."

"Watch this day, learn, and remember," Sorrano repeated Owl's words, the vision streaming back into my head and as if having déjavu, I recognized his voice.

"Is this... is this where I was then?" I thought, not realizing I had posed the question aloud and struggling with the overlap of the memory and current circumstances.

"Yes, but here," answered Sorrano, indicating the fire pit and stones, "wasn't here... then," he continued, pointing around the grove.

Perplexed as a pigeon lost in a looking glass, I slumped down on one of the stones as Andrea and Bashira entered the grove coming to the fire circle where Andrea sat on the stone beside me - wordless. Her eyes wide with astonishment, she was as dumb struck as me. Andrea's face flushed with a stunning radiance; the blissful visage described during powerful spiritual encounters like the faces of the Fatima children when they saw the Virgin Mary. Ministers voice the benediction saying, "may his countenance shine upon you and bring you peace" yet I wondered how many of them had seen this first hand. Whatever had transpired, Andrea was in a beautiful state of grace.

Once we settled comfortably, Bashira moved around the circle to Sorrano where the pair scratched a swale in the soil with their talons. Nestling their great forms into the earth, they crouched down caringly so that their eyes met ours and we could communicate easily in a seated position.

"Let me explain what brings us together," Sorrano began, brisling his feathers as if searching for what to say first, "and where we are now." He said sweeping his extended wings around the changed grove to the fire pit. "You believe you had a vision James; it was MUCH more. You journeyed back in time thousands of years and while there, participated in a critical moment of unfolding life. The trees in this grove are descendents of 'Little Oak' whom you cared for. See," he said, pointing to a limb broken in the storm, "their heartwood carries the colors of the dawn. I met you in that world as Owl, 'Watch this day, learn, and remember,' do you remember? The sound of my voice reconfirmed your memory's truth. You did watch," he continued, "but what you think you have remembered for only the past few days, has been much, much longer. You learned a deep appreciation for the interconnectedness of all life, which you have borne in your spirit these thousands of years, just as these 'Coyoté Oaks' carry the sunrise and 'Little Oak's' love for it, in theirs.

"Yes James," Sorrano interrupted my mental conjecture about how past and present connected. "There are many mysteries to resolve, but be patient with your questions. You came to the Tall Wood back on an extraordinary morning, the day when The Great Counsel gathered by these stones; though they did not bring you there, they knew you were coming. You found your way traversing the band of light that separates yesterday and tomorrow through your openness during your meditation. A Counsel of Elders exists on every planet but The Great Counsel advises and oversees their development helping to sustain the web of life throughout the cosmos. The Great Counsel sent us to meet the heart that was open enough to find its way here."

"I was Coyoté who met you," Bashira revealed with the same wry smile she gave on the trail. "The Counsel had just finished when you came upon the fire pit," she continued, with an undisclosed esteem sparkling in her emerald eyes. "You did not see them but all the Elders saw your respect for the sacred Circle and your relationship with other life."

"The Circle of Seven Stones around the fire is a powerful place," Sorrano detailed. "It is a Nexus where time, dimensions, and space join. It exists nowhere, yet it leads everywhere. Right here, we are but a step away from anywhere in creation. The stones symbolize seven fundamental qualities that are the building blocks of creation often referred to as: the Seven Rays of Divine energy sent forth to create, the Seven Archangels set before the throne, the Seven Realms of creation, the Seven Chakras of human consciousness, the Seven Bands of color in the rainbow. The names are infinite for The Seven is in all. The Counsel of Elders comes to this Nexus at pivotal moments when creation's life is threatened. Together, they evoke these qualities as needed to restore the balance."

Sorrano extended his wings for a moment as if pausing to stretch, letting us absorb his comments. The story was fantastic, I didn't know if I dared believe it, yet here we sat in my grove, with these amazing beings and an unbounded gateway before us.

"I see a light around you, are you Angels?" Andrea asked breaking the hush, in the innocence of the moment.

"No, we are mortal like you," Bashira said smiling at Andrea, "but like the Angels, we are here as messengers. Your eyes are not playing tricks; you do see an aura around us but there is light in everything including you. Because of your human propensity to focus sharply on what is immediately in front of you, you miss the whole view. Observe softly without judgment."

With a new perspective, I could see the glow; Andrea's was a warm golden with bands of indigo whereas Sorrano emitted pale blue. Bashira's aura contained a soft pink band intertwined with emerald green around her body. How could I have overlooked such ever-present splendor?

"We are messengers," Bashira continued. "Our immediate duty is to obtain your cooperation for the Counsel."

"With all you know, what on earth could we do," I said, baffled that our role could have any importance as Andrea and I looked at each other in doubtful shock.

"You have done more, 'on Earth,' than you know, you've shown your courage, your compassion, and your willingness to consider new ideas," Bashira replied in a consoling voice. "The Counsel will provide all you need."

"Tell us how we can help." Andrea responded enthusiastically.

With her words, the bottom fell out of my stomach. Anxiety replaced the tranquil repose and my mind raced through the past days. I hadn't come to grips with the information they had just provided and now they asked us to cooperate blindly with beings beyond comprehension.

"Wait a minute," I broke in, "Perhaps it is my 'human propensity to focus sharply on what is immediately in front of me,' but I need to know much more."

"As well you should," assured Bashira.

Her eyes projected an understanding that redoubled the comfort of her words. The two looked at each other with a nod of agreement as if my reaction required prudent disclosure. Sorrano determinedly reassumed his crouched position as if preparing to explain an intricate matter.

"Bashira and I are from a planet called Satoria," he began methodically. "After many millennia of positive development, it is now utopian. It was not always that way. Satoria is similar to Earth in many ways but life has different forms there. Higher mental faculties appeared early in our evolution yet unfortunately, wisdom did not. Satoria, all its inhabitants, and even the mineral kingdom, were sentient and self-determinant. Millions of years ago, the life forms on our planet fought for dominance just as they have in Earth's history until the Avans, one species among the many on Satoria, became the ascendant species. We are Avans. In our early years of dominance, we were a greedy species. Not content to live within the natural system that produced us, we sought to control the planet and all its inhabitants ignoring the protests of those who shared the planet with us. Eventually, we no longer heard them at all." He concluded sitting in silence for a moment; his emotion evident.

"The sentient connection between all lives," Bashira commenced in perfect rhythm, "plant to animal, animal to animal, minerals to all of us, broke. Our greed precipitated a complete separation of natural processes. Satoria, and all her life, nearly passed into extinction fated to become a desolate tomb of silent rock whirling in the dark abandons of space." Then sighing she said, "When we finally realized that our negative belief in our superiority had nearly destroyed us, the Great Counsel had to intervene and save Satoria."

"We didn't understand the effect our actions had beyond our world." Sorrano interjected, looking pleased with Bashira's contribution. "We were completely unaware that all things are connected, the stars, the planets, even galaxies are all like beads hanging upon the same fragile veil. When one is affected, it changes the state of the whole and to our shame, the chaos on our planet caused great destruction in worlds far beyond us. As if shattering beads upon the veil," Sorrano said raising his wing skyward and seeking to regain his logical composure, "it literally blew worlds apart that hurdled from orbit and out into space. Some crashed into other planets, including Earth, changing their life course forever. The actions of one group must never cause such a catastrophe again. This is why the Counsel seeks your help, to intervene on Earth before actions here cross a similar event horizon."

"As daunting as this request must seem, it only needs your willingness to begin and if you will help, guidance will follow." Bashira implored, a tear in her eye confirming her sincerity. "Our request is a lot to consider." Bashira said wearily, turning to her mate in the face of our inundation. "Maybe we should answer their questions first." She concluded, waiting patiently for our inquiries but with a story of this magnitude, my questions seemed trivial.

"Well James, I don't think we're in Kansas anymore." Andrea quipped. Nonetheless, we were in Kansas, making this all the more unfathomable. Fortunately, Andrea's lightheartedness allowed time for my questions to surface.

"If you averted further disaster through the Counsels intervention, what is life on Satoria like now? Why then are you so concerned about Earth, and how did you get here, and how...? I asked, the questions now pouring out of me.

"Whoa, one question at a time James," Sorrano exclaimed stopping me. "Let me say a little more. After the catastrophic events of the past, we on Satoria had to listen again. Listen to our fellow Avans, to the other species, and most importantly, to the planet herself. We had to learn that we were not the Creator and adjust our will to the Creator's. We had to trust that everything had a purpose and a destiny of its own with which we were not to interfere. Over time, we advanced our technology making sure it was in harmony with natural forces, and that it furthered the lives of everything it affected." Checking almost naïvely to see if he still had our attention, Sorrano continued. "I know that isn't all that you asked and I don't mean to lecture, but this is important. Our wisdom had to catch-up with our knowledge. Now finally, there is no waste or want, and every Satorian, Avan or other, understands, and respects, the balance of life. It is our responsibility to help Earth, because our past altered the course of development here. We are all interrelated though it is more complicated than I can explain."

"So Avans are large birds like you?" Andrea asked the obvious.

"Not exactly..." Sorrano replied hesitantly seemingly searching for how to answer. "This ties to your questions James. Avans evolved from animals similar to the predecessors of your birds but over time, many adaptations occurred. Avans developed mentally much faster than they did physically and we began to use mental abilities to perform previously physical tasks; for example, we learned to transport ourselves instantaneously by using our thoughts. Since we didn't use our wings, over the thousands of years, they became less prominent. Our appearance here as great birds results from something else, a kind of resonance effect. Have either of you ever heard of formative causation[7] ?" Sorrano asked.

---

7) The theory of formative causation advanced by Ruhpert Sheldrake is that all previous forms of self-organizing systems; e.g., living things and crystalline minerals, tend to invludence, and stabilize, similar present forms across time and space by what he calls the morphic resonance. Thus, the forms tend to stay the same.

"You mean like morphic resonance?" I replied, not fully sure I understood it.

"Well I haven't," Andrea spoke up. "What does it mean?"

"Hum...let me think of a simple...." Sorrano paused brushing his wing across his beak as if seeking an explanation. "Maybe a music analogy will help. When James plays a G string on his guitar, it creates a field of vibration that causes all the G strings in the room, or field to vibrate along with it."

"I'm sorry, I'm not laughing at you," Andrea apologized, blushing red and trying hard to hold in her laughter to Sorrano's complete confusion. "I do understand what you mean. It's that 'G-string' has another meaning in this world and when James played, I try not to think of the G strings vibrating that aren't on guitars."

"I'll stick to our example then," Sorrano said, still bewildered that there was anything funny about his example. "When we travel to Earth, we encounter the resonant fields of forms here. Since we are more like birds than any other life form on Earth now, when we appear on this planet, the resonant field of all the previous bird forms influence the way we materialize."

"What do you mean materialize?" I asked, feigning my intellectual comprehension.

"When we travel using our mind, it is really our energy, or light body, that changes locations." He replied. "It contains all the information needed to recreate a physical body wherever we arrive. What your scientist Sheldrake calls 'morphic resonance,' that is the resonant field of previous birds, influences the shape in which our physical bodies reappear. So, since we are bird-like beings on our planet, we look like birds on Earth." "So, did you travel to Earth through this Nexus using your minds?" I curiously asked.

"No, our mental ability was sufficient for the trip." Bashira returned in response. "Only the Elders use the Nexus because its scope is so vast.... Only the most advanced can accurately navigate to a specific destination. Without real skill and knowledge, one could end up anywhere in space, time, or dimension without much hope of finding a way back. We don't have the insight or acuity to use the Nexus."

"Aren't you part of the Counsel of Elders?" Andrea asked, surprised by their limitation.

"Bashira and I are young and rather inexperienced." Sorrano replied modestly. "You might call us advanced 'work study students,' not wise enough to be part of the Counsel. Through our teacher Malchizadec who escorted us to Earth, the Great Counsel entrusts us with various tasks as we learn," he explained showing his admiration as he then stood up to continue. "It is he who will guide you in this work, though he is currently elsewhere coordinating an impending matter." Sorrano said, punctuating his words with emphasis.

Time had slipped by listening to them unveil their purpose; early morning had turned into late afternoon as we learned intently and they looked tired. If Sorrano and Bashira describe themselves as young, inexperienced, and lacking wisdom, I couldn't imagine what influence Malchizadec would have on our path. That puts me down near an ant larva I thought.

"Ants are highly intelligent creatures you know." Sorrano projected into my noisy mind

"Oops." I bowed with an acknowledgment of my inter-species bigotry.

"Malchizadec is nearly 3,500 years old," he continued, replying to my inquisitive reflection. "He is a shapeshifter who easily changes forms and we are fortunate that he accompanied us. Wise beyond his years, he is an Elder with tremendous power and healing gifts. On Earth, he is what you call a Shaman."

"Our journey isn't through space alone," Bashira continued expanding on his comments. "We also shift from one dimension to another; the iridescent colors you see are a resonant afterglow from its effects. The tension of staying in our light bodies except when contacting you, also adds to our weariness. We need to rejuvenate in physical form for a while and no one must know about us; it could endanger everyone putting our plan at risk. So James, can you give us a secluded shelter?" She concluded, clearly showing their fatigue.

Agreeing that we'd keep silent, they accepted sanctuary in the barn loft, a place that would give them room to move comfortably. Andrea and I looked up as we started to leave at the lush covering lofted above our heads, absorbed in the timeless ambiance that had immersed us in the grove. Walking into the vineyard, I looked back amazed that the grove appeared the same as it always had -- a group of medium sized hedge trees. How the tall cathedral-like canopy that covered the Fire Circle could exist on our property mystified me, but from this day forward, I would call them "Coyoté Oaks."

"What happened with Bashira before you entered the grove? It looked like it was something big." I asked walking towards the barn with Andrea.

"When I looked into Bashira's eyes, I seemed to expand and all separateness vanished." Andrea said, respectfully as the peaceful air returned to her face. "The Monks in India told me about this, they called it *samprajnata samadhi*, but experiencing it is almost indescribable. It was a deep oneness with the trees, the soil, and every creature with no separation, all being... one. A web of energy flowed everywhere like a golden rain and I was a node of vibration connected to every other node on the web, exactly as Sorrano described, like beads hung on a veil.

"The trees call you the 'Friend of the First' you know." Andrea said sharing what she learned from the trees in the grove. "They revere you James and feel honored by your presence. Apparently, your story has an equivalent legend passed through generations of these trees about one human's kindness that saved the first of their kind. Bet you didn't know you're famous in arboreal circles," She said with an amused smile.

The end posts of the trellises caught my eye as we came to the vineyard.

Made of hedge, I chose them for strength and durability but their ruggedly powerful figures, like aged sentinels, stood an extra watch in the vineyard, as if guarding the ends of each row. They were made of "Coyoté Oak" and Andrea's message from the trees made me wonder as we walked on, if my choice might not have come from the ancient bond I now understood between us. Before I knew it, we were climbing the stairs to the hayloft to discover Sorrano already perched high on a rafter near the peak of the ceiling and Bashira on top a stack of bales delightedly gathering loose straw into a nest.

"The Counsel is pleased with your willingness and has planned a Rite of Introduction to honor you both." Sorrano said as his penetrating gold eyes peered down from the roost like an oversized barn owl. "We have also been asked to assist Malchizadec so we would be grateful if we could remain here for the duration of our assignment." He continued, swooping from his roost to land in front of me. "I wasn't sure if I had adequately explained your importance to this work, as they say -- 'You can lead a fish to water but you can't make him drink.' Now if you'll forgive us, we need to regain strength. To help repair the world, we must repair as well. Tomorrow will be a very busy day." He candidly added. Sorrano recited the old platitude without a twitched muscle, or a waver in his piercing glance. I wasn't sure if he had misquoted, or if he was testing my reaction, but either way, he had underscored his point.

The sun was low on the horizon and the humble grove of hedge trees, the Coyoté Oaks, had hosted revelations beyond my imagining. Revelations that augured there was much more to come. I had started this day determined to find answers about my treasured feathers, and the bird that appeared to be their source. Never had I expected what we discovered nor could we fathom the implications revealed. Our evidently inter-dimensional guests' daunting intention to "help repair the world" had our attention. Maybe I was a "fish out of water" but I was hesitant to drink. I had yet to assimilate the path down which we seemingly had been lead. Fully engrossed at the grove by possibilities much greater than ourselves, we had forgotten to eat for the entire day. Though tired and hungry, their unflappable focus on the interdependence of life stayed with us as simultaneously we decided to eat a can of cheese ravioli and avoid the pangs of conscience.

CHAPTER 6
INITIATION

After our "hearty" supper, exhausted from the extraordinary day, we showered and crawled into bed. Tomorrow real life returned as Mason and Jake would be back to help and I had no idea what to tell them about this weekend. Living in these disparate realities, we speculated about so much that the Avans told us, Malchizadec, The Counsel, and what a Rite of Introduction meant. I needed rest but my mind wandered the vaulted cathedral canopy of the grove, and I drifted to sleep intrigued by the adventure that dubbed me "Friend of the First" by the Coyoté Oaks.

A blue-silver ribbon of light draped across the sky. In contrast to the vision on the hill, it engulfed the horizons, swirling freely beyond all distinction of yesterday from tomorrow and eliminated it. Both time and space were permeable while side-by-side Andrea and I lucidly watched as if we were two points of awareness looking upon infinite moment. Whether insight, or illusion, we beheld this vision together. White-gold spherules of light, like a pensile golden shower that neither dropped nor dispersed, glistened across the expanse. At each coupling of these lumens, silver and gold, they purled unfettered until unfolding from the tumult appeared a faint flicker of form. Side by side Andrea and I watched and wondered as eddies ebbed and flowed, congealed and coalesced. Whichever the scale, microcosmic or empyrean, side by side we sat witness on the border of formlessness and creation.

Before us, an omniparient artist shaped an impalpable lace, woven with cavity and cord. Each knot that joined the weave, as Sorrano described, held a beaded jewel in which we could see the reflections of every other jewel. The fabric, spun of light, was in every way interconnected and beautiful beyond description. Recognizable shapes appeared where the weave became dense, until within the adjoined brocade, we saw the landscape of life. Hills and valleys, rocks and trees and every kind of living creature unfolded from the ethereal veil. Amid this unfolded panorama, Andrea and I stood hand in hand near the ridgeline of a dense jungle where the sound of drums resonated from deep within the trees and echoed off the rock bluff across the river below.

The compelling rhythm invited us forward on the narrow trail. Pushing back the lush undergrowth as we walked, the warm moist air dripped the fragrance of moss and blossoms. A gentle breeze rustled high in the branches, where large beaked toucans glided precisely through vine-tangled treetops like missiles guided to their mark. How easily they flew. Every plant and animal joined the lively orchestra, each performer one of nature's virtuosos playing at fortissimo. Hand in hand, we moved through the pulsating umbrage to the constant throbbing of the drums.

The touch of Andrea's hand was different; it registered as my own. The fabric spun of light enfolded and interconnected us with everything we witnessed, including each other. When one of us touched a leaf, tree, or insect, we both merged with its awareness feeling the sum and substance, the quintessence, of each encounter assimilating it into an expanding mindfulness. "I am that. That am I. I am THAT I am." The words murmured in my head and for the first time, I understood them. Elation swelled and a river of compassion flowed from our common heart to every crevasse of creation. Our heart, one heart found in many, clocked a timeless cadence, the unbounded love of the Creator for creation.

Treads upon the trail had changed. Knowing completely the tiny lives beneath each footfall, we strode conscious that our crossing affected every worm and wort, mite and microbe within the sodden soil that cushioned our step. Aware of the lives in balance, we set each footstep gently, with resolute intention to bless each being that granted this passage. As if impressing a royal seal to wax upon a letter, we marked our course imprinting gratitude and adoration upon the hallowed ground. Amidst this gait, we sensed a tacit presence, enfolding the others but muted by the strain of grievous sorrow. Whatever the source of this apprehensive consciousness, it engulfed us. Yard by yard Andrea and I trudged forward crushed by the weight of this being's suffering, the anguish of enormous proportions that swept through us. What was the source of this pain? The feelings came from everywhere as elation turned to sorrow. Unable to take another step, we yielded to our fear, loss, and worry, crumbling to the ground to weep.

Slumped in submission, my mother came to my mind and I remembered the last minutes of her life. She had been unconscious before her death lying in bed day after day as her body slowly eroded and betrayed the verve she once possessed. Before passing, her spirit awakened. As if to check on, and ensure the well-being of those she loved, with her last ounce of strength she allowed us time to say good-bye. My mother's passing was peaceful, the completion of a life well lived, these feelings felt premature, as if a death was immanent but this life was unfinished. Then I understood that the alarm flowing through us was a mother's fear that her last efforts for her offspring would fail. A mother who knew that her demise would cause the death of all she loved.

"A mother is dying." Andrea said, rupturing my introspection, "We have to try to help. I can't stand feeling her pain."

We looked in the undergrowth surrounding us for the suffering organism certain this creature must be very large to match the magnitude of our emotions. On hands and knees through the underbrush, we crawled with the hope we could allay this pain, stopping only to listen to the cry for help that compelled us towards the misery. Through thickets and briars we searched, nowhere could we find the ill-fated source of distress. Our helplessness mirrored the being's struggle, its burden of sorrow and excruciate sensations inundated us until the shadows fell upon our spirits and dusk had crept across the land.

"Where are we James?" Andrea asked, "What is this place?"

"I don't know," I answered remorsefully, "but we should go up to the ridge and take a look while there is still light," I added, guessing the broader view might show our way.

A rock knoll jutted up above the trees from the side of the saddle and from there we could see the horizon in every direction. Lush rainforest extended across the rolling hills as far as we could see and we rested as the sun's golden orb nestled towards the Earth's edge. As the sun slipped downward, perhaps in our fatigue, we felt as if we melted into the soil beneath us. We no longer sat upon the Earth but merged into the globe as if we were the eyes of the planet looking out upon the sky. To our surprise, we felt movement. We joined the planet's rotation, rolling slowly as if over on our backs with the sun sinking beneath our belly, we glided effortlessly in orbit around the shining sphere. The vast distances of space shrank as we danced in relationship with our celestial neighbors. The sun, the Moon, and Venus were all next-door it seemed. The myriad of bright stars and galaxies were nearby villages. At home in our solar system, the fabric of light, the *prima materia*, interconnected us with every element of the celestial vision.

How could everything interrelate so seamlessly and we mortals be so unable to grasp it? Perhaps it was as Bashira said, we see only on what's immediately in front of us, which makes us feel separate, alone in the world and lost in the universe. Out of this core of loneliness comes our fear, and from fear, the justification to lash out, to protect ourselves, which in the end only solidifies our solitude. Ending up alone, we rationalize that fear is our just and true companion. If others only could experience this I thought, what change it would make, oh what a different world it would be.

As quickly as I discerned it, the view from the ridge shifted. The verdant unscathed forest dispersed and in its stead, we saw a pestilent panorama, a land torn as if it were under attack. Huge regions of the forest were burning with plumes of smoke trailing skyward. Deep craters gouged the rolling hills. Open pits and strip mines looked like giant cankers oozing yellowish bogs of pus in their bottoms. Everywhere, a cloak of chaos sprawled across the earth, its malignant mayhem putrefying the air and water with the stench of chemicals and death. This was the dying presence we sensed, *Gaia*, Mother Earth, the living sentience of our planet. The feelings of a sentient planet were unsettling; we could assimilate the experiences of animals and plants. Perhaps like the Avans, we carried the illusion of human superiority and accommodated "lesser" forms with our human centeredness. In contrast to a living presence of planetary proportion, we were the tiny lives mere microbes by comparison. This sentient planet may be aware of our thoughts and feelings just as we discerned those of smaller beings but to us, planetary consciousness was too big, too expansive to comprehend in return. We could only recognize its sorrow. "What do you want us to understand?" I shouted out in frustration and a swirl of light responded, quickly taking the shape of a woman dressed in a long flowing gown. Her beauty cloaked behind her sadness, she looked directly at us with a laden smile.

"Thank you for caring." The woman said. "For eons, I have born life in my womb, nurturing it at my breast as the treasure of my being, but my children have forgotten."

"Are you a Goddess?" I asked naively, lost in her receptive, unwavering presence.

"I am to be loved, not worshipped." The woman smiled and said. "Some call me the Queen of the Forest, but I am greater than the forests, a living system created by the same hand that created you. I am *Gaia*, the Soul of the Earth in which everything on this planet lives, and has its being. Just as your bodies are cells and organs, I am atoms and ants, molecules and mushrooms, plants and animals; all are a part of my body, including you. I am the air you breathe and more than the sum of all you see. There is much to tell but you must hurry for others await you." She concluded and with that, she faded.

Andrea was speechless, her face revealing the encounter's affect. I took her hand and we started down from the rock knoll looking around for the others that the Earth Soul told us were waiting. I saw no one. The scarred landscape at our backs, we started towards the trail. The shadows were long, covering the valley below with the blanket of twilight and the evening breeze grew cool. As we reached the trail, I heard the drums in the distance beckoning us towards the dense forest and shelter.

Knowing that darkness was rapidly surrounding us, we hurried silently along the trail, walking in the rhythm and direction of the drums. They were loud; their deep crisp thunder smacked against the escarpment above us, ricocheting in the loose bark that vibrated on the trees beside the trail. It seemed we should find them soon. Night animals were waking in the twilight as the fearsome sound of predators replaced the unitive voices. Our footsteps hastened but wandering worried and exposed, we were prey.

"Where are we James?" Andrea stopped abruptly and emphatically asked. "Is this a dream, or what is happening? We don't know where we are, or how we got here. I'm getting really frightened."

Not knowing what to say, I began to answer when a panther leapt from the underbrush with unworldly speed and bounded past me. I shifted to protect her, but the predacious black marauder dragged Andrea into the thicket instantaneously, as if the shadows themselves had swallowed her. I could do nothing. All I could hear was her screaming and then silence, swift, cold, deadly silence.

"Andrea," I yelled at the top of my voice. "Andrea," I screamed my voice cracking as I charged into the bushes where the panther vanished.

Silence, I heard only silence. Then strewn across a small clearing in the brush, I saw bones, human bones, Andrea's bones. Their flesh stripped clean, they looked like chalk marks scattered on an ebony canvas without a trace of her, or the jungle cat. Only naked bones remained, seasoned by the pungent horror that she was gone. Stunned and trembling uncontrollably, I wandered alone in the blackness when a great crush slammed me to the ground and I felt sharp claws tear into my shoulder. Intent to fight the panther with my last bit of rage, I fought to roll over but when I managed to turn my head upward, I saw a huge eagle with outstretched wings above its quarry, its talons lancing my shoulder to the ground. I swung my arms to free myself but it plunged its beak into my torso, ripping my heart from my chest and I was a helpless prisoner to this fate. Is this what I am to understand? I pleaded, as a faint glimmer hovered around me.

"I have been forgotten," *Gaia* gently whispered, "kept in dark slumber by ignorance and greed until my death is nigh. You have watched creation's veil unfold from the formless and learned the heart of many lives. With my last strength, I awaken, not to save myself, but to save those who live within me. Love among my children brings balance. Forgiveness invokes the nourishing rains of Spirit. Understanding restores life. Invite hope, for I am the ground beneath the firmament and all the lives between; in my demise will be your own. Remember these words of a crying planet." Then there was only blackness, obsidional blackness, and death....

"Huh! Huh! Huh! Open your eyes! James, Andrea, open your eyes. Huh! Huh! Huh!" an unfamiliar guttural voice repeated.

I felt groggy, as if my eyelids were made of lead but vaguely I saw a gathering of people around a fire and sat up grabbing my chest with a jolt. Dancing around the fire was a man dressed like a bird, an image that was disconcerting. Startling me further, a hand reached around my waist, it was Andrea awakening to the scene, and both of us were unscathed.

When I started to speak Andrea pressed her finger over my lips and pointed at seven stones that encircled the fire; we expected Sorrano and Bashira but they were not there. Mesmerized by the overpowering rhythm of the drums, we watched a figure dance by the fire who appeared to be a Shaman garbed in a temiak, an Eskimo coat made of bird skins. Flamboyantly dressed, his face camouflaged with a feathered mask, he wore a plume-like headdress atop his head. Bells and metal pieces jangled furiously around his waist in tempo with his strides and two large black talons curled down over his feet scratching the dirt hypnotically as he danced.

"Ummm, put you back together pretty good," a voice boomed towards me as the dancing ceased and the drums fell instantly mute.

"Emm, put you back together...pretty!" The voice behind the mask continued, this time directed at Andrea.

The strange birdman bent down in front of Andrea and peered into her eyes as if he were looking through a knothole in a fence. Then he stepped over to me, stuck his beak to my nose and gawked iris-to-iris. I could feel his glance move inside me as if he were scanning my cellular structure, as if he were scanning my soul.

"Good, good, good, ready now! Rites of Introduction complete," he said with a squawk, flapping his wings once over both of us.

Returning to the fire, the Shaman threw something in the flames creating a puff of smoke and continued his ceremonial dance. The drumbeat resounded with his first step as if created by the impact of his foot upon the earth. With thundering tread, he circled the fire three times and then turned again to the flames reaching into his pouch and pulling out a small packet of herbs; he lifted his hands to the sky and with his deep guttural voice chanted a prayer in his native language. In a dramatic swing, he hurled the prayer bundle into the fire causing a swirling column of smoke to shoot skyward and with startling speed, it towered beyond our sight. As if the smoke collided with, and cracked the edge of space, streaks of light streamed outward. Seven distinct color beams shot forth from the point of impact like lightning stretching across the dome of night to form a giant starburst. Where the strands joined, there was brilliant white light and for several seconds the heptagonal pinwheel spun above us. Just as quickly, it contracted into the swirl of smoke, descended toward us to the fire, and the column disappeared.

The fire illuminated the seven stones that each held two representatives. We rested on the ground between the stone circle and the fire pit; beyond the stones were several more circles of people where the bird-like Shaman, deferring his authority, took a seat. Each face throughout the group, from more cultures then I could recognize, held the idealism of youth etched within the wisdom of the ages. Past the outermost circle, a strange figure stood in the shadows of the forest that appeared like a bird taking a human form. It was the same figure I saw in the jungle vision after the Tall Wood; almost the reverse of the Shaman, its stance was similar to Sorrano's but taller and with a human countenance. A faint aura of light surrounded the tall figure giving it a beautiful lavender luminescence, which caused me to wonder if it might be Malchizadec.

"James Davidson. Andrea Davidson. Come forward! Do you accept your places?" a booming colonial voice questioned.

Addressing us from across the fire was a tall ebony-black man with the regal carriage of a king dressed in a leopard skin loincloth and pounding the ground with a long staff as the beadwork draped around his neck shimmered in the firelight. Andrea and I clambered to our feet and staidly walked to the center by the fire.

"I am Navu, Zulu Chieftain, and Elder member of this Counsel," he said, his deep baritone voice filled with confidence. "This is Earth's Counsel of Elders, one among many across the stars," he continued waving his staff slowly in a circle above the crowd. "Your Spirit animals put you together well. Do you know of your Spirits' work?" he asked, the clarity of his diction clashing with his primitive appearance. "Andrea, James, you have both undergone what some call 'Shamanic Initiation.'

"Each person gathered here is like you," he began with a sweeping gesture, his long arms moving outward to include the crowd and then drew them to his torso. "They have found, and experienced, the mystical core of their beliefs," he continued, his eyes reflecting the firelight as if the glisten came from deep within him. "The Creator left many doorways, every door is narrow, but no matter the faith or tradition, once we step inside, the Presence that sustains us is the same. You two have come through the doorway many times; now it is time to bring what you have received back into the world. Your initiation today, harsh as it may seem, was a healing. Simply explained, the Spirit animals must destroy you and tear all frailty from your body, mind, and spirit, to rebuild you without the wounds of your past.

"Andrea," he said gently turning his cavernous brown eyes to her. "You are a flower cut before its bud burst into the sun. You did much to restore your health and beauty, but much pain remains in your core and regret permeates your aspiration. It drives your healthy idealism and desire into perfectionism. Those burdens are now gone," he concluded with a flourish.

"James, your sorrow is more subtle," he whispered in a low voice placing his hand on my shoulder. "You longed for the creative life you once lived. Its absence hung stones upon your heart and dimmed the color of your life.

71

The spirits have tuned the music in your soul for a new audience that even now gathers unknown to you. Life is about to confront you both at full throttle and your complete healing was necessary to endure it.

"Welcome to this counsel, we will have much work to do." Navu said with a grand bow and pointed with his staff to a place next to the Shaman.

Andrea and I seemed to know how to join in the common spirit around the circle, uniting in meditative prayer. Where my meditation experiences stilled my mind, this was different, active, intensely focused, and noisy. It reminded me of being in a beehive; I could hear the thoughts, and heartbeats, of everyone present. After the first few minutes, the heartbeats fell into a common rhythm and the thoughts sounded in clear tones that came into unison and then gradually widened into one harmonious chord. The resonance started within our group and expanded until I could hear the voices of all the lives around us. Every creature bestowed its voice and essence, to the healing work of restoring balance and life to the crying planet.

Time didn't exist as we all joined in the eternal moment. My eyes closed, I listened intently to the reverberation flowing through me, content to remain in this state forever. Once I opened them again, I was astounded to see a dome of pale violet light enveloping several acres around us. The luminescence was viscous, tangibly circulating down from the dome's apex to the fire pit then out towards its circumference. The sinuous current moved through me, revitalizing every cell in my body continuing to build in speed and turbulence until it seemed to quiver like a pot just ready to boil. Navu arose from his stone, moving with great determination to the movement's center and then extending his staff into the core; he raised his other arm.

"From the point of life within the heart of the Creator,
let life stream forth anew into the hearts of all.
Let life expand upon the Earth."

He eloquently proclaimed. The brilliant substance shot out with the utterance of his last word spreading from horizon to horizon, enveloping every tree, stone and sentience with gleaming vitality. The aurora lingered, fading slowly like a sunset, until we settled in total darkness.

Andrea threw her arm across my chest and pulled herself close. We were lying in our bed again; neither of us said a word knowing our thoughts were the same. Initiations are not accolades doled out to mark achievement; they are the beginning of hard work to come. We needed the comfort, grounding, and stability of each other's embrace but instead, a cacophony of moans, wails, and screeches suddenly pierced our serenity.

Something has attacked Sorrano and Bashira I thought. It was 5:30 A.M.

Bolting from bed, we ran feverishly to the barn. The sulfuric stench of heavy crude assailed my nostrils as I swung back the double doors in the pre-dawn darkness and though I couldn't see, I could hear the clamor and commotion inside; the frenzy was out of place. The foul odor grew stronger and things smelled rotten in Kansas. Entering the barn, I made my way carefully along the wall trying not to step on the riotous source of unknown squalor. Initiations foster expectations, some placed upon you, and some of your own choosing. Whether they lead to distinction or disgrace remains a choice. Shuffling in the noisy darkness, I found a light switch near the horse stall and with one small flick of the toggle; I got one giant surprise. This initiation was only the beginning.

CHAPTER 7
THE BARN

Oil soaked, injured, and burned sea creatures of all sorts covered the barn floor. There were ducks and seagulls, pelicans and sharks, jellyfish, octopi, nudibranchs, seals and dolphins. More mysterious than how they got there was how the many of these sea dwelling creatures were able to survive on a dirt barn floor. I went up the steps climbing into the hay-loft certain Sorrano must have something to do with this and as my head poked up through the floor of the loft, a wet fin flopped across my face accompanied by a loud grumbling roar. Disturbed by my sudden intrusion, a sea lion ambled over to a nearby straw bale amidst a marine menagerie that sprawled across the loft floor continuing to voice his opinion along the way.

I climbed on through the loft door to see Bashira shifting quickly from animal to animal, bending down compassionately over each one, and moving her wing down its length. As her wings passed, the oil seemed to wash off and soak into the loose straw; she did this with one creature after the next. Once free from the black ooze, the soiled animals vanished. Those with serious burns and injuries seemed invigorated by the cleaning, but remained in the barn's cacophonous collage. Bashira's careful inspection, reminded me of a nurse performing triage at a disaster scene.

"Yes James, that's exactly what I'm doing." Bashira said as she turned to me. "Can you help me here?" she asked. "This straw is becoming saturated. Can you spread some fresh for me?"

"How are these animals able to survive here?" I asked, noting their aquatic acclimation as I went to the stack in the corner of the loft, rolled down a few bales pulling off the twine, and spread a layer of straw where she requested.

"We're bringing these animals' essences or light bodies here, the same way we travel and then reconstitute our physical form." Bashira explained. "Once revitalized, they return to their natural environment where their essence recreates a physical body without injuries. It's sort of healing at the sub-quantum level. The light body doesn't need physical water while it's here because it is pure energy."

Having only a vague grasp of the advanced science she explained, I returned for another bale remembering Sorrano saying he could 'lead a fish to water but couldn't make it drink.' Whether I was the fish or the water to which he referred, from the current goings on in the barn, they clearly could lead a fish anywhere with or without water. When I pulled the bale down, it opened a pocket-sized room built within the stack. I assumed one of our friend's kids created the fort just as I used to build such strongholds in the hayloft of my cousin's farm. Then a small, dark haired, head emerged from the shadowy hollow shattering my nostalgia. Cowered in the straw portal was a traumatized, shivering, oriental girl, whose petite form cloaked whether she was woman or child in the dim light. I moved towards her not thinking that my sudden advance would frighten and cause her to blench back into the dark hole. Andrea by this time was climbing into the loft with a dismayed look but fortunately, she had the foresight to bring a flashlight; motioning her to come over I stepped up the stack of bales and spoke reassuringly into the portal to pursue the girl's puzzling presence.

"Who are you talking to?" Andrea asked.

"Shine your flashlight in here," I said, directing her to the entry as I cautiously leaned into the cavity.

The girl crouched in the back of the straw fort huddled next to an old oriental man with slate gray hair, crystalline blue eyes, and an incisive smile. My jaw dropped open, with the flashlight I could clearly see the face of the same girl I'd spoken to on the ship in that horrible dream. She was the one explaining their plight in the hold of that dilapidated freighter and the old fellow had hungrily asked me for food.

"Is California?" the young woman asked, timidly looking up at me.

"No, I'm afraid you've missed it by about 1,600 miles." I smiled and said moving a couple of bales away to make their exit easier. "My name is James." I continued as I stretched out my arm to help the old traveler. "This isn't California, but you're safe now. Please come let us get you warmed up. This time I bring food."

Together, Andrea and I helped the two refugees out of the haystack and over to the ladder down from the loft. Bashira gave a knowing nod and continued her remedial care as I slipped down the ladder first to steady the beleaguered pair when they descended. The man came first; about half-way down, he lost his grip and fell backwards plopping tangible proof that this was something other than a dream right into my arms. This was real. He was skin and bones; I could feel each rib sticking out with empty hollows between them as if they were notches carved in an alabaster statue. Though he was weak from hunger, his muscles remained firm exposing a life of hard physical labor. I moved him near a stall fence where he could brace himself while the girl came down the steps. She descended taking care not to fall herself until I helped her the last distance. Again, her body was drawn and weak. Andrea bounded down the steps and I realized how much we took our health and strength for granted; it was so different to see someone struggle with simple tasks and in that moment, I was grateful.

"This way," I beckoned, taking the patriarch gently by the arm, when Andrea and the girl came along side, we walked slowly across the yard.

"My name is James," I repeated, "and this is my wife Andrea. What are your names?"

"I Ch'ien Li, this Grandfather, Hahn," the girl replied in understandable, though broken English.

"You must be hungry. When did you eat last?" Andrea asked, seeing their frail steps.

Grandfather Hahn didn't seem to speak English and conversed with her in Chinese as we carefully guided them up the steps of the porch, and into the house. Ch'ien Li didn't know but thought they had been at sea for at least a week without food. I pulled the chairs out for Ch'ien Li and Hahn, a courtesy to which they visibly were not accustomed, seating them at the kitchen table while Andrea started to prepare a meal putting a pot on the stove and heating some miso soup, a rich soy broth, to which she added a couple of eggs as it boiled. I found a few blankets to wrap around our chilly guests, put on a kettle of water, and prepared us all a hot cup of green tea.

"We better start you with something light that won't upset your stomach," I told Ch'ien Li who was engrossed with every nuance of the kitchen.

I remember how helpless that heartbreaking dream felt when I heard the people on the ship say they were coming to San Francisco. It was their journey of hope, one for which they gave everything they had, and much of their future as each émigré would work off remaining debt once in America. Their smugglers falsely promised them safe passage, proper documentation, and a job when they arrived but their gaunt presence, confirmed all my uneasiness. I tried not to let my face reveal my doubts, for the flame of hope burned in their eyes even with all they had endured; I was not going to extinguish it. Thinking to myself that they were lucky not to have reached San Francisco and their patrons, I asked how they ended up in my barn.

"Not know," Ch'ien Li said, attempting to describe the inexplicable. "We on ship, then floating in sea. We in ship's hold can't see nothing. It night, ocean very rough and we hear metal scream. The ship turn over, we pushed deep below surface like that," she said snapping her fingers. "We tumble and thrown about for...." Ch'ien Li paused struggling for words in English to express her emotions. "Grandfather hold my hand, know I very afraid. Grandfather and I way under water; very cold and black. We feel bubbles rise around us, know must swim up, follow bubbles. Took long time come surface, lungs hurt very bad. Arms and legs burn, start go numb in cold wet darkness. Grandfather find piece of crate floating on ocean surface, we struggle and pull ourselves up on it. Nobody else from ship make it, nobody! We alone on ocean, oil all around, oil, fuel, and…. I must pass out. The next thing, wake up in pile of straw. Not know how."

Hahn took a slow sip of his tea and set the cup carefully back on the table before he turned to Ch'ien Li and spoke emphatically in Chinese.

"See light, like sunrise, see light first," Hahn announced, surprisingly in English.

"Grandfather say he awake after I pass out," Ch'ien Li continued translating his full account. "He grow weak and about to collapse when a pale light …how you say… color of plums surround us. Same light in barn. He say Light of Heaven bring us here." She said as her Grandfather said something more, causing her to blush as she translated.

"Same light come on night I born. Mother die having me, I survive. Grandfather say light save me and name me Ch'ien Li, means…'Heaven's Light,' as thanks."

The rich aroma of the miso filled the kitchen perceptibly wetting the appetites, and anticipation of our Chinese guests. Andrea placed a large tureen of soup on the table, filling small bowls in front of Hahn and Ch'ien Li, and recalling a modicum of her Mandarin lexis, invited them to eat. It seemed with each spoonful strength flowed back into their bodies and vitality returned to their faces. Through Ch'ien Li's translation, Hahn explained that they originated from the Junggar Pendi region of Xinjiang Province, an arid flat plateau in the far northwestern area of China near the borders of Kazakhstan, Russia, and Mongolia. Both seemed delighted that we were interested in them personally and I was curious how they had come from the inner reaches of China. I was certain it was an interesting story but this wasn't the first morning mystery; the mélange in the barn still baffled me and Bashira needed me in the loft.

One-step away from the table, Lorenzo shot from beneath my descending foot with a squeal that knocked me off balance onto the floor. Moving directly to the door, the indignant little gremlin reminded me that I had forgotten my attendant's duty in the excitement as I picked myself up to the grins of everyone seated at the table.

"Lorenzo, you're in for another surprise if you go to the barn," I said as we exited, but after that incident, he wanted no part of me sauntering instead around the corner of the house.

"Good morning James, would you mind moving the tractor and trailer out of here?" Sorrano asked, as I entered the barn's meandering milieu of aquatic visitors.

I found the marine multitudes had changed and both Avans were on the ground floor tending to a group of dolphins that looked as if they were crushed between the ships hulls. Following his request, I crawled up on the old John Deere still parked in place since the auction, and moseyed it onto the yard. Immediately upon my return, Sorrano cautioned me out of the way and a great luminance started to fill the area where the tractor had been. Within a few seconds, a humpback whale filled the entire back half of the barn. The light even suspended the whale as it had all the other creatures. There was a crackling sound like one hears from electrical lines on a moist night as another luminance began to appear closer to us.

The crackle became very intense resonating so loudly that the tools hanging on the wall begin to rattle until the amorphous lumination finally took shape. It was another great bird but taller in stature and emanating a lavender luminescence like that filling the barn. He seemed familiar and I realized he was the bird-like man in the shadows at the edge of the jungle circle. To this point, I had been living in two separate worlds; the "Dreamtime" that took place in the far reaches of some spirit world or, perhaps my imagination, and my daily life complete with Andrea, Lorenzo, and a computer. Suddenly Hahn, Ch'ien Li, and now this Avan, had all hurdled from one world into the other. Andrea and I walked both worlds together, but now we stood where worlds collided, and they were colliding in Kansas.

"James, this is Malchizadec our teacher," Sorrano said confirming the arrival of the new Avan.

Malchizadec gazed at me intently for a moment; his eyes were like two deep amethyst jewels, his coloring much more vivid. Then, nodding his head slightly in acknowledgment, he went straight to the whale. Gouges and gashes stretched along the sides and across the head of the grand leviathan. Dark sticky oil covered its entire body as it gasped for breath. Moving from the head, Malchizadec came down to a long gash on the whale's side, the light seeming to concentrate from the tip of his wings as he waved them slowly above the wound. I could see the flesh growing and mending the huge cut before my eyes; for some time, the Avan medical technicians scurried around the whale sealing every wound and regenerating the tissue. The great beast revived. Its breathing became slow and regular, its long torpedo-like body seemed to relax and extend as if gliding through the corporeal light medium that suspended it until the luminance around it began to fade and as it did, the whale disappeared.

Calm returned to the barn and I noticed the sun was up; dust particles stirred by the commotion, danced in the horizontal light that streamed through the gaps in the east wall. Animals appeared in waves, received treatment, then vanished again in the flashes of lavender light, and no one had spoken a word for hours. Sorrano and Bashira looked exhausted but not Malchizadec, if anything, the flow of light left him stronger.

"I know the speed with which things have unfolded in the past few days hasn't given you time to comprehend them." Sorrano said breaking the silence and apologizing for the rapid series of events. "You have done well James. I prepared you as best I could but many things are about to occur through which Malchizadec must guide us all." Sorrano concluded, extending his wing towards Malchizadec.

The deep royal purple feathers on the crown of Malchizadec's head flashed as they caught the strands of sunlight. His jewel-like eyes exuded the poise of a hardened warrior, tempered by the wisdom of more seasons than I could imagine. With a confident gait, he took a few steps towards us and stopped. The light around him intensified, his torso and wings drew shorter as his legs extended; the immense raptor's head shifted and its beak transformed into a nose. His height diminished by a couple of feet until standing before me was the gangly Shaman of the Tall Wood. With my own eyes, I saw a bird shape shift into a man who I now recognized in both his forms.

Andrea had returned to witness the metamorphosis and was standing agape near the door. Lorenzo had also found his way to the barn but unlike his first fearful encounter with Sorrano, he had tuned in on the present magic. Lorenzo was floating on his back a few inches off the ground suspended in the healing light just like the other animals, his legs extended in unruffled repose and I could hear him purring all the way across the barn. He was a cool cat taking leave in kitty heaven.

The bird turned man, motioned us to come sit with him. The three of us moved to a couple of bales lying at the end of an empty horse stall and sat down, when I heard the crunching brattle of tires on the driveway gravel. I had completely forgotten it was Monday morning; Mason and Jake were coming to work!

"It will be fine," Malchizadec interrupted raising his hand to halt me as I started to speak. "Inform your friends of what's going on, like you believe it, before they walk in and see it for themselves."

How could I possibly tell Mason? I went out the barn door perplexed and headed for the encounter anticipating his predictable cynicism. Though Mason was a good-hearted person, the wounded soldier in him was still wary of any new ideas. He scoffed at anything with the slightest hint of the paranormal. I didn't know if he had ever pronounced the word paranormal or even if the current events were, but they were certainly mysteries, and far from normal. How would I introduce the subject to a true unbeliever? I rounded the corner at the back of the barn to discover Jake pinned against the wall by an angry sea lion barking furiously at him.

Mason was running across the yard with his rifle ready to blast the beast in full battle mode. I quickly stepped in between Mason and the sea lion to block his shot. Hoping that one of the birds happened to be listening to my thoughts I said, "I'm going to need a little help here," in my head.

I focused on what I thought were the light bodies of Jake and the sea lion, and passed my hands across the bellowing beast as the Avans had. The sea lion calmed down immediately and "woggled" back towards the barn door. Mason charged up fully agitated, I stretched out my arms and passed my hands down in front of him, he relaxed too dropping the gun back down to his side. Jake, who had nearly pressed himself into two-dimensional form against the barn wall during the sea lion's engagement, watched my passes, the retreating beast, and his father's de-escalation with bemused reservation.

"What...? A sea lion? What was that?" He expressed emphatically stepping away from the barn wall and back into three-dimension relief.

"You mean the sea lion?" I asked in return, hoping he had overlooked my childlike attempt at wizardry.

"No," he retorted, "what you did! What did YOU DO to the sea lion, and Dad?"

"Let's go to the workshop," I said walking that direction, "there are a few...." This is going well I thought. I'm up to my neck before I've even begun.

"What's our mission for the day Chief?" Mason inquired, plopping down on the couch with his usual ease but the look on his face was anything but customary. We all knew the day was different; it was my job to tell them how different it was going to be.

"Your mission, should you choose to accept it," I replied jokingly, hoping the mission wasn't impossible, "Is not to shoot anything today, not birds, badgers, or even a beluga whale." That drew a perplexed look. "Remember that feather I showed you last week?" I asked, noticing their nod of agreement. "Well, I found the bird it came from, or maybe I should say the bird found me. I think you might need a few explanations before you see the rest of what today might serve up, a few things have changed around here."

Without stopping for questions, I attempted to summarize the inexplicable dreams and weekend experiences but I could see Mason's bullshit button was about to go off.

"I know..." I countered. "You'll see, they're here, in the barn, now."

The questions were coming fast and furious at this point until Lorenzo pushed open the door, walked across the room looking exceptionally unflappable and jumped up in Mason's lap, which calmed the inquiry until Andrea also appeared through the doorway.

"So, are you going to try to convince me of all this hokem pokem too, Beautiful?" Mason asked Andrea suspiciously.

"Believe it or not, Mace, it's really true. Unfortunately, I've got a class to teach in twenty minutes and have to go," she said, giving me a glance to acknowledge that I had my hands full.

Andrea had forgotten it was Monday too, I could only wish her luck with her duties as she headed out for her workday "reality." Real life was closing in. I wasn't sure how well we would do merging our mortal mundanity with these miraculous musterings when I noticed my freshly illuminated feline sit up and stare at the door.

"Holy sh..." Jake let out, as Mason's face went pale and his laid-back sprawl snapped to sudden attention.

"Good morning Mason, Jake," Malchizadec said, stooping over as he came through the door into the workshop.

Malchizadec's human form was smaller than his Avan body, yet he still stood a good six inches above the doorframe. Unlike the feathered cape I had seen before, he had on a long *dashiki* with a colorful African print remaining barefoot as he stooped through the door. I could see a resemblance to the great bird in his long face, which was more sagacious than

84

handsome, but most noticeably, his eyes remained violet exuding absolute command and confidence. Mason and Jake politely nodded with ashen faced astonishment, and remained speechless.

"There will be more animals and we're going to need straw. Do you have any more James?" Malchizadec asked frankly, ignoring his flabbergasted audience.

"We have quite a stack left out in the vineyard don't we?" I asked looking at Mason. "Why don't you two haul that up to the barn? We'll probably need to buy more from the neighbors." They agreed, still staring at Malchizadec as they left like they had bumped into a movie star.

"I want to give you a better understanding." Malchizadec began, as he sat down where Mason generally landed.

Despite his diminished size in human form, the sofa looked like it belonged in a child's playhouse beneath him. Even more striking in dialogue, was the depth of his acuity, it was clear that he knew everything about me, and what brought us together. His authority engulfed the workshop lending credence to the thus far mysterious "project."

"What you and Andrea each experienced as a frightening dream a few nights ago," he continued, "was a real event. The only way to show you the degree of suffering and pain in this world was to have you actually experience it. You were on that freighter when it sank. The freighter, used for smuggling, was fully loaded with thousands of barrels of crude oil when the tanker overran it; everything, including the human cargo spilled into the ocean. All the people on board drowned except for Ch'ien Li and Hahn. The injured animals we are treating are the ones we could save from the environmental emergency the wreck created. The tragic result of greed on a grand scale."

"How could anybody be so irresponsible?" I said, trying to control a growing twinge of anger as I realized it was no accident.

"It was not irresponsible," Malchizadec replied. "It was a choice. A choice based on the lust for power. A company by the name of Oil Resources and Transportation Incorporated owns both ships leasing the freighter, and other dilapidated ships to third parties that carry all manner of illicit goods including human slaves. This also allows them to hide assets for the personal profit of corrupt corporate officers."

"ORTI, I'm familiar with them!" I interrupted, as my anger surged. "That bastard! People like Mallory need to be stopped by any means. They are enemies of humanity." I fired off stopping my tirade when Malchizadec raised his hand abruptly.

"There is no enemy! There are only those who do not understand!" Malchizadec said looking me straight in the eye with chilling resolve.

I went silent. How could a company like this, not be an enemy since they put no value on anything, not human life, not our environment, not even the life of the planet? Malchizadec, seeing my consternation, clarified that the reckless incident was common practice with firms operating around the globe where profit is the only motive to satisfy their shareholders. In this case, when the freighter became a liability, they simply arranged the accident far out in the darkened silence of the open sea.

"But what about Mallory, he controls the company. He's responsible." I insisted.

"There is no enemy." Malchizadec replied resolutely again.

"What should we do then?" I asked cynically completely dissatisfied with the answer but realizing he was not going to alter his response.

"Right now, we must care for the innocent; the creatures victimized by this act, and not lose the thread of life that sustains each one of them. Focus action on what one can do now. Our action today will determine our future course." Malchizadec replied, looking at me with great patience and motioning me to follow.

"I brought Andrea and you to the Counsel last night," he confided as we walked back to the barn. "I arranged your Rite of Introduction and know the fear you felt during the initiation. Do not to take that lightly! You were there, as was I. The Counsel of Elders on Earth has known of impending disasters for centuries, futilely seeking to awaken humankind. The Great Counsel has responded to their effort. That's why you and I are here, why your initiation was imperative."

"What do I ha…." I blurted out only to have Malchizadec stop me again.

"In time James, it will be clear, in time." He replied, his demeanor conveying that the time for questions was over.

The droning two-cylinder putt of the John Deere echoed from the barn walls as Mason pulled it up with the load of hay. They had loaded the trailer with unusual speed. Ch'ien Li and Hahn were moving the oil soaked straw out of the makeshift veterinary ward as we approached, piling it well away from the building so we could burn it. They made a quick recovery for such sallow, spent, spirits as I had witnessed earlier. The miso soup may have helped, but I suspect it was the "Light of Heaven," as Hahn described it, that had restored them, for this was the mien of miracles.

"Hello" Jake said, in a puzzled pitch with a nervous curiosity about Ch'ien Li.

Coming around the corner of the barn as he hopped down from the trailer, she acknowledged him by nodding her head with a shy blush, but tried to look busy with the sullied straw; he responded by immediately toting the first bail towards the awaiting menagerie within. I ran up quickly to prepare them for a mind melt inside the door. Reaching for the latch, even in the bright sunlight, a violet glow radiated through the cracks in the barn and I knew it was just a glimmer of the electrifying medicine show they were about to encounter once we stepped inside. Mason and Jake walked in slowly, reverently watching the lissome moves of Sorrano and Bashira, and the astounding power of Malchizadec who had returned to his Avan form.

"Where's the water? I mean we're in Kansas; don't these critters need an ocean?" Mason blurted out after minutes of staggered silence. He had a way of bluntly cutting to basics.

Stating the obvious incongruity of the event cut the tension of too much solemnity. Along with the barking of sea lions, the twitter of osprey, and the songs of blue nose dolphins, the room roared with laughter.

"We're working with the light bodies of these animals, not their physical bodies; that is why they don't need to be in the water. Healing the essence and returning it to their physical body, is all that's needed," Malchizadec explained to Mason who seemed to accept what he had earlier dismissed as "hokem pokem."

A moment of laughter gave way to hours of focused work. Mason, Jake, and I carried bales and spread straw while Ch'ien Li and Hahn cleared away the old. We worked in a smooth rhythm flowing from one task to the next as the animals came and went, to and from, the resplendent clinic of the ramshackle barn. Throughout the day, I noticed another rhythm developing in brief hopeful glances between Jake and Ch'ien Li. Occasionally both would smile, and then hurry on, pretending they hadn't noted the other's glance. Finally, the consortium of critters, as Mason called them, thinned to a remaining few, and Malchizadec announced we had completed our day's task. It was time to rest.

The flash of shifting headlights streaming from the road through the asymmetric knotholes of the old barn wall surprised me; the day had gone by quickly. The beams swept the room with a dancing pattern of lights as if the light bodies of each animal present today made an encore cameo appearance. It's probably Andrea coming home after her last class, I thought, realizing Mason and Jake had stayed long past their normal quitting time.

"Well, a longer day than I intended," I turned to them and said, "would you like to stay for dinner and we'll figure out what I owe you for the extra hours."

"It's on me - off the books - Chief. I mean I'd pay to see this." Mason replied as Jake nodded in content accord.

The barn had hosted a dance of activity all day and the lull gave us all a chance to rest. At any good hoedown though, most of the action is off the dance floor in the corners where people get to know each other. This shindig was no exception as the respite precipitated a rise of good conversations. Hahn and Mason flooded Sorrano with suppressed questions about everything to which, Sorrano graciously rejoined communicating fluently with them in English or Chinese. Interestingly, Mason and Hahn understood one another. The bits of language Mason had taken into the bush in Viet Nam had seemingly percolated through his protective barrier of rage. Jake and Ch'ien Li started their much-awaited tête-à-tête, excited that their glances were mutual. Lorenzo, knowing a good barn dance when he sees it, stayed, reassuming his supernal repose, afloat in Heaven's Light.

"Well, come on in when you're all ready," I said, unable to pull the group away, and went to the house to meet Andrea.

The barn was well over a hundred years old. Built by my bygone ancestors as part of the homestead around 1850, it had survived many farm residents. Countless calves and colts, pups and kittens had started their earthly sojourn within its walls. Like all barns, it was the grounded center of life for all its inhabitants giving shelter and storing sustenance. Yet for all the events it hosted in its long duration, today was certainly unlike any other. Today, the barn had hosted Mason witnessing the wondrous.

CHAPTER 8
A GOD NAMED JOE

Our old Victorian two-story house was like an antique jewel wearing the soft romantic glow of a different time. Built by my Great-Great Grandfather in 1901, some years after settling the land, it maximized function; like a rose cut diamond of his time, it had simple elegance not based on fire or flash. It was a grand house by comparison to their first sod house and its modest appointments made it an accent on the prairie. There was far more room in this farmhouse than the two of us needed but the extra space allowed for entertaining and there was plenty of room to put up Hahn and Ch'ien Li. I searched the freezer in the walk-in pantry for some staples from which to start. The pantry had a built in china closet, the cabinet and drawers of which opened to both the dinning room and the pantry, so the cook could easily place and put away dinnerware. When Great-Great Grandpa's large family built the house, they must have considered it a handy adaptation.

In addition to the kitchen and dinning room with bay windows, the main floor had a large parlor with a hallway going off from it to my office and the master bedroom. Double pocket doors cordoned off the grand entryway, which led from a wrap around front porch used only by guests unaccustomed to our usual kitchen entry. A curved staircase, with a railing even grown-ups liked to slide down, swept upstairs to five extra bedrooms. My favorite appointment though, was a frosted window in the front door that pictured a pair of swans floating on a pond. Swans join for life and with all that our bird-like guests had revealed, I questioned if we had not joined for much longer.

The car had pulled into the yard but Andrea had yet to come through the door. Today was her late day; I assumed she had headed out to the barn thinking I may still be there. I just needed a good idea for dinner and hoped Andrea would appear soon; she could turn laundered lint and corn-cobs into supreme cuisine.

"There's someone here to see you Chief." Mason said sticking his head in the kitchen door with an uneasy grin as he wrinkled his eyebrows up and down. "This is Janell."

A shapely woman with coco bronze skin, sandy auburn hair, and striking gold eyes stepped into the kitchen with indomitable grace. I could see why Mason was disarmed. His eyes rolled towards the barn and shaking his head from side to side, he seemed to indicate that she had not been near the barn. Her long legs and short skirt though, visibly distracted Mace as she walked a few steps forward. I on the other hand began to re-alize the magnitude of the secret we were trying to keep, the first stranger was here in the room and there were sure to be more. How would we keep the birds safe when they were much harder to hide than the serene pair of frosted swans on the front door? A twinge of suspicion crackled up my spine and tightened in my chest, a hot flash shot across my forehead and suddenly, I felt very uncomfortable.

"Thanks Mace, take care of <u>everyone</u> <u>outside</u>," I said trying to mask my anxiety and hoping he would get my inference for caution.

"Are you James?" she asked with a polite reticence in her voice that ve-neered her resolve.

"Yes, can I help you?" I replied almost shyly.

"I'm Janell DeLaque," she enunciated in French flare as she crossed the room with the aplomb of a walking runway model. "I wrote you about the dream," she continued without disrupting her confident advance. "Is this a bad time, or do you have a few minutes to talk?"

"Sure," I responded with a courteous nod, thinking exactly how bad a time it was. "You must be very tired. Please have a seat while I get us some coffee." I said vaguely remembering that her email mentioned her coming.

Janell appeared to be about thirty and, even though she was fatigued from the long journey and stressed by the unsettling dream, her exotic beauty was distracting. I wondered if the journey would grant absolution or if instead, she had arrived in the midst of events that would precipitate pure madness. Either way, she was here and my problem was to discern her intention.

"You've come a long way…. I mean, all the way from Florida?" I began, placing two cups of coffee on the table.

Today's events resolved the dream for me but I wasn't sure what it would mean for her or, whether I should tell her that two of the people in her nightmare were standing right outside so I encouraged her to start. Janell looked relieved to be able to talk but just as she started to speak, Andrea rushed through the door looking haggard, and then noticed our company.

"Andrea, this is Janell the person from Florida who wrote us about our dream." I interjected. Andrea seemed distracted but grasping who Janell was, she composed herself and joined us. Janell sat back in her chair slightly stymied by the interruption and sipped her coffee. "This is my wife Andrea," I said dutifully completing the introductions and thankful not to be having this conversation alone.

They exchanged a few pleasantries but even though Andrea deferred to the situation at hand, I could sense that she had much more on her mind. Both of them were under stress in contrast to the positive portent of my day so, I envisioned the room filled with the viscous glow wielding my novice skill to relieve their troubled spirits and I hoped the healing would follow.

"You seem like you're ready to burst Janell, please continue." I reassured as Andrea gave me an understanding glance.

"Yes, please go on Janell. I interrupted you and you've come all this way," Andrea graciously conceded.

"We all know the dream, so I won't bother to restate it," Janell began with flawless articulation that masked a Caribbean lilt. "The reason I felt I had to come in person is deeper...much deeper. I've never seen anything like the wave of response that poured into your posting. Nor do I understand how so many people could have had the same dream right down to the rust on the bulkheads. This sounds crazy but everything in me says this is bigger...bigger than I can describe." She paused searching our eyes for any response.

"I don't know what is happening," she resumed, "but I've had all the way from Florida to think about it and I'm certain we are part of it. That's why I drove all this way, to see your face and know if you had the same reaction. It looks to me like you did! Do you sense the same looming purpose?" She stopped, her long fingers spread, she reached her arms out wide and shook them with emphasis, as she continued, "or...am I... *boufée delirante?*"

Janell's discerning read of my face and dramatic gesture caught me off guard. I didn't know what "*boufée delirante*" meant, but her gesturing conveyed that she questioned her sanity like me. There were answers to her questions, and she intuitively knew that I had some of them. However, I promised Sorrano not to reveal their presence. I never imagined when posting the dream that it was about real people and a catastrophic event, or that they would step from the dream world and come to life in my own. If Malchizadec was our guide, I wanted his advice about what I should, or could say, because I knew first hand the turmoil Janell was feeling. Still submerged in her thoughts, Andrea seemed to be struggling between listening politely to Janell and bursting herself.

"Before I try to answer questions Janell, is their something you need to talk about Andrea?" I asked, addressing her noticeable worry.

"No, mine can wait, I received more harassing phone calls today, that's all" she replied as if dismissing her preoccupation.

"It sounds to me like you should call the police; some people will stop at nothing. You had better find a good lawyer and protect yourself." Janell responded with surprising directness, instinctively sensing Andrea's predicament as well and quickly assessing the matter with little forethought.

My thoughts went to the earlier conversation with Malchizadec about enemies, ORTI and Mallory. I knew Janell was right but it was all too coincidental, why was Andrea receiving these calls at the same time as the dream, and the arrival of the birds? Was there some warning here we were overlooking? I needed answers, if there was no enemy, what "did I not yet understand." I understood nothing. Under the guise that I had left Lorenzo stranded in a feeding stall, I excused myself briefly in search of answers.

"They're not there," Mason yelled from halfway across the yard as I walked determinedly towards the barn. "Sorrano said we should all – everybody – meet at the grove after we eat. By the way, what's the grove?" He added, seeing me stop dead in my tracks as he and Hahn sauntered towards the house.

"He means the clump of hedge trees at the end of the vineyard," I explained.

"Not much to see in that clump of thorn wood, why would they want to meet there?" Mason asked.

"Hard to figure, you know, we'll have to wait and see, but I promised supper so we better get on with it." I answered, not knowing what the gathering would be to which they invited us.

If the birds intended to bring everyone into the same experience, I chose not to explain more and turned my attention back to hospitality as the new acquaintances continued to swap their stories. Speculation about the dream and the ship Hitam Emas had grown as Andrea and Janell were still talking when I reentered the kitchen. Andrea suggested that the nameless sinister calls might somehow connect to the ORTI group since they were into all sorts of chemical manufacturing around the world.

"Companies like that are like ghost governments, they shouldn't be allowed to have that much power. That shouldn't be; they're enemies to us all," Janell spouted as if she were personally abused by such power.

Andrea must have shared what we had learned about the ship and its corporate owners. I thought of Malchizadec's admonishment about "enemies," but chose not to counter the flow of their conjecture. Instead, I invited Janell to stay for supper and mentioned that Mason and Jake, along with two other guests would be joining us. In no time, the coals were ready and so were we. The evening was perfect for a barbeque and before long the smoky aromas brought everyone around the grill enticed by the bouquet of my ever-changing marinade. I wasn't sure what the dietary regimes of all the guests were; after today, I wasn't sure of my own, but we needed to eat after the hard days work. Janell walked out with paper plates that, upon seeing our Chinese guests, promptly fell to the ground scattering across the yard in the breeze like rousted field mice.

"I thought you might remember them but I wanted to be sure," I said bending down to help gather the rolling river of plates. "I guess this means we have a match," I said, waving for Hahn and Ch'ien Li to join us.

"Yes, it's a match, but how is it possible? It was a dream." Janell questioned, understandably more rattled by their presence than the sprawling dinnerware.

"You are meant to be part of it just as you thought, as for 'How is it possible?' that has been stretched a lot around here the past few days and you're not that 'boufoo' thing." I reassured her. "By the way, what is that?" I asked.

"It means you have hallucinations, kind of like you're psychotic where I grew up." She said and then abruptly changed her focus to Ch'ien Li as she came closer.

"This is Janell DeLaque; she had a dream about you." I said to Hahn and Ch'ien Li. "Janell, this is Hahn and Ch'ien Li ..." I stopped, realizing that I didn't know their last names and that I hadn't even told them about our dream.

"Chang, I Ch'ien Li Chang. This Hahn Siu, Grandfather. It's nice to meet you." Ch'ien Li said, glowing with pride that she had properly used a greeting she had likely practiced long before their trip here.

"Yes, we dreamt about a freighter and tragedy." Janell said, trying to make sense of it all and unable to stop her inquiry. "Did you see any of us that night? It was so real."

"Not know dream, know shipwreck. We there." Ch'ien Li replied pointing to Hahn and herself. "We see big crowd…many people, look down in cargo hold." She continued. "But people too far up see faces. All foggy, see darkness and ocean."

I had no idea about the crowd, I thought as the conversation ended. I only remembered being terribly alone and feeling helpless as I stared into that hold. The sense memory of the stench revisited my nose and I shivered as I recalled the cold, obsidian-like blackness that followed in the watery depths. As frightening as it remained for me, the experience must be much more traumatic for them; it felt good to fill their plates with home cooking, to be able to offer a little comfort to our uncommon guests and hear the conversations flourish between morsels around the picnic table.

"Well, I didn't suppose you'd be serving grilled fish tonight." Mason said at the table giving me a rye look.

The joke went right past Janell who had quickly merged into the group, but everyone who shared the miraculous day got it. The look on Mason's face indicated his interest in Janell's attention and that he had more yarns up his sleeve.

"Sorry Mace," I interrupted as he was starting with another of them. "I want to prepare her for tonight, that's only fair, don't you think? Janell, you'll want to add this to your how is that possible list too."

I began what I thought was a plausible explanation but as I heard myself speak I recognized how ridiculous it must sound. I realized that, if I hadn't seen the Avans myself, I wouldn't believe what I was saying either.

"They look like very large, vividly colored, birds. You'll meet them and they can explain." I concluded.

"Yep, biggest chickens you'll ever see." Mason retorted with the first volley of prankish puns. "After that we'll take you out for a little traditional Kansas cow tipping." He continued heightening the ridiculousness of my account.

"Since childhood, I've had very powerful dreams about all kinds of things," Janell began with dramatic emphasis. "I pay close attention to them, even if they're about chickens. Tonight, maybe I'll learn why big chickens cross big roads." She continued, peppering him right back.

A creamy orange crescent moon was creeping up the eastern horizon casting an apricot glow on the few high clouds spread across the night sky. There would be no storms tonight. I looked forward to going back to the grove and let the jibes slide by. The fireflies danced with florescent abandon about the yard as if a legion of fairies were performing in our private dinner theater. Lorenzo normally chased the lightening bugs futilely but tonight, after his illumined repose in the barn, he was content to witness the presentation. It seemed Gaia was smiling in thanks for our kindness to her creatures. I finished my meal with a keen satisfaction and a deep appreciation for my callow, but unfolding awareness.

After dinner, I led the group across the farmyard and out into the vineyard towards the grove. Andrea looked at me with a knowing smile. I could hear Mason in the back of the group restating his confusion that we would meet out in the "thorn wood" as he had described it. Stars and the crescent moon filled the night sky providing just enough light for our walk through the vines. It was a tepid night with a gentle breeze as soothing as warmed milk and an owl intoned salute as our procession moved quietly along. We were halfway down the trellis rows, the young grape leaves shimmered in the dim light and the "Coyoté Oaks" lay some 50 yards ahead. I didn't know if others were aware of it, but I could sense we were crossing over into magical time. Once again, we were travelers from one world into another and this time I couldn't wait to get there.

Reaching the grove, I entered the cluster of humble hardwoods and as before, with each step the canopy above ascended into the now familiar cathedral-like boughs. I expected to hear Mason erupt with astonishment at any moment, but only silence followed me on the path. Silhouetted by the firelight, Sorrano's great form stood at the edge of the grove waiting to greet us. Bashira and Malchizadec were standing by the kindled fire discussing something very intently.

"What's going to happen` tonight?" I asked hastening forward to greet Sorrano.

"We'll both find out together." Sorrano said giving me a perplexed look. "Malchizadec wants to teach us more about our undertaking." He concluded while the group joined us with awed expectancy around the fire and the Circle of Seven Stones.

"Welcome Janell, I have waited to meet each of you and now the circle of seven is complete." Malchizadec began, clearly prepared for our arrival. "Mason, Jake, Hahn, Ch'ien Li, Andrea, Janell, and James, your presence is not coincidence. Tonight I will explain more of our purpose, but first, everyone please walk slowly around the Circle of Stones. Look carefully at each one and let your innermost self listen," he finished directing us to the stones.

Walking clockwise in single file around the circle, we passed each stone, which bore its unique marking; a glyph carved into its face. I wasn't sure how to let my "innermost self listen." Malchizadec directed us to keep circulating in the flickering light until I noticed that each time I passed one specific stone I heard a tone. The glyph on that stone seemed to vibrate when I passed, emitting the enticing resonance.

"Did you notice anything about any particular stone?" Malchizadec asked stopping our circumnavigation and everyone nodded that they had. "Then go to the stone that called you," Malchizadec concluded.

I recalled what Sorrano told me about the stones in my first encounter at the grove, when he explained about "The Seven." I went straight to the stone that had resonated with me remembering that each one symbolized a unique quality of energy, the qualities of a Ray as he called it. One by one, each of us walked to a different stone. The resonance of the stone I chose must indicate my relationship with a particular Ray, I thought.

"Yes James, that's exactly what it means." Malchizadec replied aloud.

"The Circle of Seven Stones around the fire is a powerful place." He explained, addressing the entire group. "It is a Nexus where time, dimensions, and space join. It exists nowhere, and yet it leads everywhere. As we sit here right now, we are but a step away from anywhere in creation. There is no power in the stones themselves, but they symbolize the seven fundamental qualities that are the building blocks of creation. Many religions, cultures, and philosophies refer to them as follows: the Seven Rays of Divine energy sent forth to create, the Seven Archangels set before the throne, the Seven Realms of creation, the Seven Chakras of human consciousness, the Seven Bands of color in the rainbow. The Seven is in all. The Counsel of Elders meets at this Nexus. Together, they evoke the seven qualities as needed to restore the balance at pivotal moments when creation's life is threatened."

I was amazed that he repeated precisely what Sorrano had taught me and likely as he had taught Sorrano. Malchizadec's voice was calm and powerful as if he had been teaching all of his 3,500 years. Each word seemed carefully selected, not only to convey its meaning, but as if it were a carrier wave transferring knowledge at levels beyond his eloquent phrasing. He was clearly a master teacher and I had so much to learn.

"Each of you heard a tone from a different stone," Malchizadec said taking a moment to asses our readiness, "a specific note that is unique to you. That's because each of you carries within you the talents and temptations associated with the energetic quality, or Ray, symbolized by that stone. Like the Counsel of Elders, the seven of you as a group will learn to evoke these seven qualities to assist in the work that has drawn us here. There is no head to a circular table and so it is with this Counsel. Every position, each quality, is of equal importance which means each has its time of prominence. Listen to, and respect every voice amongst you who speaks from the inner resonance, the same resonance that evoked the sound from the stone. Still, someone must instigate and coordinate matters. James if you are willing, you have all been wisely chosen for this task, and you must choose wisely in the work that lies ahead."

"I heard the thing hum. I don't know anything about seven qualities or what a Ray is, and what's this work you're talking about?" Mason asked with unusual interest.

"Of course Mason and it is most appropriate to begin with you," Malchizadec replied. "You embody the qualities of the 1st Ray." He paused deep in thought for a moment.

"Mason, do your remember the decision you made lying wounded in the brush back in Viet Nam?" Malchizadec asked. Mason, astonished that he perceptively knew about his time in Nam, listened nervously.

"You fought with everything you had as all your comrades died." Malchizadec continued. "Bullet after bullet punctured your body yet you kept trying to defend your men. Do you remember? Do you know why you lived even when everyone else died?"

Mason's lips pursed as his eyes moistened and with a slow serene sob, Mason began to undulate. I feared the memories might be too much, knowing his torment. Malchizadec quietly waited as wave upon wave of emotions emerged.

"Do you remember why?" he gently asked again.

"Yes," Mason whispered choking back the lump in his throat, "even though I knew we had lost, that I hadn't saved my friends, there was still something left for me to do. I had to survive. I willed myself to stay alive... no matter how long it took."

As he spoke, Malchizadec walked over and shrouded Mason with his wings enfolding him with the violet glow. Mason's feelings flowed, the long guarded emotional and psychological wounds washed clean. Just as

I had watched physical wounds heal on the animals in the barn, Mason's emotional wounds were healing too.

"The 1st Ray is the quality of will or power." Malchizadec said bending down towards Mason. "Your strong will made you loyal to your fellow soldiers, and determined to live despite your loss, and your wounded, broken body. It is the deepest and best part of you, which you bring to this Circle. Welcome home Mason, welcome home," then he paused to let Mason reflect in silence.

"Hahn, your qualities are those of the Love and Wisdom, or of the 2nd Ray." Malchizadec began again. "Here in Ray order, are the qualities for the rest of you: James, your active intelligence personifies the 3rd Ray. Bringing harmony out of conflict is your ability Jake. Ch'ien Li, you have a scientific capacity that has spurred your curiosity since childhood. Devotion to ideals is at your core Andrea and whether in an Ashram in India, or at your gym, you strive to represent perfection. Janell, you have the ability to organize in detail and to merge the vision in your mind's eye with the physical world. It is the purest form of magic. I will not detail these great qualities now, as the best teacher will be your self-observation; these Ray traits already appear in your lives. Each has the power for good or evil. As you become mindful of them, their potency in your life will increase so you must always remain keenly aware of your intention.

"Remember, there is no order of more, or less, importance in these Rays." Malchizadec continued, knowing it was our human nature to discern a hierarchy. "These are the basic colors on the Creator's palette if you will. Though for each of you, your soul is the dominant quality, you also contain the other Rays in your personality, mental processes, and emotions. We are all individuals. Observe the various qualities in yourselves; learn how the positive and negative aspects of your Rays appear in your life. These strengths overcome weaknesses as you integrate your soul's purpose and ability."

"You mention the Creator, is this idea of Rays a religious teaching from your home world," Janell asked with rapt attention, her golden eyes dancing with energy like the flames in the fire as she sought to organize the information.

"No," he replied emphatically. "Religion is the solidification of the manner in which sentient creatures have tried to explain the Creator and find their place in creation. You might have noticed that nearly all religions teach that they are the real and only truth. Often they favor the culture in which they originate. The teaching about the Rays is an esoteric science. It is esoteric in that it is not what you see at first glance. Currently, you can't measure these energetic qualities with any instrument in your world but you can see their effects once you begin to look for them. It is science in that you can learn to use them effectively and everyone can get the same results if they follow identifiable procedures with the same discipline, like any other scientific experiment. You might call them applied formulas that precipitate specific results. The dictums needed for their use is then a spiritual science. By applying these qualities precisely in their proper relationships, the formless became the formed, and that which is now, evolves into that which is to come."

"That sounds spiritual to me. Like the religious stories we have been taught, but different?" Mason barked, showing that some of his skepticism remained.

Malchizadec paused again looking slightly perplexed. Then, he closed his eyes, spread his wings, and began to emanate the violet light. The light expanded to encircle our entire group and as it did I saw a vision in my mind of an apple. The image was vivid and I experienced it with all my senses. Malchizadec instructed each of us to note what we saw in our mind, and list its most important characteristics as we experienced them. I jotted down an apple with bright red skin and a little yellow stripping. In addition, I listed the shape, the exquisite aroma, the size, and flavor as its characteristics.

"Now, please tell each other exactly what you saw in your mind's eye," Malchizadec requested.

Mason said he saw a peach, Hahn a plum. Ch'ien Li reported seeing a persimmon while Jake perceived a pear. Janell vividly observed a mango

103

and Andrea said she didn't recognize what she saw, but it was some kind of fruit similar to a papaya.

"I projected the idea of my favorite fruit to your minds," Malchizadec continued. "We call it a Pedeo, or Custard Fruit. It is unlike anything you are acquainted with. Each of you received a vague impression that your mind filtered and translated into something you could recognize. In this case, your mind's filter reproduced your favorite fruit, except for Andrea. You saw an image very similar to the actual Pedeo.

"Now, imagine that I had not told you the source of the impression and that each of you were trying to share your vision with other people who had not experienced it directly. You each might be thoroughly convinced that your perception is the correct one and try to bestow your knowledge of it by repeating the list of characteristics you remember. Then as those people, who lack even filtered knowledge of the Pedeo, passed information to others about the fabled fruit, they would rely exclusively on the list of descriptors they had heard. Since they don't directly know of the Pedeo, they might even give it a different name. Over time, people would add, exclude, and modify the descriptions as the information passed from one generation to the next. Eventually, even you would scarcely recognize your narrations. Think of the disagreements if people who had heard differing descriptions shared their understanding. It would be as if people had now enmeshed the legendary Custard Fruit in the dance of dogma. Without direct experience, people have only their belief that the lineage of knowledge they've received is correct. So much discord, so much division comes out of the desire for connection with a beloved impression.

"What's some silly fruit got to do with religion you ask? Well nothing, the example is to demonstrate how the mind encounters something beyond its familiarity, like experiencing the Divine Presence. The powerful event changes when one tries to describe an ecstatic union in static terms. Every religion has at its core an ecstatic interaction between the Creator and a human individual. The individuals who experienced these events did their best to record faithfully a description they could share with others. However, their minds filtered and interpreted it, to make it comprehensible to them. Some saw the Creator as a great Father, others a Mother. For some the Creator was the sum of all form while others understood it as an endless void liberated from form. There was one *Pedeo*, a simple image, in my mind, that became seven variations when transmitted to each of yours. Imagine the complexity of trying to grasp the impression of an infinite Creator. Still each religious tradition is the result of some individual's, or group's, encounter with the Creator's Presence and their sincere desire to share the experience with others. The dissensions come when we argue over which description is the most correct.

"What I am trying to teach you about the Rays is a science, not a religion because you will have first hand information of it. You will learn to implement their effects with skill and wisdom, not just repeat a description of them passed from generation to generation until it has lost its potency. I urge you to keep your personal knowledge of God and look for the similarities in other people's encounters with the Divine. That will help us all come together and perform our work."

"But who, or what, is the Creator, the true Supreme Being?" Janell interrupted. The orange glow of the embers painted her coco skin but her passionate inner appeal for deep understanding burned most brightly. "What is the Creator's name?"

"Janell, it is that desire for detail that personifies your Ray quality." Malchizadec answered with a smile. "I don't know the name of the 'One in whom we all live and breath and have our being,' any better than you; perhaps it is nameless. I can tell you how we stopped the misunderstandings on our world."

"Wait a minute. You were going to... well, what about the work?" Mason interposed.

"Yes Mason that was my intention tonight. We don't have much time left this evening so which would you like to know about first?" Malchizadec stated, pausing for us to consider his course.

We all looked around at each other while Sorrano walked up to Malchizadec. Janell seemed temporarily satisfied that Malchizadec would say more but I could almost hear her mind still trying to name the Creator. The high canopy reflected the soft firelight down on Sorrano and Malchizadec as they conversed. Seeing the Avans together in the flickering glow seemed as if we were half way between a dream and waking, too surreal to believe and too powerful not to. Sorrano's demeanor suggested that he was presenting his thoughts carefully to his superior and waiting for him to make a decision. His youthful exuberance was in clear contrast to Malchizadec's staid discernment but it was equally apparent that they shared a mutual trust and absolute respect for one another. Personally, I wanted details about the present anomalies, and what was coming next but Janell's question intrigued everyone else so I deferred to the decision of the group. They, after all had not had the conversations we had shared with Sorrano and Bashira.

"Why don't you finish with the God stuff? You've got me curious." Mason piped up with a deferring smile towards Janell.

"Very well," Malchizadec acquiesced, "as Sorrano resolutely pointed out to me, these will all tie together eventually. Sorrano and Bashira will convey more information about us to all of you individually as they get the chance and I will address our operation together later. As you wish, I will 'finish the God stuff,'" Malchizadec confirmed, resuming his sole stance near the fire and prepared to teach.

"Sentient life evolved much earlier on Satoria and, as our appearance suggests, in a different form." He began again. "The great questions nonetheless, about our meaning and place in the universe, were much the same as yours. Over millennia, great thinkers and philosophers struggled with these queries exactly as they have in your cultures. Our planet also had many different cultures. As the centuries passed, within each tradition, there were individuals whose pure hearts and ardent dedication drew them into the Creator's presence. So close were their spiritual encounters that afterwards their face would shine with a bright light. Those who would meet these shinning individuals were awestruck and called them the Radiant Ones. They inspired and reflected the wisdom that they received by grace to their cultures, some to Avans, some to other species. However, just as you experienced trying to convey the vision of the *Pedeo*, those who learned from the Radiant Ones could not grasp the full meaning of their unitive communion from the descriptions alone. They did not have their own personal experience by which to understand it. Instead, they clung to the phrases as they had first heard them. Over time, they raised the words to be absolute truths, rather than the best individual efforts of each Radiant One to share the experience of the Divine. This saddened the Radiant Ones because they saw the same love of the Creator in each other and sought only to help others share the experience. With all their wisdom, they were unable to change the minds and hearts of those who had come to worship their words, in place of trying to encounter the Creator for themselves.

"When the Radiant Ones died, the words they left behind gained even more importance as others began to study them and make interpretations. Great factions formed around various orators whose renditions took on a life of their own. The original teachings of the Radiant Ones, and the path they suggested, became less important than the fervor surrounding the various interpretations. The dissension split everyone apart as groups tried to convert each other, stating that their doctrine was the one true path to the Creator. Arguments, cruelty, and wars broke out with each group calling those who disagreed, the evil enemy. So much destruction, all committed in the name of the Creator. For several thousand years, Satoria tumbled into ever-darker shades of chaos and all the while, those in combat believed they were spreading the light of order.

"Satoria, once a place of harmony and great beauty, was in ruins. Avans had attacked each other, and every other species turning our technology to the tasks of war and destruction. In doing so, we brought us all to the brink of annihilation. Amid the destruction, a few survivors, victims from all sides of the unholy wars, found common shelter in a cave far from the bleak rubble fields that once were our cities. They sought only rest and safety forgetting their mistrust of each other and the battle of beliefs that had divided them for millennia. Each one of them silently asked with the purest part of their hearts, for understanding. They asked to find a better way, a way that would end the separation, suffering, and slaughter for every being, not for themselves alone.

"During their steadfast supplications, the shadowy corners of the cave
brightened. The grotto in which they huddled filled with a viscous light
that swirled through them like living water. The light flowed from one
color to the next in shades and hues no one had ever imagined; as it
poured through them, their injuries mended and the sadness fled. Each of
them realized that they were in the presence of the Creator. The light was
everywhere. When it concentrated on one rock at the center of the group,
one member humbled herself before the stone and asked, 'By what name
shall we know you that we may thank you and call for you in our time
of need?' After the question, the light drew tightly into a brilliant point
and then burst into millions of points throughout the cavern. Each shown
as brightly as the first yet glowed with an individual warmth and hue. A
voice filled the illumined chamber. 'By which of these would you know
me? Am I more in one than in another? I am as incomparable as the most
cherished pearl and as common as a grain of sand. I am within all things
and all things are within me. I am the dessert and the sea, the famine and
the feast. The Avan in flight flutters enfolded in my wings as does the
wind in which it soars.' The myriad sparks began extending towards one
another until a gossamer veil hung throughout the grotto. The voice assured, 'I am that. That am I. Know me in all things, call me by their name
and I will hear you.'"

Malchizadec paused for a moment the emotions rising in his breast.

"That small group thousands of years ago on Satoria changed the course
of our history," he continued, gathering his composure again. "We call
them the Lucid Ones because, in their humility, they allowed the Creator's
light to shine through them without reflection or obstruction and thereby
corrected the misinterpretations that had grown from the Radiant Ones'
teachings. By their example, they saved the planet showing others that
the Creator lived through everything. It precipitated a change in every
creature on Satoria and made it possible for the Great Counsel's guidance and aid because the Lucid Ones respectfully asked that all might
heal. Remembering the Creator's words, 'Know me in all things and call
me by their name,' and recognizing that our nature was to name things in
communication, the Lucid Ones addressed the Creator by the most common name they could find on the planet that had neither gender nor rank;

a name used in every culture and creed. If you were to do the same on Earth, it might end the strife between ideologies. Perhaps you might call the Creator, a God named Jo or Joe"

Malchizadec had finished for the evening and the fire in the middle of the pit dwindled to its last embers but a spark had ignited within us. We left the grove without needing to say another word; the challenges ahead seemed less significant. Walking beneath the gossamer veil of stars, I greeted the millions of shinning points that stretched across the night sky. Perhaps as the lights had in the cavern of the Lucid Ones, each glowed in return with individual warmth. Creation was listening. "I am that. That am I," the voice had confirmed. "Know me in all things, call me by their names and I will hear you." It assured. The Creator was listening, waiting patiently for our lucidity to let the light shine through and we marveled at the work of "A God named ____."

The Coyoté Oak: Burgeoning Wisdom

CHAPTER 9
THE GATHERING STORM

A consummate coiffeur, Lorenzo lay curled in the center of the bed licking his paws as Andrea and I entered. He briefly looked up to acknowledge our presence and then returned to the important task of maintaining proper stripe alignment on his left and right front paws. This ritual required several hours every day and seemed particularly crucial right before sleep. A cat of distinction must never be caught with tousled toes. I mused to myself, "One must look their best should the need arise to saunter to the food bowl during the night, or encounter an errant mouse in need of a thorough trouncing." Normally, I would remove him claiming the territory for Andrea and myself but tonight, the house was full and it seemed best to leave him where he wouldn't disturb our wearied guests. Mason and Jake had driven home, while Hahn, Ch'ien Li, and Janell would be staying with us for an indeterminate time. With a full house, I imagined just how it might affect our daily routine but everyone blended well, smoothly handling the surreal sonnet playing out before us. I looked forward to a long night's rest even if we had to share the bed with Lorenzo. Andrea laid her head on my chest, and we surrendered to sleep.

BAM – BAM – BAM like claps of sharp thunder, the terrible thumping snapped me upright in the bed. My heart was racing fast enough to bludgeon its way out and it felt as if something had yanked me up by my chest. Andrea awakened with equal alarm. Then the thumping came again.

"Do you hear that? I think there's someone on the front porch," Andrea said with curious concern.

"Who could it be at this hour?" I muttered scrambling to my feet and halfway remembering to slip into a pair of pants before I made my way in the dark to a front window.

There were three cars parked about halfway up our drive that I didn't recognize. My spine felt wormy and my heart continued a second lap on the anxiety speedway. I was having a dream minutes before, in which I was on a Ferris wheel that kept going and I couldn't get off it. It seemed psychological, as if the wheel's cycling highs and lows symbolically reflected the experiences of the past days. I was glad to get off the endless ride, but reluctant to turn on the light revealing my presence until I knew this ride wasn't trouble on the other side of that loud bang at the door. Covertly I peered out the side window in the parlor relieved to see a Sheriff's patrol car parked next to the walk. An explanation for the strange cars lined up on our property was imperative. I guessed the Deputy might have some clue about them so I turned on the light and opened the front door.

"Good evening Mr. Davidson, I'm sorry to bother you at this hour but there is an emergency. Is Andrea Davidson available?" The officer asked and introduced himself as Sheriff Dan Blackwell.

"I'm Andrea, what's the problem Sheriff?" she said walking across the room out of the darkness as she pulled on her robe.

"You are the owner of Perfect Form, is that correct?" he asked.

"Yes..." she replied hesitantly.

"Ma'am, I'm sorry to report there is a fire at your business. Can you and your husband come with me?" Sheriff Blackwell interrupted.

"I'll get my things," Andrea said flying out of the room to finish getting dressed. I invited the Sheriff in, groped about to turn on the light, and offered him a chair as I excused myself to find a shirt. Racing down the hall I met Andrea already dressed and coming back.

"I'll ride with him, you bring the truck," she said hurriedly passing me.

"Tell him about the phone calls and… ask about these strange cars in our drive, we need to know..." I said to her back as I heard the door slam behind her.

The Sheriff slowly pulled his car down the drive past the parked cars and I noticed him shinning his search light on the license plates. The night visitation awakened everyone in the house and lights popped on in the upstairs hallway. Now that the Sheriff had gone, I could hear footsteps above me as the creak of the banister announced their descent on the stairs. Hahn was gesturing cautiously to Ch'ien Li who said they were very afraid the Sheriff had come because of them. Janell overheard the conversation from the top of the stairs and offered her assistance. Angst deflated the earlier air of excitement and marked all our drowsy minds with concern.

"Please make yourselves at home. I don't know how long we'll be gone," I said. "Make yourselves breakfast and watch the home front. You're free to use the computer if you need it."

With that, I went out, got into my truck and fumbled to start it in a robotic state of fixation. The stars still shown brightly in the night sky as I drove the blacktop road to town. A few hours earlier, I had felt such deep peace as I looked at them but now, like a storm rolling in, there was no peace in me; I was angry and in shock. I felt like an egg being poached, cracked, helplessly undulating in the boiling water and, hardening by the second. My deliberations became dark and sinister; my designs were all about revenge. As if a coal black hurricane raged within my skull, my mind sorted and categorized all the possibilities, I was certain this was no accident. Mordant spasms of seething retribution replaced the fear I had felt earlier. My foot lay hard on the throttle and I was completely unaware of my speed when I finally noticed a familiar curve in the road. The tires begin to screech as I lost control and slid sideways on the shoulder. I steered into the slide and managed to straighten the vehicle out, only to shoot from the road over a patch of Sumac and down into a broad grassy ditch where the truck slowed to a welcomed stop. The engine was still running; I saw no damage. I was alive and felt lucky to be so. It took several moments to calm myself from the chilling experience, but the irate ramblings continued in my mind.

"Be careful what you think of James," said an accustomed voice. I looked over to see Sorrano peering in the driver's side window.

"Sometimes these taloned telepaths tweak my last nerve," I said to myself.

"James, please pardon me for listening," Sorrano apologized, "but you were thinking so loudly I worried about you and came right away. You were easy to find with that cerebral fracas. What has happened? Can we help in some way?" He asked with an almost irksome serenity.

"Andrea's business is on fire," I told him realizing that they were unaware of the night's events. "She has received several threats over the past several days. Now this? That's why I'm so damn mad."

Sorrano opened the back door with his talon and hopped carefully into the truck's cramped back seat. Extended diagonally, and scrunched in as best he could, it looked like an uncomfortably tight fit.

"I'll ride with you to the edge of town." He directed pulling the door shut. "You might drive a little safer if I'm along," he said, his wing scuffing across the rear window of the extended cab as he tried to motion me to drive ahead.

In gear, the truck rumble bummed slowly up the steep rutted slope towards the road and at last, back on the blacktop, we cautiously headed the six remaining miles into town. Sorrano, packed like a live pheasant under glass in the backseat, as I tried to pay more attention to the road than to my thoughts.

"You have an opportunity here," Sorrano said.

"What do you mean; are you naïve or something?" I retorted, irritated at such a Pollyanna response. "This is a catastrophe. If someone did this, they are certainly an enemy."

"Yes this is an evil act if what you believe is true," Sorrano continued, "but, when Malchizadec told you 'There are no enemies, only those who

114

do not understand,' he didn't mean there is no evil. He meant we must not separate ourselves from others by calling them an enemy. When we make someone, or something, our enemy we are enticed by the first seduction of evil. We can justify all sorts of hideous acts when we believe we are wielding them against our enemy. Having an enemy is being an enemy." I was speechless. In no mood for a lesson, I seemed to have lost my interconnected insights more easily than I found them.

"It's a mirror," he continued, "only an illusion that there are two sides. The same hatred reflects in both directions. You can't fight evil with evil for then, only evil wins. Whenever you truly apply spiritual knowledge, darker elements will draw near and try to destroy your progress. You have an opportunity here to find another path. Let the dark ones self-destruct by refusing to let them engage you. If you don't play, they go away."

Looking at Sorrano in the rearview mirror, I was still thinking he was a completely idealistic greenhorn when he started to speak.

"I am new to this planet James," Sorrano said cutting me off, "but not new to this work. Please hear me out. Evil wants your attention, your mental energy and your emotional engagement. It feeds on that energy…. Deny it that, and you deny it success."

Though I didn't want to, I listened; it was impossible to argue against his impeccable commitment to truth and though I knew he was right, I was brawling with the amassing hurricane in my head. We pulled over about a mile outside town where I could see the column of smoke rising and a red-orange glow in the area Perfect Form should stand. Sorrano oozed out of his backseat containment and vanished. The small berg that lay ahead was like many Kansas towns that, once touched by history, had outgrown its agrarian roots and remained unable to find its future. It struggled for balance between strip malls and a sagging economy. I drove on considering his challenge to me. The phrase "out of the frying pan and into the fire" felt all too real. Life was pushing me out of the spiritual feel good theories nest, to learn how to fly through fire.

At the stoplight on Elm Street, I turned right and drove through the historic buildings of an old cavalry fort on the edge of town that lined the access road leading to Perfect Form where a police officer stopped me at a barricade. Surrounded by onlookers, the firefighters were working frantically just ahead so I parked where he directed me and stepped out into the hubbub and commotion. Andrea walked towards me her hair burnished by the tawny orange flames that emanated from the collapsing embers. The light being behind her, I saw only her silhouette, but I could imagine her disillusioned expression. As she came near, I held out my arms and gave her a hug.

"The fire crew thinks it was an accident," she said disgustedly. "…an accident?" she repeated. "They think the winds came up overnight and blew a spark onto my roof starting all this."

"Did you tell them about the threats?" I asked with my own exasperation.

"Yes!" she emphasized, showing her agitation with their assessment. "I called the insurance company. Both the company and the fire investigator are looking around now, when they can get close enough to the building. It's very unsafe."

A concussive explosion came from the building as Andrea finished, proving how unsafe it really was and disputing the accident theory. The firefighters closest to the flames were scrambling up from being knocked to the ground and trying to form new fire lines while a dozen of their comrades rushed over to help them. Pandemonium ensued as officers scurried to move non-essential trucks back fearing more explosions may follow. Everywhere spectators were jostling around weighing their choice between finding the closest possible view and becoming the next casualty of the emergency.

"Is there something explosive we should know about?" one officer yelled over to Andrea.

"Not that I know of," Andrea yelled back. "It's an exercise room … an office. That's all," she replied.

"You'd have to be crazy enough to fill'em with hydrogen for exercise mats to blow-up like that. I think this fire had a little help. Sure there is nothing else?" the investigator asked coming over to us.

"There's nothing. The place uses solar panels for heat and there is no gas," Andrea reiterated resolutely.

Like a well-tightened latigo, that brings safety to a long hard ride, the strength and deep resiliency of her character emerged to shepherd her. There, etched in the light of the flaring debacle was a woman who handled it, who reckoned with reality, and of whom I could not be more proud.

The back wall of the building collapsed sending a plume of sparks and ash into the air; the heat of the fire was so intense that the old brick cracked and crumbled. We could hear the snap as bricks shattered into pieces giving up the last droplet of moisture that had once bound their clay. It had been a beautiful old building with an inviting ambiance and a character only achieved through decades of meaningful use. That would be no more, now it was a pile of rubble to cart away. I didn't want that to be true of her business too.

"James, I couldn't stop shaking all the way to town as I rode in with the Sheriff." Andrea said, grasping my hand. "All I hoped was that we could salvage something. The Sheriff tactfully tried to prepare me for the upheaval and the probability that everything was lost. When I saw the building, shuttering in the inferno, well...inflamed is how I felt. How did it come to this?"

A cloud of acrid black smoke blew over us, the last vestige of the exercise mat that was now a boiling pool of liquid plastic splashing fiery globs as debris fell into it. I looked into the hellhole of percolating chaos, the sea of spectators that had gathered around the predawn conflagration, and I was unable to voice a single word of hope in response to Andrea. All I could think of was how vulnerable we were. How had it come to this? I didn't know.

"Before you came," Andrea continued, "I stared at the flames like you, unable to move or say a word, my emotions boiling as intensely as that puddle of plastic. Rage and revenge were surfacing when two questions crystallized in my mind: Will these emotions make it better or worse? Will they defend me, or spread hatred?"

Andrea surveyed the disastrous landscape with a stoic acceptance that didn't imply defeat. Another dream she had worked so hard for was gone but she was still an idealist and wouldn't stop until she found another way.

"A strong resolve came over me to focus on the tasks here and now instead of my emotional reactions." She added. "I needed to call the insurance company, and realized I'd left my purse in the Sheriff's car so I went back and while there, Bashira appeared. She looked at me with so much compassion and helped me find my center. Very calmly she said, 'You've made the right choice, there is no point focusing on revenge, it only serves your pride. The right time for release and healing will come.' Then she disappeared."

"Sorrano laid a little wisdom on me coming here too," I said, knowing I didn't need to go into the content of his message and asked about the Sheriff.

"I did tell him about the threats," she said. "He kind of hemmed and hawed a bit but his slow talking, down-home banter doesn't fool me. He's clever, very deliberate, and almost a little intuitive like any good detective should be."

A large section of the sidewall fell inward towards the fire as Andrea finished her last word and a platoon of firefighters turned their hoses on the fount of sparks that shot skyward. All we could do was stay out of the way and listen to the sizzle of the embers drowning in the constant deluge from the hoses. The tall plumes of smoke had turned to bellows of steam that now glowed in the pre-dawn light. The blue-silver ribbon of light along the horizon once again defined the boundary between yesterday and tomorrow; but who Andrea and I were yesterday would most certainly not be the same tomorrow. Change was falling on the heels of change and coming faster than I could adapt; all since that first morning when this band of light catapulted me into an unplanned adventure, into unforeseen alternates of reality. Our vision was broader now, our goals surpassed ourselves and our perception exceeded our senses. What would unfold in the coming days from the devastation that lay before us in this moment? Embers, ashes, and aimless aspiration were all that remained of Andrea's work but "seduction of evil" or not, there was no enemy to fight.

The fire had been squelched when we decided to go home for a little rest and return later to do a search for anything that might have escaped the flames. Our soot covered, soil worn bodies were trudging towards the pickup, when the fire investigator interrupted. Saying his suspicions had changed considerably with the "explosive developments." Without apologizing for his pun or the incorrect assessment of this being a roof fire, he asked if we could be available to answer some more questions later in the day.

"We'll be back in a few hours." Andrea answered turning towards the truck. "Why is there Sumac sticking out of the grill?" She asked as she saw a large bouquet of the resolute shrub protruding from the front.

"We'll, I did a little off road driving on the way here. I wasn't coping very well either," I said nonchalantly, hoping the subject would end there.

Andrea crawled into the passenger seat and lay hear head on my lap unable to view the row of old buildings that now seemed empty, as we pulled out onto Elm St. for the drive home. We were as drained as juiced lemons and the tiredness hit us after we slumped into the cab, the few hours of sleep weren't nearly enough. Feelings rumbled deep in her core like magma held in check, until with volcanic force, the teardrops erupted like emotional lava flowing down her cheeks onto my lap. Perfect Form was gone but the desolation of this night would linger.

"Tell me more about the threats." I asked rubbing her shoulder as I slowed for the stoplight.

"It hardly matters now," she said, pausing to sit up and wipe her face. "Yesterday, a black SUV with dark tinted windows was watching us all day long; everyone noticed and felt very unnerved. Phone call after phone call came in offering more money and advising me to sell as if they could push me aside. I wasn't about to cave in. No one should be able to bully people that way and I made it very clear that I would not sell. Looking back, I should have told someone, but I never thought anyone would go to these extremes for my little property."

"Do you know who it was, or why they wanted it?" I asked.

"There are rumors it's a chemical company that plans to build a plant," Andrea said, "but no -- they didn't tell anyone. I guess a slew of money makes it easy to hide behind lawyers and remain anonymous. The first calls came the morning after I had that dream. Hearing Janell talk about the dream brought every subtle threat back into my mind. The last thing the caller said was how sorry he was to hear about my neighbor's misfortunes. He hoped I would remain safe in that neighborhood. I didn't know what he was talking about!

"I found out tonight that two other storeowners who refused to sell had trouble," she continued after a mesmerized stare across the green sea of wheat waving in the early light. "An intruder robbed Ralph's Antiques as he was closing his shop yesterday and he was badly injured. Sally's Home Boutique also had a fire earlier tonight that destroyed much of the store; I guess I was next," she said with a prolonged sigh. "It feels like I'm dealing with the mob or something...the phone harassment, people following us, and now assaults. I never thought.... I'm scared; what else is going to happen?"

"No was the right answer," I said giving her an assuring rub, "I'm glad you stood up for yourself but like Janell said, maybe we should have called the police. I hope the Sheriff, can get to the bottom of all this."

"Yes, but it's the city Police's jurisdiction. Dan's is a county officer and may not be able to do much," she said exhaustedly and then collapsed back onto my lap.

This time I rounded the curve carefully that had served as my launch pad earlier and the rest of the drive home went smoothly while Andrea rested. I hoped we could slip in quietly and get a couple hours of shut-eye before we had to start answering questions. I slowed down to turn into the drive noticing that the three cars remained parked there but dozens more with license plates from all over the country had joined them. The autos looked like a pod of pilot whales that had beached themselves overnight. Parked in every reachable location and in the most harried fashion, they looked as if they struggled ashore to die by dawn's light in our farmyard.

"What is all this," I exclaimed in a grouchy tone.

I didn't have the energy to deal with whatever was waiting for us by the dozens and this day promised to be full of fire related responsibilities. I steered carefully through the aggregated autos parking as close as I could to the house. No one stirred around any of the cars, which seemed strange. Janell was on the porch waving her arms towards the cars and shaking her head.

"I don't know what they're all about but they've been coming in small caravans since you left." She said shrugging her shoulders as if to head off our questions. "I slept on the couch in case someone came to the door." Then turning to Andrea she asked, "How bad is the fire damage?"

"It's a total loss," Andrea said while she walked into the kitchen with us following.

"We're really shot," I said. "We've got to sleep a couple of hours and go back to town; so would you mind finding out why these people are here when you actually see somebody?"

"What do you want me to tell them?" Janell asked agreeing that she take over in our absence.

"Nothing for the moment," I said. I hadn't thought of that. "Find out what they want and we'll figure it out."

The sun had risen when I started for the bedroom after Andrea. Paranoia hit; what will happen if this fire was deliberate? These could be stolen cars out here and someone trying to frame us. Pretty weird idea admittedly, but nothing was strange at this point. I decided to give the Sheriff a call before I lay down. Sheriff Blackwell assured me that he had run the license plate numbers of the first three cars last night and nothing appeared to be amiss. Nonetheless, he agreed to come out later in the day and check the situation. I felt a little more at ease and burrowed my head into the pillow next to Andrea who had all ready fallen fast asleep. I hoped I would be so lucky.

"Wake up James," Andrea said, sitting beside me a short few hours later.

"So you drove all the way from Toronto?" I heard Mason ask outside on the porch amongst other conversations. I didn't recognize the new voices as the clock rudely blinked 8:45 A.M. as if to remind me how short the night was.

"It's time to find out what's going on here." I muttered as we stumbled into the kitchen where Hahn, Ch'ien Li, and Janell waited at the table as if they already knew.

"You better get ready for this." Janell said handing each of us a cup of coffee. "I should have guessed this; these people are all exactly like me. People sent hundreds of emails about your dream and I know some of them are in the yard right now."

Hahn set his tea down with an audible sigh, resolutely got Ch'ien Li's attention, and passionately gesticulated as he began speaking in Chinese.

"Grandfather feel very strong, must honor why people come." She translated. "Not let feel disrespected. They make big effort to come here." She finished and then paused as if she was formulating her own thoughts. "Maybe they here help too! Need find out how people are like us. Now, excuse please." Ch'ien Li added, then got up and with a determined air and turned to go out the front, not the back door, without explaining further.

I agreed with the inscrutable patriarch and couldn't but help notice that Ch'ien Li's English was improving with surprising speed. She seemed to drink in every word any of us said and quickly incorporate it in her vocabulary.

"Mason has been out talking with them for a couple of hours." Janell continued. "Apparently they've been waiting for us to get up, sleeping in their cars, or wherever they could. About 7:30, waves of cars started coming until they stretched a half mile down the road in both directions. We've got to get organized and fast."

I took a couple of long sips of my coffee while Janell went to get Mason. I wasn't ready to say anything to the crowd and frankly didn't know what to say if I did. Understandably, Andrea's mind still seemed numb from the fire's aftermath.

"Lot's of people out there Chief." Mason said as he came in. "Gettin' kinda freaky around here don't you think?"

"There's no doubt about that. Your mission today Mace, along with Janell, is to find a place for all these people. You know the ground, so try to arrange them somehow." I said. "Stall everyone until this evening; but most of all, don't let anyone near the barn or the birds. I don't know how to avoid the crowd, but I need to meet with Malchizadec before we go back into town."

"First off," Janell said to Mason jumping right into the task ahead, "we need some way to keep the crowd safe and not milling around waiting. Are we going to need food, water, and sanitation? This can get ugly fast if we don't have a plan."

The quality of everyone's approach struck me more than the content of their words. I heard them, but, as Malchizadec had described, the Ray qualities of each person stood out. Mason's driving will, approaching people directly, Janell's command of detail and ability to systematize it, Hahn's compassionate wisdom, and Ch'ien Li's scientific curiosity; each one's capabilities added to a total solution.

"Once you've decided how to manage everyone, just go ahead with it." I said and headed towards the barn to find Malchizadec ignoring the crowd of several hundred people.

I noticed three winged figures circling high above the farm. At first, it looked like Red Tail Hawks soaring on updrafts above the hill from the size of their images in the sky, then I saw them fly through a bellowing cloud; they were far too high in flight. It's the Avans. I went into the vineyard towards the grove calling to them in my mind. The thicket was far enough away from the farmyard commotion and would be a safe place to converse. Coming near the trees, I felt the shift in awareness followed by the regal metamorphosis as I walked onto the shaded ground. Before entering the grove, I looked skyward to see that only two birds remained in flight above the hill and hurried inside. Sitting on the stones with Malchizadec, were Jake and Ch'ien Li. Unsure what I was interrupting, I entered quietly until Malchizadec acknowledged me.

"Please come sit down James," Malchizadec said waving me forward to the stone where I previously sat. "They have some questions. Jake, go ahead."

"Last night," Jake began, subdued and sullen, "my father's experience brought back sad memories of growing up in a house at war with itself. I wanted peace and harmony so desperately in our family and tried every-thing I could think of as a child to help mom and dad get along. With the fire at Andrea's business, it feels like I am back in the middle of another conflict. This time it's even stranger and I'm not sure how I can be help-ful."

"From the time you were a child you have seen yourself standing in the middle of a war of opposites." Malchizadec replied looked compassion-ately straight into Jake's eyes. "You perceived conflict, but as you have listened to the guidance of your inner voice, that perception has come into question. Imagine yourself standing in the center of a ring. As you look to all sides, it appears as if opposites surround you, one side bal-anced against the other. Still the ring is one; it is only your perspective that makes it seems as if there is a pair of opposites. Your mind and body once seemed like opposites but you learned to bring them into alignment through your disciplined study of Aikido. Now, your personality is integrating; that is, coming steadily under the direction of your indwelling soul. Thus, you perceive the illusion of a new pair of opposites. One calls you to a higher path, the other to your own self-interests. You will find a middle way that brings harmony and serves both as one. That is characteristic of a 4th Ray individual.

"The difficult part," Malchizadec continued, "is the tendency to become discouraged when one can't decide when faced with two choices. This is one of evil's greatest devices. By keeping you focused on the futility of your choice, disparagement delays the alignment with your soul, your connection to the Creator. Hopelessness and apathy result. However, this is also a moment of great promise. When you feel torn between opposing forces, align with your indwelling Self and remain detached from either pole of the duality. Then notice as your true Self begins to take over the task, illuminating your mind and restoring hope. Do what you know, learn all you can and the rest will be provided. Willingness and right intention are all that is required of you," he concluded.

Wearing a pair of fashionable jeans and a light sweater from Andrea, Ch'ien Li was scrutinizing the trees while she listened and silently mouthing Malchizadec's every word, imitating his speech pattern as he spoke. I couldn't help but notice how charmingly she assimilated her new language and culture.

"Ch'ien Li, I know you didn't come to the grove to talk with me." Malchizadec continued, discerning her curiosity. "You wanted to see if the change you observed in the trees last night was truth or illusion." Ch'ien Li nodded her head in agreement with a shy blush. "Your keen interest in understanding the form of the world around you characterizes the 5th Ray of concrete knowledge which is the core of your being. What you saw here, and see again today, empirical reason cannot explain; that is, you cannot measure it with your senses. That is your dilemma is it not?" He asked. Again, she nodded affirmatively.

"Here in the grove," Malchizadec resumed, "you have seen behind the veil of form where reductive logic fails and parts no longer explain the whole. Yet, what you see around you is true. To resolve the conflict in your concrete mind, continue to train your mind as your grandfather has taught you. Similar to Raja Yoga, you have focused your mind intently to achieve contemplative states. You must go deeper, past the abstract mind of the soul and connect with spiritual mind, which is the source of insight. Learn this and you will do much to bring hidden certainties into physical understanding.

"Now James, we appreciate your concern for us," he carried on seamlessly. "We will be fine. As you know, we are quite able to remain out of sight. The crowd looks to you for direction. They won't benefit by knowing about us, nor is that their purpose here. Steer them carefully by using your bare attention; by that I mean, use single-minded awareness of the moment as you speak to them without emotional distortions. All will go as it should. You are all much stronger than you know."

Malchizadec faded dramatically away almost as if to emphasize his point, leaving us alone on the stones. We walked calmly back to the farmyard absorbing the information he had tailored for each us as though they were nourishing drops of rain on thirsty soil. As we neared the farmyard, Mason, Hahn, Andrea, and Janell walked out to meet us. I could have used more guidance on how to manage it, but nonetheless, the crowd waited, filling the yard from the house to the barn. In all the hubbub, I had to find my bare attention.

"We're going to organize them into smaller groups, kind'a like tribes," Mason whispered, adding to my distraction while the crowed milled around us, "tell'em to pick a color and follow the banner when you talk."

With too much to comprehend, my mind went blank as I crawled up on the tractor; grabbing the well-worn wheel for support, I took a deep breath with single-minded awareness and tried get their attention. At least 500 people filled the farmyard with still more walking in; I looked over astounded at the reaction the dream posting had evoked. The faces I gazed upon were all looking to me for direction. Overwhelmed by the task of distilling our common purpose, I quieted my worry and listened as a calm voice inside me said: "Let it begin."

"I imagine all of you are as surprised to be here as I am to see you," I started. "Like you, I don't exactly understanding what has brought us all together, but we seem to be bound by something... well... phenomenal..."

"*Hitam Emas*" someone yelled from the back. Murmurs and commotion spread across the assembly like a tsunami coming ashore. Everyone knew that name. Worried by the sudden reaction, the volatility of their anger, and the fear that motivated everyone to drive many miles to come here, I felt woefully unprepared. Again, I took a deep breath and tried to remain singularly focused. It was time to defuse the anger and fear, and transform them into a positive purpose.

"Yes," I improvised, "I had the dream too. It made us all feel helpless and afraid." I motioned for Hahn to come over beside Ch'ien Li and me without mentioning them to the crowd. "It was an awakening for all of us." I continued. "The dream was real. Its events really happened." Affirming my words, people began to see Hahn and Ch'ien Li and with equal speed, a hush fell over the group. "We came together because we experienced the tragedy through our dream." I said feeling a reassuring power come into my voice. "There is an urgent need to stop such exploitation. We came together because we want to make things different, because we need to help restore our planet, and because we must mend the rifts that divide all of us who call it home. Does that sound like the reason you are here?" I asked.

"Yes," the answer roared back from the unlikely barnyard assemblage.

"Yes," I reiterated. "This is Hahn and Ch'ien Li," I introduced them. "As you can see, they survived the shipwreck, our nightmare at sea. Everyone else perished and the greed that caused that tragedy continues to afflict lives all around the globe. You're here because you have chosen to see that, but have felt helpless to stop it. If we all search our hearts to see how we can help each other, maybe we can find a way to make a difference. I don't have the answer, but perhaps together we do. I've witnessed miraculous occurrences since the bitter dream awakened us and these events

127

have transformed that night's terror into hope of things to come; your presence here validates that hope.

"Some of you have traveled a long way." I said, pointing to the raised banners flashing pure bright colors against the beryl blue Kansas sky. "Please follow the banner of your choice to a campsite, make yourselves comfortable and get to know one another. Starting today, we exchange a nightmare for a new dream, a dream of a better world that affirms life rather than demeans it. We have a vision that cherishes all the Earth, rather than separates and degrades it. We carry hope for a planet that will shine again like a bright blue jewel in the veil of heaven. If you share THAT dream," I concluded, "I'll see you tonight on the crest of the hill at sunset."

Crawling down from my provisional podium my legs felt more like rubber than I remembered climbing up. My "bare attention" had widened and the nerves I had ignored as I spoke left my steps a little shaky as I made my way over to Andrea. I saw Mason and Jake heading out to place the colored banners around the campsites with the crowd calmly following.

"Where did that come from?" Andrea said, unaccustomed to my new role. "Your speech brought the whole situation together. Right now though, we better get back to town." Andrea finished, shifting our elation back to the rubble field of chagrin.

Our band of seven would continue in our absence, to host the disparate nomads drawn together on our farm. Upon arriving and standing over the charred remnants of the now, "Imperfect Form," our thoughts swirled through the myriad of dissimilar events packed within the past days. Excitement, trepidation, and uncertainty swarmed the atmosphere like a gathering storm. It was hard to understand how such polarity, both good and bad occurrences, could so abruptly dominate our lives. Any of the events were implausible in any given life, for all of them to exist simultaneously in ours, defied reason. The fire investigator informed us that the fire was deliberately set with chemical explosives and military precision. One more implausible act that left little chance they would ever catch the perpetrator. Together we looked around for anything that might remain

128

from the fire but as the investigator said, it had burned clean; it appeared there was nothing but soot covered memories and ashes piled in a mound of ruin.

"I want to save a few of these old bricks to remember," Andrea said kicking the cinders back. Kneeling down, she stacked a few of the saturated clay blocks. "Would you look at this? I can't believe it wasn't destroyed."

Andrea stood up holding a green jade dragon she brought from China. Her favorite figurine, Andrea kept the finely carved treasure in her office as a reminder of her healing transformation those years ago. Now it punctuated the importance of her work as she passed the healing on to others. As Andrea had, the jade Dragon endured a firestorm and ascended from the ashes like the Phoenix. Destruction had come upon us and when we had finished searching the debris, we loaded a few burnt memories in the truck knowing that as we moved on, more changes followed. The fire may have destroyed Perfect Form but it tempered our spirits. We were ready for the sunset and the tribes upon the hilltop. We were ready to embrace whatever transformations would ascend through this gathering storm.

CHAPTER 10
SLITHEREENS, SLIMERS, AND SLOTHS

The top of a hill at sunset is always perfection. Cloudy or clear, wind or whist, the flaws in nature only enrich her palette. The flaws in humankind, though colorful, do not always better the batter. I knew everyone in the mix this evening had the dream in common, but the people had come to our farm for their own very individual reasons. Many of them probably thought I had answers. Did all these people come simply because I had spoken about the dream first in my computer posting? If so, I imagined some were looking for a way to strike back at injustices they had suffered, while others might be seeking to smear groups more powerful than themselves. Whether they slithered, slimed, or were just here to hang around, I didn't think the modicum of understanding I had acquired to date, was enough to guide anyone. Most of all, despite my inspired moment on the tractor, I knew I didn't have the wisdom to know what information I should share with them and, other than the birds, what facts must remain secret. I felt like a character in a cosmically twisted western movie who needed answers by sundown.

The farm had quieted down though people had continued to stream in all day. Mason directed everyone to several areas that dotted the hillside like small villages. The spread of tents and people across the land looked like a gathering ground for a rock festival; by default, I was the master of ceremonies. It was afternoon and I could see families picnicking around the pond and children, playing ball further up the hill. Thankfully, Mason and Janell had the cars parked neatly out of the way reestablishing order out of the chaos. The birds weren't circling in the sky, so assuming they had returned to the barn, I could slip out for some advice without exposing them to unnecessary risk. Nonchalantly, I walked out making sure no visitors observed my trajectory, narrowly opened the barn door and slipped inside. The ground floor was empty and quiet. I supposed Malchizadec, Sorrano and Bashira had taken refuge in the loft to avoid discovery from any errant guests so I mindfully ascended the ladder softly announcing my arrival.

Poking my head up through the floor, instead of the usual lavender glow, shadows met me. Sunlight glimmering through the cracks in the old barn wall formed a striate pattern across the floor revealing only the stack of bales across the loft. I crawled through the doorway calling, "are you here?" My question faded into dusty silence until something wet and sticky fell onto my shoulder completely saturating my shirt. It stank. A giant sloth hanging upside down by its claws from the aged cottonwood rafters above me had relieved itself on me. Repulsed by the strong odor I peeled off my now filthy Hawaiian shirt put on fresh for the hilltop gathering thinking -- so much for the musician look -- and stepped out from under the great ball of hair pending further deposits. The birds were nowhere around. Then something moved in the darkness by the bales.

"Excellent, it worked just so," a voice boomed from the shadows.

Standing upright in his Leopard loincloth, out from the blackened shadows of the loft, stepped the tall ebony form of Navu the Zulu, the head of the Counsel of Elders. With cool exuberance, he approached me carrying a panther tucked under one arm and a Black Mamba snake coiled around the other.

"Frisky little 'bobos' these ones," he said striding over to the excrement on the floor.

Navu was perfectly comfortable in the setting but seemed to be operating at a primal level; highly intelligent and focused, his speech had a much less of a Colonial African accent than before. I was so surprised at his presence I didn't know whether to say, "Hello," or "I've got shit of my shoulder." Neither came out, I just stared agape.

"Grab that one quickly," he said pointing behind me.

Without thinking, I latched onto a tail heading underneath the straw.

"Well, I'm dead. That's no tail!" I exclaimed, discovering I had attached to a six foot Fer-de-lance. "This is an - e x t r e m e l y – dangerous and - d e a d l y - snake isn't it?" I asked in a shaky voice.

"Oh yes, and she has nasty moods; very difficult." Navu replied with far less concern than I would have liked.

"What am I supposed to do now?" I asked as the long viper turned its head towards me.

"Give her this when she opens her mouth." He said throwing something in my direction.

I caught the small bundle carefully with one hand but the movement was enough to startle the snake, which promptly launched a strike at me. Her jaws stretched wide exposing two sizable fangs that were reaching for my flesh with alarming speed. Almost by reflex, I tossed the tiny packet into the snake's throat, diverting her attention temporarily and quickly dropped her to the floor. As I stepped back - well back - my emotions fluctuated between fear and elation unsure whether I had performed a compassionate act or dodged a painful bullet.

"So hard to get them to take medicine." he said. "When they get sick they are stubborn to die."

With that, he taunted the Mamba still coiled around his arm, tossed a similar bundle in its mouth and set it on the floor near the other snake.

"We give them a few minutes and see how they feel," he said and took a long sniff of the excrement on the floor. "Yes, Mr. Sloth better now, can go home soon!" He accentuated by stroking the inverted patient.

Moving without even a pause Navu reached into a small bag around his waist and started spreading a suave like gel across the panthers left hip telling me the panther was a much better patient. She believed he could make her better. With the suave applied, he laid the big cat down on a pile of straw and authoritatively seated himself on the stack of bales.

"So James, what to know did you want?" He asked laughingly, as he silently waited for me to respond.

"I was expecting to find Malchizadec..." I started, disarmed by his un-characteristic jumbled speech. Navu acted with power and authority, this seemed quite different.

"Yes - but not now. To show your work, it is time. Many eyes you draw. The birds are near and safe." He chuckled and pointed out the hay door. High above the hill the three birds circled on the currents of the wind.

"They hide in plain sight. Can you the same do?" He inquired in the twisted dialect.

"What, fly?" I replied, thinking how absurd my question sounded.

"No, hide in plain sight," Navu answered back. "So James, what do you really want to know," he repeated in much clearer diction.

"Well, all these people. I was hoping Malchizadec would give me some idea what to say to them, really what to do with them." I continued, getting frustrated with the diversions when I needed some support even though I knew he intended for me to learn something that still escaped my reason.

"Easy, easy," he answered. "They came for healing. Give it to them."

"But I don't know how to heal," I argued back.

"She thinks you do," he said pointing to the Fer-de lance.

"But, I didn't do...," I tried to assert again when I heard him cut me off.

"Yes James - you did! Now come, sit," he maintained, motioning me over to a bale. "What you really want to know is how to hide in plain site! Not so you can run away, but so you can work effectively. You can't do much as a healer if everyone looks at you as a phenomenon, a guru, or a freak." He exclaimed with the clear, commanding demeanor I'd witnessed at the Counsel that night of initiation.

"Sometimes… best play… fool," he resumed in his halted, crazy sage patter, this time with a grin. "It keeps people from attaching to much importance to a personality. Now, let me tell you a little more about healing, and about you," he said regaining his composure but giving one more wry glance. "That is… if your time it is worth… you think?

"James, when I asked you to act," he said, emanating his Zulu nobility once again, which strangely enough fit comfortably on a hay bale throne in this Kansas loft, "you reacted immediately and did not let go even when you realized that you held something that could kill you. When she struck, you followed your instincts giving her the medicine without retaliating or diverting to protect yourself. A true healer responds even in the face of his or her own peril. You act like a healer; you are a healer.

"Hold on." Navu said cutting me off as I was about to object. "I know you don't believe you did anything but the medicine bundle you think solved the snakes' problem was only a bundle of tied grass and mint, nothing medicinal in it."

"It sounds like trickery. That doesn't seem like it would heal anything." I responded still skeptical that I had anything to do with the serpent's recovery.

"Listen, I will explain -- with no tricks of course." He replied disarming my uncertain willingness. "There are three elements in healing. First, the patient must be willing to heal; that is, the very soul of the patient must feel it has more to gain by giving up the illness than by remaining ill. Second, healing requires faith that the treatment will bring about change; one must trust that it works. Finally of course, one must believe in the healer and be fully assured that they can execute the healing method. These elements are true, no matter whether the healer is a surgeon or Shaman, a faith healer or a *Curandera*. Malchizadec works with the light body of his patients, my healing comes from old African traditions but when these three elements are present in the patient's mind and emotions, the spirit restores the vitality of the body."

I thought about the three elements as Navu stretched his long form back against the haystack. Neither Andrea nor I had been fully willing to let go of our old wounds before the initiation. We clung to them, and the injustices they represented, like treasured pets even though outwardly we seemed to have healed. The Spirit animals that had destroyed us in the jungle bypassed our defenses and healing was the natural result.

"You watched as the panther, sloth, and these two slithereens transformed." Navu continued as if he knew I had connected my thoughts to his message. "The loss of their habitat disheartened these two snakes. They were dying because they were so homesick they would not eat and no longer had the will to do so. The stubborn serpents suffered so; they would rather fight to die than fight to live. Then, with a target for her anger, the snakes struck out and by tricking her into eating, you caused her belief to change. Healing was a natural outcome. The sloth was too tired to climb back into the trees. If he could rest upside down hanging by his claws, he would get better. He could not muster the might to hoist his clambering carcass up the trunk even though staying on the ground he would die. I only made him sleepy with a few herbs and hung him by his claws from the rafters. When he awakened and relieved himself, flushing his worries on your shoulder so to speak, Mr. Sloth believed he would get better. This panther felt the burns on her body and could not overcome the pain even to care for herself and lick the wounds. A little slime smeared on the injuries did the trick. Her pride was stronger then the pain, so as she cleaned herself up, she engaged the healing process."

Navu stood up and with his commanding gate went around the loft gathering all the animals into one place. Then standing upright before them he clapped his hands and in a calm authoritative voice proclaimed "Goduka," which caused the animals to disappear immediately, not leave, but disappear.

"Sometimes you have to tell them to go home." He said as he gave out a hearty laugh. "They listen best in Zulu.

"So what did I do to heal them?" He whispered, stepping over and moving his face directly in front of mine. "I let my spirit listen… listen to theirs and reacted without thinking, without concern for personal danger, or attachment to the idea that the healing depended on me. You did the same. Healing is always an intercession by one spirit for another without the interference of either ego. The hard part is keeping the ego from sticking its nose in. If it is out of the way, the Creator does the work. You must learn to hide in plain sight, so to speak."

"What about the lavender light?" I interjected. "It is always present when Malchizadec works, isn't that the healing force?"

"Ahh… the 'Tempest Light,'" Navu replied noting my observation. "No, the Tempest Light, what Hahn calls Heaven's Light, is a side effect, a florescence that happens when the energies of the Creator flow through spirit. It means things are being shaken up and reordered. Truly, it is a clear light, it is the Ray of those involved that colors it. Malchizadec is a 7th Ray soul, some call that Ray the Violet Flame, so his involvement tints the light with the lavender or violet hue. The glow appears because the Creators energy vibrates the substance of spirit causing it to emit light, the same way physical atoms give off photons when excited by heat or electricity. It is the confirmation of change in process. It's important to recognize the Tempest Light but it's easy to overlook in ourselves. It shows the Creator is busy." Navu bent forward and blew sharply on my hands. "Take a look at your hands for instance."

Looking down at my hands, I saw a golden glow surrounding them like a big baseball glove that extended outward for several inches. The energy rippled like waves blown in the breeze.

"Did you do this?" I asked fascinated by the warm rich glow.

"No! It's like electricity -- been there all along. I only stirred it up. You see, you didn't even notice it looking from the inside out." He said laughing at my surprise.

"So what about these people, how do I give them healing?" I asked again.

"Hide in plain site." Navu said still grinning broadly at my interest in the glow. "Let your head give them information based on what they know and can understand. Let your heart give them love without conditions. Let your spirit do what it already knows and don't interfere. The Creator will take care of the rest. I know you came for Malchizadec, but you and I have much to do together. It was time to begin.

"Janell," Navu said, projecting his voice towards the steps behind me. "You've been hiding away there for sometime. Are you coming up?"

Two wide golden eyes peeped over the edge where the stairs came through the loft floor. Mortified that Navu had spotted her stakeout, Janell slowly clambered up the steps and shambled over beside me looking like a disobedient toddler fearing reprisal.

"I was looking for James, that's all." Janell said ostensibly fearful of Navu.

"May I see it?" Navu asked without introduction, looking directly at Janell.

"What?" She replied defensively.

"The scar you've been hiding from the world so long." Navu gently rejoined. "It's time to free you and remove the mark."

"But…" Janell sighed, starting to cry as she pulled up the left pant leg of her shorts to reveal a large "D" branded on the outside of her upper thigh.

"Are you ready to let it go, and all that it means?" Navu asked intensely. She nodded but remained fearful of Navu's approach.

"I am not the one to heal you." Navu continued. "You have no faith in my magic; James can release you if you're willing."

Flabbergasted by his statement, this time I roared an emphatic "BUT…"

"Let your spirit do what it all ready knows and don't interfere." Navu repeated, unmoved by my protest.

I looked at Janell, who appeared as unsure as I felt, and noticed that unlike the strong, capable, and intelligent woman, I usually saw, there was a mis-alignment. As Bashira had mentioned, my human propensity was to focus on what was right in front of me, Janell presented herself nearly perfect physically, what I typically observed was her intelligence and attractive-ness. This time I let my perception widen, as I did so, Janell resembled something like a comet; there was a dense, bright body, with a wispy tail of effluvium. The lavender glow of the Tempest Light around Janell's body dimmed on her left side and streamed off to the right as if it were blown off center. At the end of the tail, I saw another bright concentration and something in me recognized it, a voice inside said, "Invite her spirit back. It has moved from her body fearing the pain that left the mark."

"Janell, place your hand over the scar," I began, as I walked up. "Are you willing to give me this scar and the fear it symbolizes to become whole again? Your spirit remains afraid." Janell looked at me as if she had never heard those words.

"Yes, but no one has ever been willing to… I mean… I don't want to harm anyone else." Janell said, timidly placing her trust in me.

I closed my eyes and imagined the golden glow around my hands expand-ing to connect with the lavender aura of Janell. As I did, I felt them warm until they were almost hot and could feel the energy tingling through them. Placing my hand on top of hers, I invited the displaced concentration to her side to return. In my mind's eye, I could see the shining focal point move slowly back in line increasing in brightness as if her entire being was reintegrating. I opened my eyes realizing the change had vivified the remnants of Janell's displaced light body which now shown with a grow-ing violet luminance. Exactly as I had watched Malchizadec do, I focused on her light body, passing my hands over the area where the scar persisted while asking the Creator to heal her body removing the mark from body, mind, and soul.

"I can't… It couldn't have… It can't be gone…," Janell exalted, lifting her hand to reveal smooth supple flesh where the brand had been and passing her fingers across the fresh bronze skin in astonishment. "Now I belong to me," she said in an assured whisper. Janell resolutely reached out, kissed my hands, which were still warm, and threw her arms around me in a thankful embrace.

"Yes Janell, it's really gone and behind you now," Navu said, giving her a gentle glance. "You can grow again." Turning to me he continued, "You see James, when the spirit is ready, the healer appears. The sun is getting low in the west and you have much to do this evening. You two had better go." Navu concluded, opening his hand in front of his heart as he bowed majestically with a playful salute.

The sloth's gift mandated a quick shower and a change. After my rapid cleanup, I realized I hadn't asked Navu how he came to be in the barn, but one thing was certain, that night of initiation was no dream. Navu was real and he must have transported somehow from that far away jungle. Did he know how to use the Nexus? I wondered. Curiously, Janell said nothing more about the scar, though the healing in the barn continued to dominate my thoughts along with speculation about the source and meaning of the wound. When she was ready to tell me, I assumed she would, but if that day never came, it was enough to see her restored.

"James, James. Are you listening?" Janell burst out brimming with enthusiasm. "I came to tell you about the data I collected from the questionnaire. "Look at this," she said handing me a copy. "They're nearly all like that. I don't know how, or even exactly what it means, but look how many have written they want to help repair the world. These people care about life on this planet. They're here to help! Oh." she said, stopping her excited chatter. "Thank you for your help! I will not forget…. Someday, I will tell you what you released me from."

Janell's foresight had concisely discovered what was on the minds of the people around us and organized its useful essence. Their latent sense that things must change for the benefit of all, was seeking expression. The dream was activating them. Now it was time for me, as Navu directed, to give them a chance to heal themselves and help repair the world. When I had changed, we went outside where Mason had stepped into the role of folksy maître d', with Will Rodgers' charm, he was showing another group how to find their way through the farm and where to park.

"Are you coming," I yelled over to him.

"Yep, I ain't about to miss this dance. Hope you can 'cut this rug' better than you two-step though Chief," he said as the four of us walked together up the hill.

"How, or what are you going to do?" Andrea asked.

"I was told by Navu in the barn a moment ago to give them information they can understand, love without conditions, and to let my spirit do what it already knows without interference. I think I'll try that." I said without thinking or editing my words to which Andrea looked at me with a sudden start.

"Who is Navu?" Mason asked at a loss.

I tried to describe the Zulu chieftain and summarize his lesson, but it was impossible to portray his quirky training techniques. Janell nodded affirming my comments and I was relieved that we were near the crest of the hill and I would have no more time for explanations, no chance to reveal accidentally Janell's secret or my efforts to help her.

"What did he do to you two?" Mason asked giving a muster master's review. "You're both kinda fluffy and glowy... all lavender and gold... like you're them iridescent violet and daisy mascots at a local garden show." He concluded satisfied that he had defined our anomalous afterglow.

"Must be an after effect of the healing work he was doing," I said deflecting attention and trying to learn to hide in plain sight. "I'll stand with the sunset behind me and maybe no one else will notice," I said jokingly, but it was my intention.

"There're folks here from other countries you know. Why would people come from that far away?" Mason asked sincerely. "Are we prepared for this?"

"I know, it's unbelievable how far one Internet posting has spread, but it is what it is." I replied, thinking here's another problem I hadn't thought about and hoped the force that motivated them to come would work its purpose.

The Internet posting had drawn a trickle that turned into a flood and the flood became a wave of humanity that washed up upon our hillside. High magic was at hand and I could feel it. Just as in the jungle, I heard the voices of tiny lives beneath each footfall, the worms and wort, the mites and microbes, the grass and wild flowers reaching out to us. The trees rustled melodically with the breeze and birds twittered in excitement. Were we ready to take on this evening's task, was I, or was this some grandiose ego trip about to delude me? I wasn't sure, but Navu's words returned to my mind, "Let your spirit listen to theirs and react without thinking about what will happen."

Meeting Hahn, Jake and Ch'ien Li about halfway up the hill, all of us slightly afraid to let the smiles creep across our faces as the seven of us joined. Simultaneously we knew that what was about to happen felt right and good. Walking on together, each footstep was gently set with intention to bless each being that granted us this passage impressing our course with gratitude and adoration for this hallowed ground. Atop the hill we were the proverbial "rag tag band of refugees out to save the world," and perhaps at the deepest level about to save ourselves. It was time to speak, time to give the Earth a voice.

The conversations throughout the unlikely gathering subsided as I walked to the crest of the hill and it seemed I was about to destroy a vacuous silence at my first utterance. The crowd had grown from those gathered earlier around the tractor, but they looked at me as one face with fixed attention awaiting my response. I looked around letting my spirit listen to theirs. The large cadre flowed down the hill engulfing the lone hedge, the "Coyoté Oak," that grew upon the slope where my gaze happened upon the form of Owl perched atop the tree; this time I could see it was Sorrano. I turned further to see Bashira, as Coyoté sitting on the adjoining hill across the saddle. One lone bird, Malchizadec, circled in the sky above us. It was time.

"I didn't know why you were here when you arrived. Now I believe I do." I started, confident of what was about to happen between us. "Some common truths and a common experience have drawn us together. The dream that awakened us gave no answers, but made us ask better questions. We looked into the hold of that decrepit ship, heard the cries of human suffering, smelled the stench of greed unchecked, but for us it was a vision, only a vivid dream. Hahn and Ch'ien Li lived that horrible night at sea. Though they survived, everyone else perished and the causes of that tragedy continue for many, all around the globe. We know that a dream woke us up, not from a night's rest, but from a slumber of acquiescence and apathy. We know that our nations, races, and religions do not listen to each other and that their members often fail to embody the ideals taught in their traditions. In fact, many have used those ideals to divide, suppress, and even kill in the name of the Most Holy. We know we have stopped listening to the impassioned cries of the Earth, to our fellow creatures, and indeed to each other. We have stopped listening so long we have gone deaf. Today we can hear again. A dream woke us up.

"A few days ago," I continued the passion rising in my heart. "We saw despair too frightening for our eyes. We were blind to the toxic haze that spoils our sky, the lesions in our soil, and the venom that flows where once there was bright water. We didn't see a million mothers' tears shed for children that they could not feed or shelter from pestilence and war. We overlooked the homeless, cast upon our streets and did not notice their growing numbers. We turned away from sights that bruised our hearts. We refused to gaze on harrowed habitats destroyed to meet our need for energy, food, and water; we overlooked the animals and plants left extinct in our wake. We averted these sights until we went blind but today we see each other. A dream woke us up."

I finished as the setting sun squashed wide on the horizon knowing
the enchantment of the hilltop would speak more powerfully than my
words. I stood speechless for sometime when I noticed tiny threads of
light extending, first from a few people, then reaching out from one to
another and blending in the most complementary casts. As I peered over
the crowd, the soft radiating light began to show from others. The light
spread throughout the group, as if drawn by a weaver's shuttle to lace the
woof and warp of candescent cloth that stretched across a master's loom.
Drawn together by a fearsome vision, we were now bound together by
light. It was beauty without limit. One by one, like fireflies around the
pond each woman, child, and man ignited in an iridescent tapestry tinged
of countless colors, shades and hues. The Tempest Light showed bright. I
let my spirit listen, reacting as it directed I turned to the west, to the melding colors of the setting sun and gestured for everyone to sit down.

"As you watch the sun sinking towards the horizon," I directed as the
wave of movement flowed across the settling crowd. "Imagine you are
sinking into the Earth beneath you. Relax, and let your presence settle
comfortably into hers. There is no separation; you are part of her grand
essence. Your breath is a swirling of the wind that swaddles her being;
your eyes are but a porthole through which the Soul of the Earth gazes
out upon her course. Let your conscious mind calm and become only
that porthole through which she may peer. Let your self merge with the
Earth's and allow her deliberations."

The threads of light had expanded, swelling up like fountains in a choreo-
graphed display. I moved to the back of the group and sat to avoid blocking anyone's view. The entire slope of the hill shimmered with dancing
radiance as the sun merged with the horizon. Just as before on this knoll, I
felt the rotation of the planet spinning along her route through space. The
vastness of the solar system shrank into an intimate community where I
knew my neighbors Sun and Moon. The fountains of light like an auroral
dome covered the group and extended outward merging with the glow on
the horizon. The luminance rose towards Malchizadec where it glistened
with violets, lavenders, and plum colors as his wings soared over. The

substance of spirit was excited and we interceded one for another, persons, earth, and sky. A dream awakened us and called us together, but from this moment, essence binds us. Quietly united, within us an inner voice invokes; "May the Tempest Light flourish in the Creator's work."

The Coyoté Oak: Burgeoning Wisdom

CHAPTER 11
A BARRISTER'S BOND

The top of a hill at sunset is always perfection, a fleeting foretaste of cosmic creativity displayed for our imagining. Last night, persons, earth, and sky melded in that imagining and its portent of promise drew me back for this morning's sunrise. The red-orange ball had not risen when I decided to return to the crest where my first encounter had unfolded a few days earlier. I quietly made my way through the growing encampments; the country space I cherished was a sleeping village, a collection of characters seemingly plucked from the ethers and assembled for some yet unknown purpose. They longed to affect change in a world they felt had lost meaning, compassion, and life. A revolution was happening in their lives, here, on our land. This morning on the hill, I hoped a voice inside could chart the course between last evening's impassioned encounter, and a reasonable endeavor to occasion such a shift.

"I'm joining you this morning," Andrea said, slipping her hand into mine as I was half-way up the hill and losing ground to worry.

"Good, two heads may be needed to find our way home again," I answered pointing at the sprawl of tents below.

"What shall we call it?" Andrea asked with a smile looking down at the canvass cloister.

"The tent village?" I asked.

"No," she continued. "Since you found the first feather, something has been struggling for birth. First, the events only involved us but they have steadily emerged from ill-defined apparitions into certain substance. Yesterday it reached critical mass encompassing many more people; last night, it crossed the event horizon. Everyone found a positive vision and a common purpose. It is born, it's an organization, a living thing now and it needs a name. What shall we call IT?"

"Any ideas?" I asked turning to Andrea.

"I was hoping you had some," she replied.

"I haven't thought that far ahead." I continued.

By naming something, one crosses the last frontier of denial where it becomes an entity unto itself. It surfaces from the depths of quiet imagination and takes root on terra incognito to grow its own form. A Chinese proverb says that how something begins determines its character until its end. Naming it would mean it has begun.

"It seems so important that all the ideas I have come up with seem trite. Fine Feathered Friends won't work right?" I quipped with a grin.

"Probably not," she winced.

"It's hard to believe that only last week we looked out from this hilltop on just our land," I continued. "Now it's a village with people who think we can change the world like it's… just our Earth."

"That's it" Andrea exclaimed! "Just our Earth is THE perfect name."

That could work, I thought to myself, but the acronym would be "J.O.E." Malchizadec ought to find that amusing. As we neared the top of the hill, the sun splashed the first warm rays of morning across the slope. It seemed fortuitous that we named it in the place, and at the same hour, that all these events had begun. JOE had promise we could hardly wait to share and the beauty of the morning only added to our exhilaration.

"Good Morning" a voice said to our left.

We hadn't noticed anyone nearby but there, sitting wrapped in a blanket, were Jake and Ch'ien Li. They wore that nervous blush on their faces that comes when others first notice a relationship. That expression that holds in uneasy balance, the anticipation they feel for each other, and their concern that others accept it. Andrea and I likely wore a comparable expression balancing our enthusiasm about the new name JOE, with the surprise of meeting them.

"We have something to ask you," Andrea called out.

"Come on over" Jake said with a beckoning wave welcoming our approach as an indication of our tacit acceptance.

I suppose it was. Immediately taking the cue, Andrea stirred through the details of our discussion with the prowess of a magician preparing to unveil a dove from beneath a handkerchief.

"So... we thought a good name for this organization might be 'Just Our Earth.' What do you think?" She said, finally releasing our conjuring into flight.

We were as nervous waiting for their approval as they had been waiting for ours. They gave each other a slightly puzzled look; I guess they hadn't expected any decision making this morning. Ch'ien Li repeated the name in Chinese and then smiled.

"Very good name," she said with clear confidence.

"I like the name but what it is going to do?" Jake finally responded. He had his father's knack of grounding heady ideals with a teaspoonful of reality.

"That is the next dilemma," I replied. "We'll all get together in the workshop and do some brainstorming later this morning." I concluded leaving them to enjoy the morning light and the fresh buds of their romance.

"Something is happening James! Ever since it started it's been, ready or not, here it comes." Andrea emphasized, as we started down the hill. "All we can do is do our best and trust the rest. There is no way we could have prepared and planned for what has happened already. This is the point where we have to have faith that we are being guided through it all,"

"You're right. None of this is happening through our doing," I agreed and her idealistic grit was what I needed to hear. "But, if 'things are as they begin,' is JOE's beginning the union we felt last night or, the terror of the shipwreck? If it's the latter, this may not be an easy journey. One thing's for certain, we need to set this up right so trouble doesn't follow down the road." I concluded feeling as though we had inhaled the first life giving breaths of our newborn idea.

A slither of mist swaddled the far valley below us, following the creek bottom's winding course. Towering through the fog, reflecting the opening beams of daybreak, a windmill turned in the soft breeze as if inviting Don Quixote to dispatch one more futile foray. In the early light a hodgepodge of activity was developing, people were waking up when we walked down through the campgrounds; some were cooking breakfast on portable camp stoves, others were packing up ready to return to their work and family. We stopped and talked with many folks and introduced the idea that we intended to sustain the connection we all had experienced. Many expressed a desire to stay and lend a hand setting things up, to shape whatever form our effort was going to take. There was a tremendous talent pool in this accidental assemblage but putting it to good use would be a challenge. Their enthusiasm was infectious and after an hour or more of conversations and creative suggestions, we finally made our way back.

Janell was flipping banana pancakes at the stove when we came into the kitchen with Lorenzo attentively positioning himself in her path every time she moved to remind her that he was available for handouts. "Sit down and eat," she instructed, carrying a platter full of cakes over to the table where Hahn sat with his eyes widening, as the aromas of banana, melting butter, and maple syrup mingled in the kitchen air. Seeing his anticipation, Andrea picked up the platter and passed it over to him telling him to dig in. Lying on the table beneath the platter was a morning paper

Janell brought back from town and Andrea's eyes fixated on the paper. "Consolidated Chemical Clinches Contract with City," the headline read. Her face became more pallid with every line she read and as we silently waited, she was well into the second page of the article when there was another knock at the door. I answered to find the Sheriff again, but unlike his typical professionalism, this time he was standing too upright and wore a self-conscious expression that looked like a teenager about to ask for his first date.

"Come on in. Would you like some breakfast?" I asked seeking to normalize the awkward moment.

"I have some papers for your wife," he said, reaching in his back pocket and sheepishly handing them to Andrea. "Maybe you better read these first, and see if you still feel hospitable."

"What is it, a warrant for my arrest?" Andrea joked nervously.

"No," he replied, but it's not good news." He replied clearly bothered by his task.

"Notice of Condemnation" Andrea read aloud, after unfolding the letter. "The health department, through a warrant sworn out by the city attorney, has condemned my property....What?"

"After the fire it seems like adding insult to injury," the Sheriff said, "but the department does the job as the Court tells us and since I had met you folks, I brought the papers myself."

"Look at this! It's dated three days before the fire." Andrea exclaimed as she kept reading the notice. "Putting me out of business once wasn't enough?"

"Folks, can I give you some advice — off the record!" Sheriff Blackwell emphasized as he dragged out the extra chair and positioned himself at the table next to Andrea. "There is a lot of money being thrown around at city hall concerning this plant coming to town. City government believes this will be good for the local economy and has knocked down all the barriers to bring this to town. Your property happened to be in the way. It's not right, but with such determination in play, I'm afraid if you fight, it will get even uglier."

The clattering of breakfast forks came to a standstill and not even maple syrup would sweeten the silence. All ears had tuned in the Sheriff with acute interest, waiting for him to continue.

"The police department has arrested a suspect in town and charged him with starting all the fires but to my mind, it's too convenient," the Sheriff explained, making us fully aware that he was speaking outside of his obligations. "The suspect is a mentally challenged man, shall we say, about whom few are likely to care. He has a history starting fires as a child, but nothing even remotely sophisticated...." He concluded with a thoughtful pause.

Rubbing his chin with his hand, Sheriff Dan Blackwell's chiseled features intensified as he thought. He was a straight shooter making an honest effort to help who didn't need a hat, boots, or a sidearm, to look like he had stepped right from the old west. One of those rugged individualists who felt comfortable in his own skin, he was quite at home on the range but his reticent forethought suggested his suspicion that there was more trickery involved than this town had witnessed in his long career.

"I think a pro started these fires and this guy was set up to make the investigation go away," he continued in a slow deliberate manner. "Many people want this project, no matter what the cost, but it's not my jurisdiction. This is some dirty business..."

"Should we get a lawyer?" Andrea interrupted grasping that things may be shaping up even worse than we thought.

"Yes, and a good one. I'd encourage you to be very careful," he replied calculating his words as if weighing whether or not he had already said too much.

"This is OFF the record! I came out last evening as you requested and went up the hill with the crowd thinking I would find you. I was there when that light was playing tricks," he continued warily. "I saw… Well, I don't know what I saw. Anyway, I didn't find you." Then as if he wanted to change the subject, he said, "There seems to be a lot cropping up around you folks right now. Better do something about food and sanitation with this many people sticking around; it's beginning to look like a rock concert and I guarantee the Health Department will flush you like yesterday's dinner if you don't," he concluded.

There was a strangely polarized silence in the room. The Sheriff arrived duty bound to deliver news that devastated Andrea, eliminated the value of her property, and would surely complicate any insurance settlement. The disparity between the papers he served and his helpful comments, made it difficult to know if he was an old west champion for truth and justice, or a dutiful servant here to enforce his county obligations. I still had enthusiasm about this new enterprise JOE, but Dan's sobering admonition had tempered it. I wondered if the beginning was to define JOE's character until the end, what transitions may lie ahead.

"Would you like that breakfast Sheriff?" I repeated.

Janell followed my invitation by piling a tall stack of flapjacks on a plate for him. I couldn't help but think with the plate down in front of him that the intrigue was stacking-up just like the pancakes and getting stickier than the maple syrup. Somewhat taken aback by the cordial hospitality, he accepted and asked us to call him Dan. Between his bites of griddlecakes, we engaged in table conversation trying to explain the crowd. It was difficult to describe how people responded to a post made on the Internet and how we never expected them to show up in person, or find a common purpose, much less launch an organization.

"Those were delicious," Dan said as he finished the last bite. Rising from the table, he reached into his wallet, to my surprise handing me a business card. "Like I said, be careful," he reiterated, "if you want a good lawyer, he might be the right person for you. He's done some work for me." Embossed in elegant gold scroll on the card was *J. Remington Parks, Attorney at Law*.

The warning I took seriously, along with his recommendations. We needed a lawyer for several reasons and it was time to act; I decided to see what I could find out about J. Remington Parks before I contacted him from a web address listed on his card. Perhaps I was overreacting, but I was a little suspicious of anyone whose name started with an initial. Somehow, the G. Gordons, and E. Howards always turned out to be CIA operatives or something to that effect.

Remington or "Remi," as he chose to be called was a former U.S. Senator, now practicing law in Kansas City. His Vita revealed that for several years he was a senior partner in a high-powered corporate law firm in San Francisco. Among his former clients were several major corporations including, Luther Mallory Incorporated. There was that name again, Mallory seemed to be everywhere. Parks' current clients were fortunately quite different from his opulent past reading like a Top Ten List of major charities. This J. Remington Parks sounded like someone with all the credentials one could ask for, the connections to handle any legal work we might need, and someone we could never afford. Nevertheless, I picked up the phone and gave his office a call. The worst that could happen was he would say no. He didn't! Furthermore, he would be in our area next week and agreed to meet on our turf Wednesday, at the farm, which was fine by me.

In addition to researching Remington Parks, a further search on Consolidated Chemical swiftly revealed that they were a division of Oil Resources and Transportation Inc., ORTI. All of a sudden, we were right back at the same place. Maybe I wasn't overreacting. The dream, the ship, and now the chemical company all defied coincidence. I felt we were like that old freighter sailing in the fog, and that we were about to collide with something big enough to overrun us. The referral to Remington seemed unusually convenient too, coming as it did at the same time that he was opportunely in our area. I questioned whether he was someone we could trust, or the helmsman sent to steer us into certain disaster.

As usual, Mason would be rolling into the workshop shortly; it was time to get going and leave the breakfast delights behind. In addition to all the "JOE stuff" and resolving the Perfect Form problems, work was waiting back on our real job, the vineyard. After we discussed the new name and developed a framework for the organization with everyone, Mason, Jake, and I would care for the new planting. The young vines needed shaping, staking, and protection much like our new endeavor.

Mason arrived sprawling on the couch and I was prepared to answer his usual "mission question" but uncharacteristically, he said nothing. I had a tendency to assume that other people felt like me, a quality that had often left me surprised, and disappointed in the past. I needed to check the emotional temperature of everyone before expecting they all would sign on this time, also Mason was sick to death of "touchy-feely process" after all his years in rehab groups so I hoped I could draw out his cooperation.

"It might be a good time to talk… to hear everyone's perspective on what we've been part of... and... where do you think it should go from here," I started, looking at everyone. "Does anyone have anything they want to say?" I asked, eliciting several minutes of awkward silence.

"Grandfather has something to say." Ch'ien Li said, after a nodding exchange between the two of them. "He feel very important you know how we here. It about light like last night," she said easing the uneasy hush.

"This is first time I saw heaven's light." Ch'ien Li began speaking in first person for Hahn. "When I young boy, live on farm in Anhui province in Eastern China. It 200 kilometers from Shanghai. I take goods to town, trade with others and listen to stories from travelers in marketplace, places far away. Stories intrigue, want to see. I plan travel from home when duty to parents complete. Father and mother very old, need me work our little farm. Both die in cold winter when I fifteen year-old. Following spring I go.

"I want travel Silk Roads, the ancient trade routes connect Asia, Europe and Middle Eastern worlds for two thousand years." She continued, with more confidence. "I plan go as far west as road would lead me, look for adventure in cultures I hear about. I work for food, lodging, and money along way. I travel through Gansu Corridor and follow northern trade route. It take ten years to reach Urumqi, far northwest in China, there

Silk Road turn south to India, and Persia. Trade routes very active for centuries, people from many backgrounds travel and settle along route. In Urumqi, most were Torgut from tribes in western Mongolia."

Ch'ien Li told the story as if she was sitting around a tribal campfire recounting their ancient oral traditions. Clearly, she knew this narrative very well, like silk threads woven in her memory since childhood. Our interest captivated, I listened to her halting speech and watched her passionate animations, like a treasured cloth unveiled on our behalf.

"Grandfather was a Han, named for his tribe, he a Mandarin speaking outsider. We add 'H' to name, more better for English," she continued, looking directly at him and narrating as if the story were her own. "The trade routes brought many cultures to same place, Mongol tribes very clannish, want remain distinct. They expect their people stay with own kind. He broke rules, fall in love with Nara, my grandmother, a Torgut from Daur tribe. They met trading in Urumqi. Such relationship not accepted. When her relatives hear of their affection, they come Urumqi angry, take her back to village near border of Kazakhstan. They not see each other for over a year until Nara run away. They marry and hope put end to resentments. Not so, only fuel hatred. When family hear Nara expecting first child, they enraged. They think shame them, not allow her thin bloodline with someone from outside tribe. Her brothers feel obligation try stop. One night break in house beat Nara until they think her dead. Intend to kill child. Nara live long enough to miscarry, give birth to frail, premature daughter."

"I beat also," Hahn interrupted intent on telling some of the story for himself. "I practice speak English too," he replied to our astonished interest. "Want me feel loss of family, you say… retribution for soiling their own. Knocked out longtime… awake find baby gasping on floor. Name her Tui Li, mean Joyful Light! So happy she live I not wait for word to reach Nara's family. Leave at once, hide Tui Li in suitcase, go north far away where I work and hope stay safe. Make bond with barrister who own important farm one day allowed operate farm… my own. Thanks to him, we safe and happy, raise Tui Li no trouble. When she marry, I so happy! Hope she have love and joy I not have. That not be.

"Tui Li heart broken first year, husband die in accident on farm. She already have Ch'ien Li in belly. Tui Li's body not rise above frail beginnings die in childbirth. Infant not do well and I frantic help her. Not bear lose another person I love. I very angry to all people cause heartaches. Vow revenge. That when first see heaven's light. Light appear around Ch'ien Li, heal us both and voice whisper, 'There is no enemy, only those that do not understand.' I feel hatred drain from heart, great love for granddaughter replace it." Hahn paused for a moment rubbing the top of his head as if recalling something of importance. "I knew greater destiny saved us for a purpose." He continued indomitably. "I knew we would continue the journey west. Now we here and destiny reveals purpose. Heaven's Light saved us from the sea, and now it heals others here. It is time we help in any way asked of us." Hahn concluded with his English nearly flawless.

Hahn's story touched us all. Ch'ien Li added that they both felt this purpose and must learn about the source of their fortuity so I shared the lessons in the barn, about healing, avoiding the limelight, and the Tempest Light. Even though we might be required to play a healing role in the face of our own peril, the consensus was unanimous to go forward. The silence returned to the room. This time, it indicated the solemnity we each felt realizing that by grace, we were part of something astounding, something for which we all felt ill prepared. After a short reflection, we had only to decide how we would conduct this work, "hiding in plain sight," and what exactly was our mission? Andrea then introduced the name, Just Our Earth, and was pleased when everyone loved it. We had committed to an ambitious project, one not of our asking and this meeting's agenda demonstrated the scope of our ambition; we had to quickly make decisions that hit the mark before I engaged a lawyer's expertise.

We decided that JOE would be a research and educational organization focused on deep ecology. It would honor the interconnectedness of all creation. This ecological approach acknowledged the spiritual dimension as well as the environmental. It would give the public a way to categorize the group's work, without making it necessary to explain every aspect. We could accomplish the healing work in the background. JOE would serve body, mind, and spirit in a way that people could relate to, and understand. In particular, we wanted to find practical applications for the lessons Malchizadec, Sorrano, Bashira, and Navu were teaching us. While the Avans, birds, were currently the heralds of change and the means through which the healing events occurred, we must keep their presence secret and the group must be prepared to function on its own after their departure. Most of all, we could not be perceived as some strange "healing cult," that endangered the birds, or ourselves. We had a lot to learn.

Like Malchizadec's story, *A God Named Joe*, the organization named JOE would be nonsectarian and inclusively serving people of all creeds. The vineyard and orchard would be a pleasant face to present to the world and give the organization room to expand. The next hurdle would be how to pay for the needed, additional facilities. We decided to become a non-profit organization, set up a website, and hope we could attract suitable donors, which gave me reason to mention my appointment with J. Remington Parks next week. In the mean time, Janell and Andrea volunteered to draft a mission statement, a clear expression of the organization's purpose, while I prepared the website. Mason would take over operations of the farm temporally and finish with volunteer help. Ch'ien Li, Hahn, and Jake agreed to manage the gathering of people and the encampments. We adjourned our meeting after accomplishing much, and set to work.

"Whew, I was getting boufée delirante," Janell said relieving the tension of our long concentrated effort.

The past days had remained busy but before doing anything else, I wanted validation that we were going in the right direction. Remembering what awaited me last time in the loft, I climbed the ladder looking around cautiously. I certainly didn't want more moldering dung landing on my shoulder. Though Malchizadec had remained out of site for several days, the customary lavender glow showing through the trapdoor suggested he was present. They were all there, each administering their vitalizing treatment to a bunch of bugs. There were all sorts of creepy crawlers moving about the barn floor blipping in and out as had been the case with the other animals. Bugs, I thought, why bugs?

"'Even as you have done it unto the least of these my brothers, so have you done it unto me?' Isn't that what Jesus said?" Malchizadec asked. I never expected him to quote the Bible but it was clear by his actions that his intent was to include every spiritual tradition, and exclude no one, no creature, from compassion.

The heaving mass of insects quickly included me as part of their crawl space. Thousands of wrigglers, hoppers, and darters covered my legs and torso. Every last nerve in me wanted to start slapping, swishing, and smacking them. I wanted them off.

"What are they saying," Malchizadec asked. "Can you hear them?"

I was having trouble hearing his voice over the screaming revulsion in my head let alone theirs. Their voices were muffled and indistinct at first, but I could hear them after I overcame my neurotic impasse, exactly as I had heard the voices of the tiny lives in the jungle vision. I tried to narrow my attention to single voices out of the raucous throng. Most of them had no awareness of my presence. I was merely another upright form on which to search for food or a mate, it was subsistence thinking, "life 101." Then I noticed some discussions that seemed to rise above the subject of basic needs. These conversations were among the exoskeletal philosophers, if you will, who were postulating on the nature of the thing they were on, that is to say, me!

One scholarly centipede, gesticulating in mass with his legs, was saying that I was merely a lifeless extension of the world they knew and that the bugs should develop and use my resources. This *Manifest Destiny Group* argued that since they had found this territory, by eminent domain, they had the right to claim and use me as they wished. Other philosophic insects in the conversation asserted that I was a living being with free will and a destiny of my own.

Within this *Free Will Group*, which considered me a living thing, there were contentious divides. One faction considered my life of no consequence; I was simply a living resource available for exploitation whether that was for livestock, or as a slave. The remaining factions of the *Free Will Group*, argued amongst one another. They considered me to be, by virtue of my size, and their inability to comprehend my nature, the Supreme Being, God. These arguments ran the gamut. Speculations included; how they could use my power to gain control over others, awe and fear, the need for unquestioning devotion, and the formulation of rituals to beseech my attention, favor, and forgiveness. Whether Deity or delicacy, I was feeling completely misunderstood, and prospectively used.

"How is it being God?" Malchizadec asked with an erudite smirk.

"It's a little too alive for me. It sucks!" I exclaimed, struggling to control my expletives.

"Why don't you command them to go away," he replied calmly as I squirmed.

It sounded simple enough, so I tuned into the same state of mind that allowed me to hear the conversing hoard and impressed on their collective minds that I was not God, nor any form of Deity, and requested they leave. A wave of disappointment swept through the mass along with feelings of resentment and betrayal. Clearly, this throng didn't want to give up their beliefs.

"It's the Devil's trick!" A tiny wasp said to those around him.

"Yes, God is only testing our faith." His companions insisted.

No matter what I alleged, some group or another reinterpreted what I said to fit their cause. Being thought to be more than I am was more than I could handle. Finally, I gently brushed the hangers-on from my body hearing them cry. "Oh God, how can you let these disasters happen?"

"So James," Malchizadec began, "any thoughts?"

"Just exasperation," I replied. "Why did that happen?"

"It's the nature of encountering something larger than one's self." Malchizadec replied contemplatively. "Not only physically larger, but larger then one's sensory, mental, and emotional functions can process. Fortunately, you didn't start believing it too. It is hard to avoid the effects of such deep adulation. Glamour is just as seductive as hatred. Nonetheless, they both have the same result, separation and isolation. Are you prepared to handle it?"

"It might be easy to deflect the exaltations of a bunch of bugs," I answered, "but that doesn't compare to those of other people, let alone a crowd."

"Last night the people on the hilltop experienced something magnificent," he continued in a resolute voice. "It exceeded their senses and as they try to understand it, there is a great potential to create false Gods. As you've experienced, much can ensue trying to comprehend such knowledge."

"Can you give me an example to understand?" I asked.

"Do you remember the *Pedeo*?" Malchizadec responded. "When you look at the fruit, it is round and colorful. If you only had sight that is all you would know of it. However, with all your senses you are able to capture the aroma, the flavor, the texture, and sound of it as you bite into it. Now if I were to draw a picture of it you would lose not only what your senses have experienced, but also its round shape. It would be only a two dimensional representation of a three-dimensional object. If I were able to reduce it further to only one dimension, it would appear as a line as long as the *Pedeo* was wide."

"Then if there were no dimensions, it would appear as only a point, right?" I interjected starting to understand his point.

"Yes, that's right. All the characteristics of the *Pedeo* remain the same in reality, but the loss of each perspective makes it more and more difficult for anyone to experience the qualities of the fruit. A person simply could not understand what a Pedeo was if they had limited dimensions of information. Last night people caught a glimpse beyond their three-dimensional world," Malchizadec expounded. "They cannot accommodate it, comprehending the new knowledge, so they will try to assimilate it making it fit into what they know."

"You mean people will try to explain the multi-dimensional experience in a three-dimensional way?" I deduced.

"Right again!" he replied clearly pleased with my understanding. "Then, like what happens to the *Pedeo* when drawn with fewer dimensions, one fails to understand its nuances. As the locus of their encounter, it will be easy for them to focus on, and attribute what they experienced to you. That can glamorize and exalt you. Your challenge is to extinguish such notions as they arise. The changes over these past few days have been good even if somewhat overwhelming for you. By the way, *Just Our Earth* will serve the purpose well, though ultimately, you will provide a great service far beyond this Earth. For now, you must learn to draw attention to the task at hand while remaining invisible. As Navu told you, hide in plain sight."

Malchizadec inscrutably, always seemed to answer my questions several layers deeper than I had thought them, even when I hadn't asked. I inferred that our efforts to carry forth the work that these trans-galactic heralds had come to accomplish were acceptable, but that we, I especially, needed to watch out for the traps that such attention could bring. I climbed the hill this day to seek wisdom from that quiet voice we all hear inside ourselves when we really listen. In that still communion, I hoped to discern the clear path that enabled those who had come here to find the purpose in their journey. It seemed as though some new order was emerging from the superbly stimulating chaos. Answers had come, yet they always arrived in the company of more questions. Even with the advent of new uncertainties, as upon the hill last night, the lines of light were extending. With the determination of Little Oak, we had germinated and burst into the light of the world. Like Hahn, we now walked a Silk Road steeped in romance, adventure, and the dangers of high visibility. Hahn's barrister had steered him safely through a dangerous course, I trusted the bond with Malchizadec would guide us in our perilous portage if we could hide in plain site and keep our roots planted firmly in just our earth.

CHAPTER 12
SEVEN PENNY TRUST

"The whole is greater than the sum of its parts." Aristotle said. Exactly as a design becomes an entity unto itself when you give it a name, it also becomes more than the sum of its parts. *Just Our Earth* was becoming an entity, a whole system, unto itself though the qualities of that system engendered by its "wholeness" remained in unknown territory. Malchizadec's brief comments about JOE alluded that the system we believed we had formulated had not surfaced from our quiet imagination, but rather, it was the implementation of a crafted plan. Something was coming into being that we never could have imagined and certainly didn't plan. I presumed Malchizadec knew the characteristics that would emerge from the "whole," but we were still discovering and organizing its parts.

JOE had come into being through what the psychiatrist Carl Jung called "visionary creativity." Whether the birds were the visionaries, or were themselves part of it, I didn't know. However, it had come into all we "mere mortals" lives as a powerful, complete idea seeking those willing to be vessels through which it could find form. The process of rasping away our egos so that we could receive it had been happening for years. Hahn, Ch'ien Li, and Mason had lost everything they loved. Life had systematically stripped away much that Andrea and I cared deeply about as well. For each of us it was a painful process. Jake also suffered watching the pain of Mason's addiction and homelessness. It tore their family apart. Through the conflict, Jake learned to seek peace on the inside and bring harmony to those he loved. His dedication showed in the fond relationship he and his father had now. I didn't know all of what had prepared Janell for this task, but I was certain it was similar and would become clear in time. Her incredible ability to organize information and take action had already demonstrated her value. *Just Our Earth* was more than the sum of its parts and though it had come into the world through our "rag tag band," it now shaped our lives with an unknown purpose.

Even if the core phenomena surrounding the birds were irrefutably supernatural, *Just Our Earth* was developing very naturally. Important ideas, whether creative or scientific works, it seems, always have sort of a supernatural component. Something that makes one say, "Wow, where did that come from?" because it so exceeds expectations. It's almost as if some preexisting "whole" is imperceptibly present, seeking an outlet in our world, seeking an artist who can capably deliver it. Visionary creations are not the result of personal genius but rather, are a response to needs felt from the collective consciousness. Receptive artists get their personal egos out of the way and, almost supernaturally, allow the "whole" to impress their minds and flow through them. Life taught me that lesson as a musician. Visionary creatives are willing to surrender their skills to the needs of that "whole" and bring it to form. That was also a lot like what Navu had said about healing, especially his statement, "The hard part is keeping the ego from getting involved."

Many days had passed since our meeting in the workshop and the visit from Sheriff Dan. Since then, we had started addressing the day-to-day operations pretty well. Janell informed me that she went to city hall while in town and filed for the appropriate permits on our behalf. Mason too had taken action arranging portable toilets, shower facilities, and trash collection so the tent city would be more comfortable. For now, the waste wouldn't overrun the farm, and the county would remain satisfied. Donations of time and money came unexpectedly from the tent encampments to help cover these needs; the seven of us chipped away whatever remained. This was enough to get us started, but it couldn't provide a way to grow, or sustain us very long. The website was up and waiting to draw attention to our cause, creative projects always absorbed me, but the mission statement for JOE continued to stymie Andrea and Janell. It wasn't for lack of effort; it was because, in spite of our idealized fervor, we weren't sure ourselves. We needed knowledge of our task, not a feel good platitude.

"How did it go?" I asked as Andrea walked in and set an unusually large stack of mail on the table after a morning meeting with her insurance agent.

"They only want to settle for the materials in the building," she responded glumly, "not the building itself since the property was condemned. They're not certain that I didn't have the property burned down because it was condemned and won't pay anything until the arson investigation is complete. I'm relieved you called the lawyer, this is going to be a real mess."

"Remington will be here tomorrow morning," I reassured. "His office called a little while ago to confirm our appointment. What's all the mail?"

"Most of it is addressed to you and some is to *Just Our Earth*," she said sorting through the pile and opening the first envelope. "Take a look at this!" She yelped.

In her hand was a check for $10.00. Whether it was $10 or a $100, it was the first donation and it showed that people were interested in what we were doing. We hastily opened letters dumping out checks and dollar bills, fives and twenties; all totaled there was $2,116.07. A little girl in Cleveland had seen the website and sent us seven pennies because she loved animals.

Seven pennies was the smallest donation but clearly the most touching. The faith of a child has a sobering effect because it isn't laden with bias or political correctness. It is a pure thought with honest unedited emotions, the seven pennies were a testament of unselfish caring and her innocent hope that we will watch over the animals she loves. Everyone gathered around the kitchen table and we shared her letter with the group, and each of us bought one of her pennies to remind us that others were counting on our commitment. Those seven lackluster copper tokens of trust gave us pause and were the start of The Seven Penny Trust; a fund dedicated to the role children could play in caring for the environment they would inherit. I personally wrote her a thank you letter signed by all of us and headed out to share the good news with Malchizadec.

The loft was dim when I returned wondering what would be waiting this time but there was none of the normal activity. Stepping into their ascetic sanctuary, I found Sorrano and Malchizadec engaged in a brooding conversation, though I couldn't hear their discussion, both of them looked concerned. Something was very different; most of the straw was gone and then I noticed a yellow bundle high up in one corner where the rafters joined. With great precision, they had weaved a large mass together, anchored it securely to the crossing beams, and constructed a nest. There in the middle sat Bashira. Still this circular straw settlement was curious. By this time, I seldom thought of them as creatures much different from me. My relationship was as a friend, and in Malchizadec's case, he was my mentor. Since they had not assembled a permanent nest until now, I assumed they didn't need or want one. Sorrano and Malchizadec acknowledged my arrival, but not the surprise on my face.

"What's going on? Doing a little remodeling?" I asked trying to lighten things up as they made an oddly somber approach. Sorrano looked at me starting to speak but then deferred to Malchizadec as his emotions caught in his throat.

"Bashira and Sorrano are expecting," Malchizadec said in a strained hush with the great nest looming above his head.

"Congratulations, that's good news... isn't it?" I exclaimed but then grasped the gravity of their concern. "Is everything all right?" I queried.

"We aren't sure." Malchizadec explicated carefully. "Though Avans have traveled for many centuries, these sorts of complications haven't occurred."

"I came to ask for your guidance as we set up Just Our Earth but under the circumstances ...perhaps it's..." I said puzzled and hesitating.

"We must proceed right away despite our impasse," he interrupted. "Tonight will be fine. Bring the group to the grove this evening after the camps have quieted down. We won't be there long," Malchizadec continued, sensing my worry.

I knew his attention was on Bashira so I excused myself and as the barn door creaked closed, it felt like everything had changed. This would not be easy news to share. Even as I remembered the helplessness of being sick far from home, and feeling the lack of support when I needed it most, that didn't come close to the complexity of this. How much more at risk, they must feel.

The creak of the back screen door reiterated, as if in concert with the barn, that everything had changed. Normally I wouldn't even hear the rusty sonance, but today it underscored how the fragile situation had tarnished my naive feeling of accomplishment. We all had become an interrelated whole absorbed in performing our jobs; it felt like we were acting as a unit with each person fulfilling their niche but our interrelationship fostered a collective disquiet as I told them of Bashira's dilemma at supper. We ate in a stunned, concerned, contemplation hoping Malchizadec would explain more. In many ways, we were like children in a family suddenly learning that our elders, no matter how superior they seemed, also had frailties and that life was a two-way street.

The hours passed painfully slow between supper and the time we would meet Malchizadec. The eager conversations that normally flowed amongst us were unvoiced. We each needed introspection to adjust our idealized images of the Avans. Not without merit, we had placed the birds on a pedestal; it was time to consider a new reality that, despite their advanced gifts, they needed our kindness too. I spent the last hour alone in my office contemplating the two feathers and the obvious changes that were all around the farm, but the transformations in me were still in progress. For the moment, I was comfortable not knowing the outcome and perhaps even relishing the ambiguity.

With monastic precision, we streamed out of the kitchen walking single file towards the grove. The sounds of nature's night shift called as we proceeded across the prairie. Coyoté and Owl, Nightingale and Bobcat, each crooned with matchless voice an affirmation of their life, a song of joy and suffering, of challenge and reward. The harmony of the midnight madrigals eased the sadness and reminded me that balance was the way of life. Long trellises stretched out before us in the vineyard as we plodded our contemplative procession avoiding attention. The stars reflected along the wires, gleaming as if they were beads strung on silver thread. Quivering in the clement evening breeze, each wire hummed, adding its voice to accompany our advance. They marked our course until one by one at the end of their expanse; our fervent figures traversed the threshold of the grove and entered the portal where the mundane joined the mystical. Once again, as we walked into the heart of the grove, the thorn wood began to transform until high above us, the cathedral boughs sheltered the simple circle of stones.

Malchizadec and Sorrano were waiting in the circle where the flickering fingers of amber radiance wigwagged patterns of light and shadow on the canvas of venerated vegetation. As we entered, Ch'ien Li walked directly up to Sorrano, her diminutive size outlined against the great Avans, punctuated the strangeness of accepting their vulnerability. With courteous fortitude, she anxiously queried him about Bashira's condition trying to span the divide between the pedestal we placed them on and the insoluble situation.

"Thank you, you're concerns are correct Ch'ien Li," Sorrano replied, glancing over at Malchizadec as if taking leave to answer her questions, "and since Bashira and I are responsible for your worry, I want to clarify what we are facing. As James may have explained, we are not actually birds; these are only the forms we most easily assume here in the morphic resonance of your world, therein is the problem. Usually, when a female Avan learns of her condition, she immediately returns to Satoria, resumes her Avan form and completes a normal pregnancy."

"So will she be going back to Satoria?" Ch'ien Li asked, in a dismayed tone at the thought of Bashira leaving.

"No, and that is the cause for our concern," Sorrano continued his voice even more distraught. "Unfortunately, I have to give a bit of a biology lesson to answer this. Engrossed in our own preparations and observation, we were here for several months before contacting James. We didn't consider the possibility of a pregnancy. Avan gestation results in a live birth, but unlike humans, we are ovoviviparous instead of viviparous. That is, the female incubates an egg internally, hatching it in fourteen months to deliver a live hatchling."

Malchizadec paced back and forth as Sorrano spoke, looking more preoccupied than I had ever seen him. His wings folded back in his familiar pensive bearing, but their tips were twitching deliberately as if he was cautiously waiting to add to Sorrano's account.

"An Avan must return to Satoria within the first few months before the hard shell forms." Sorrano continued. "Once formed, the embryo is separate from her body with no umbilical connection to the mother. The embryo is then a discrete entity inside the shell, protected within her womb. Bashira is too far along and unable to return. Though she could still dematerialize and travel in her light body, the independent egg has no such ability on its own. It would simply remain behind. Therefore, in order to save our child, Bashira must give birth here and then teach our hatchling how to transform its body before we can travel home."

"There is yet a greater concern, Sorrano" Malchizadec underscored, addressing him directly, "upon which, even with all my years…. I can only speculate…. Avans are much larger than this in our natural state; I am not sure whether the egg will develop sized to fit Bashira's current body, or whether it will enlarge. If it is too large for this body, it may kill her, despite our healing abilities."

Despair swept across Sorrano's face as his innocence dissolved in the hard rain of responsibility and we could say nothing to help. Sorrano was devastated as he grasped Bashira's mortal danger, and understood that even with Malchizadec's wisdom, he could not foresee, prevent, or somehow lead them through these dire straights. Spiritual growth may come with responsibility but knowing that even for such sublime beings, sometimes it requires a stiff whack to trigger it, was more than I could absorb. The hopeful anticipation that always accompanied our visits to the grove had evaporated. In its place was a sinking muddle of helplessness and compassion.

"Unfortunately, I don't know what influence, if any, the resonant fields may have on embryonic development," Malchizadec said with an under-standing look to his disheartened apprentice. "The morphic resonance that causes us to materialize here as birds, will shape the fledgling's develop-ment the same as it affects us. There are many variables; the newborn's form may be completely unknown. I emphasize, this has not happened before and the complications are unknown."

"Is there anything we can do to help?" Jake asked timidly, in seeming doubt that our capabilities could help improve the situation.

"Well... circumstances will require Bashira to remain in the nest for several months," Malchizadec replied solemnly. "Sorrano, you of course, will have to devote your attention to her care. Certainly, they both will appreciate any assistance the rest of you can offer. I must spend more of my time to get all of you ready for your own challenges. Everyone's at-tributes will be needed collectively." He replied, pausing as if to consider how to proceed.

"I have told you," he continued, "do what you know, learn all you can and trust that the rest will be provided. We Avans also trust we will be provid-ed for even as we face our present vulnerability. In the interim, we must do what we know and teach you all we can. Understanding everyone's concern with things as they are, we must continue." Malchizadec said softly making eye contact with Sorrano, Bashira, and each of us before directing us clockwise around the familiar stone circle.

This time, the cantata did not cease when we each sat upon our individu-ally resonant stone. The tones sounded individually, cascading downward through the scale and repeating the progression several times. Intervals began to sound, major thirds, minor thirds, fifths, fourths, and sevenths, resonating two at a time in consort and revealing the temperament of their relationships. Three and four note chords formed from the intervals with each tone alternating as the center of focus. Then, from sudden silence, Malchizadec eruditely instructed us to listen carefully. A single pitch rang forth so sweet and clear it defied description. A curtain of undertones and overtones enveloped each resonance along with a distinct colored lumi-nance that engulfed the stone circle and reflected from the canopy above.

Latent within its cascade of harmonics, each tone and color held some portion of the other tones at higher and lower frequencies.

Ringing out each harmonic in an ascending progression, the arpeggio repeated faster and faster until they were indistinguishable from one another and formed a new resonance all its own. The colored hues began to fuse, until a bright beam of white light shown skyward from the circle of resonant stones upon which we sat. It seemed as though time stopped around us at the base of the column of light and sound. The moment enfolded eternity and ages passed in an instant. There was no way of knowing how long it lasted, nor any desire to know. We sat only aware of the stillness in whirling creation until we found ourselves surrounded by dense jungle with the stone circle still supporting us. Like the initiation, there were concentric rings of people like wheels within wheels; we had transported to the lush setting where the Counsel of Elders met. Then Navu appeared from the sidelines and joined the two Avans standing by the fire exactly where they were in the grove. Malchizadec began to tread slowly around the circle of stones, his shadow dancing across the lush tropical foliage of the dense jungle. Commanding everyone's attention with his ceremonial gate, he stopped to swathe each of our awestricken faces in his wings as he passed.

"My friends," the great raptor began. "There is one more song I ask you to listen to. Let your mind be still. Don't think about the answers you have come here to find, open your mind, your heart… your spirit. With all that you are… listen!"

It was quiet, absolutely -- quiet. Initially, I heard a very low-pitched sound, lower than I thought I could hear; it felt as if I was hearing it with my body and not my ears. Then I started to hear more tones, some low, some high, and in between across the spectrum, tones grew stronger for a while and then faded into the background. They all seemed to modulate in consort, one deferring to another as if each had its time to dominate. Though a beautiful constant chord, it sounded melodic as the frequencies ebbed and flowed yet always complementing the constant low resonance. High and low, we all heard this "Great Chord" clearly throughout its range and then, amid the harmonic expanse, Navu walked to the center of the circle with Malchizadec carrying a small African Flute.

Navu pressed the small ebony instrument against his lips and began to play a long sustained low tone in unison with lowest note of the Great Chord that seemed to intensify the vast resonance. Within a few seconds, he blew harder, which forced the flute's tone to jump and repeatedly with each bolstered breath, it emitted a higher pitch. Finally, it reverberated with such severity that it seemed the polished wooden instrument would fly apart. Navu's virtuoso performance would have upstaged Malchizadec were it not clear that their flamboyant demonstration had a common purpose. Each time the note had changed on the flute; different frequencies came to the fore in the Great Chord. Even the environment around us vibrated in resonance causing similar sensations in my body as Navu played.

"Everything is energy in vibration. Every *thing* is vibration." Malchizadec elucidated, his voice amplifying the penetrating frequencies. "Whether living or inanimate, vibration is the core of its form and sound is concealed within it. Every sound has a frequency - or pitch - causing it to resonate and entrain, with others in which the same pitch is found. Vibrating energy organizes in octaves and produces harmonics that resonate at frequencies that are multiples of it. Further, when different vibrations interact they produce nodes of resonance where the energy field becomes very dense. The physical forms you see are really vibrating energy fields and all their harmonics. They are densely packed nodes of resonance that your senses perceive within different frequency ranges.

"The Great Chord, which normally exceeds your sensory abilities, is the song of Earth. It is the Earth's core sound with all its harmonic elements. It is the collective chorus sung by all the creations on Earth, from microorganisms to great blue whales, from subatomic particles to the globe itself; every man and beast, plant and mineral, has their melody. Physical forms are all combinations of harmonic resonance. As long as the melodic parts remain in the same relationship, the song continues. If one note become too strong, just as Navu showed with his flute, the harmonics change, and the song changes. No single portion can exalt its place without changing the whole.

"Likewise, the song is not the same if any part diminishes. Every chord has a key, every instrument its timbre. Something greater emerges from their sum in combination. If one is taken away, the whole is tainted and its emergent characteristics transform. When enough is lost, it ceases to be what it once was altogether. It loses its timbre, its verve. Eventually it is no longer a chord and has no key. It is dead.

"The song of Earth has played for eons. A sonata with many movements, various parts raised and fell throughout the course. The composition remained the same, written to allow its parts to slowly evolve, change, and create with one limitation. Each part must complement the whole; they are inter-related, interdependent. One cannot change without changing everything. If any alteration is too great, or too rapid, the results can be catastrophic. Such misfortune has come about within the course of Earth's song irrevocably ending millions of lives, and eons of development.

"So the questions, why are we here? Why are you together? What are we ALL here to do? Simply put, our task is to bring the Great Chord back into balance. We are to help maintain the natural progression of Earth's song, as the Creator composed it, so that all its parts might change, evolve, and create. If this is not accomplished, then all manner of prophesied events will occur. The apocalyptic predictions are inevitable only if the parts of the whole remain out of balance. Jesus said, 'If thy right eye offend thee, pluck it out, and cast it from thee: for it is profitable for thee that one of thy members should perish, and not that the whole body....' Humans interpret this tenet solely within religion relating it only to them. Is it not also true of greater lives, even the Earth itself?"

I looked around to see Hahn and Ch'ien Li in rapt attention absorbing every thought. Janell was in tears. The picture Malchizadec was painting was so stark, so vivid, and so purely spoken it seemed to pierce her normally well-organized self-image. Andrea seemed angry; her idealized perspective that everything would be all right was crumbling. Jake looked worried. I was trying to resolve the disparity of being part of the problem while being asked to become part of the solution.

"Now how the h... can WE do all this?" Mason exploded, brusquely interrupting Malchizadec's treatise. "Aren't we the offending eye? How are we," he added pointing us, "halfway powerful enough to stop anything anyway?"

I looked for a reaction to his outburst wondering if those present outside our group might doubt our place. Across the many circles beyond us, there remained serenity with what seemed like a calm, supportive understanding of our need to absorb the magnitude of the task. I didn't know how, but it seemed clear that everyone present intended to help us transition from our place in the problem to being part of the solution.

"In the last hundred years, thousands of species of plants and animals have become extinct...gone," Malchizadec rejoined, pausing to acknowledge the difficulty of making this clear, clear to Mason, clear to everyone.

"They no longer exist on this planet." He continued. "Each of them was a note in the Great Chord; a note vanished that will remain forever missing. Over the course of time, species have come and gone in a natural progression. When one completed its time, another species evolved to play their melody. The song continued even though those performing it changed.

"Never in this planet's history have so many species been so quickly extinguished; the cataclysmic end of the dinosaurs is perhaps an exception. It is sad irony that the burning of oil, the liquefied remains of that calamity, now threatens greater extinction. We came to try to avert such an event. If too many living elements vanish, too many notes fall silent in the Great Chord of creation, the chord and its harmonics will collapse. Earth and all her life will collapse and that demise will adversely affect even distant worlds that resonate to the same frequency. Beneath the vast distances of space, everything connects... as it does on Earth. What changes one, changes all of them.

"You have discovered that humans are not the only sentient beings in the universe. Indeed, there are many. All things have sentience relative to their existence. Is one more important than another? Every note in a song is irreplaceable and one must not drown out another. Plainly said, humans are playing their part too loudly. They take too much of the systems energy for themselves. If the song is to continue, humans are the ones in danger. Does humankind want to be 'plucked out,' or can humanity stop offending the greater body and play its glorious part to advance the whole instead of just their kind?

"Science has given much. However, in an effort to understand, they often destroy the whole while examining its parts. For example, physics, chemistry, biology, and psychology all attempt to explain creation from the perspective of its dissected portions. Even ecology, which seeks to look at the interactions of the entire system, has forgotten to include the spirit. Religion, which addresses the spirit, too often only subjugates the mind and body without acknowledging the sum of creation. No one perceives the full composition.

"The song of the Earth you have heard tonight is but a stanza of a greater composition. Lao Tzu, the Chinese teacher, called the totality of existence the Tao. Each part of creation is a unique, inimitable piece. The personal challenge in following the Tao is to discover one's unique part in it, or Te. By living their Te to the best of their abilities, they fulfill the universe. Every note completes the song. Who studies the song of humankind and weaves its counterpoint with the song of Creation? It is our task to save what notes we can, and educate humans not to play so loudly."

"If we are effective," Navu rejoined, stepping up beside Malchizadec, "it may save humankind from fulfilling its own doom, and help repair the world. The Earth is badly wounded, fallen ill, and even now runs a fever."

Malchizadec stepped forward on Navu's last syllable to spread his wings out to their full expanse seeming to grow larger as he did so. Then, as if he had opened a transom into the cosmos, he displayed upon his feathered mantle what looked like the whole of creation. Before us, galaxies and nebulae, star systems and whirling worlds, traversed in stately succession. Each celestial part revealed the treasures it embraced in a myriad of living forms that gazed back upon us from the awesome array.

"In the greater song, Earth is but one instrument," he beseeched. "Creation spins wheels within wheels within wheels, ad infinitum, like the stone circles gathered around this hearth. Who will perform their part in consort with the greater song of life? At this moment, in this time, human-kind is not the Crown of Creation, but it is a keystone that both supports, and is supported by, all of the Creator's work. Change one part and you change the whole of it."

Then closing his wings on the galactic vista, Malchizadec earnestly appealed to our group, which without our noticing had returned and once again sat beneath the canopied grove of Coyoté Oaks. His words were fire burning in our fears but the passion he expressed, confirmed the depth of his conviction. Our exposed reticence confirmed our alarm. This was vast, larger than we could comprehend and too immense to even dare imagine.

"I know you can not conceive how you could be charged with such re-sponsibility," he continued in a much gentler tone lowering himself down to our eye level peering into each one of us for a moment, with razor sharpness. "How could you possibly accomplish such a monumental task? You are not alone. You have only to begin and accept that all you need will come.

"There are those who are dedicated to destroying the Creator's work, some though ignorance, some through their direct intention." Malchizadec emphasized in an extraordinarily resolute manner. "Some lie repeatedly so that in spite of their false conviction, it becomes difficult to discern the truth, perhaps even for themselves. There are those who have learned to lie with such assurance that they have accumulated great power; at times, even within the ranks of otherwise righteous people. They have deceived many and they will challenge you. You must live your highest ideals, fol-low your truest faith, and remember there is no enemy, only those who do not yet understand. Even so, the solution is a process, not an event. You are part of its beginning. To succeed, all you need to do is reach within yourselves with the innocence of a child, and find the seven pennies worth of trust."

CHAPTER 13
THE DESPOT'S DESIGNEE

I was right and not certain I wanted to be the visionary creative. As if a latent soul were sent from the ethers, a "whole" greater than the sum of our rag tag parts had become incarnate with a character of its own. We were its vehicle. Could we allow the needs of an idea this important to flow into existence through us? Last night's meeting with Malchizadec was as disconcerting as it was informative. After he finished talking in the grove, the meaning and magnitude of what lie ahead had an unexpected effect on each of us. Rather than feeling the strength, enthusiasm, and urgency, Malchizadec had sought to instill in us, we were struggling with a darker side of ourselves. Our fears, insecurity, arrogance, envy, anger, and criticism all seemed to creep in between us on the late night return to the farmstead. The revelations were so intense that all we seemed to see in each other, and ourselves, was the worst, instead of the best. Only Hahn seemed unaffected. This morning I was discouraged sitting alone in my office intellectualizing about what we heard, and how to respond. The isolation wafted over me like a stale draft blown from a dwelling too long in squalor and I was gasping to feel differently when Hahn and Ch'ien Li stepped into the room.

"Grandfather must speak with you," Ch'ien Li said and immediately darted out.

"Everyone caught in front of dark mirror," Hahn began as he approached me at my desk. "All can see are flaws in self and others. When Heaven's Light save us from sea, feel same. Light so bright all I see is what hide in shadows. All cobwebs, specks of dust, weakness, and imperfection glare back at me in mind's mirror. Must not confuse self with negative images in mirror. Instead, must clean house inside. It easier to clean house in bright sunlight then in shadows at midnight." Hahn gave an inscrutable smile, bowed slightly, and then left as Ch'ien Li peered knowingly into the room.

"Does your grandfather ever point in the wrong direction?" I asked rhetorically as Ch'ien Li beamed with pride from the doorway.

"Is time clean house." She replied, jokingly tapping her finger on her head. "Too many cobwebs inside."

I pointed to my heart and agreed before she left. Moments ago, I felt lost in a wilderness of overwhelming magnitude, then like a compass always pointing to true north, Hahn clarified the directions. His insightful allegory made good sense; we needed to be in the best possible shape to take on this venture. J. Remington Parks would be along shortly, so I started a list of the issues needing his legal advice. It was time to get in shape and sort things out on every level.

The list included; setting up a nonprofit corporation, dealing with all the people on the property, settling insurance issues stemming from the fire, assessing the threats made to Andrea, and our possible need for protection. Finally, the immigration status of Hahn and Ch'ien Li had to be resolved. The agenda seemed long and sundry. I didn't know if Remington could handle all of them, but he would certainly know where to direct us. These legal tasks were part of getting our house in order too.

The stained glass lamp glowing in the corner of the living room caught my attention, an heirloom from Andrea's grandmother; it depicted an eagle soaring over a mountain pass that seemed now like a precursor of our current encounters. As I walked from my office into the living room, I could see Andrea and Janell curled under the lamp's halo. They were talking with Hahn seated in one of the overstuffed treasures from her grandmother's house that had traveled with us but looked as if they had never left our country farmhouse. Hahn's discernment must have subdued Andrea's anger and lightened Janell's mood, as both were now exuberant about something. Jake was sitting near Ch'ien Li on the sofa and their engaging glances were clearly a sign of a deepening relationship.

"Please proceed with the reading Andrea." Janell announced with playful, dramatic flare and ceremoniously handed her a piece of paper from the coffee table.

"The mission statement for JOE reads as follows," Andrea enunciated, as if making a royal proclamation:

Just Our Earth fosters, restores, and sustains the harmonious interconnectedness of all beings through education, research, and compassionate intervention.

Hahn grinned immediately with astute satisfaction assuring Andrea and Janell that their work was complete.

"That puts Malchizadec's message into a concise thought that should keep us focused," I said joining the conversation. "Now, let's see if it passes Mason's BS alarm."

"Too deep!" Mason bellowed from the far corner of the living room. "The scale of it leaves me feeling kinda like Bashira -- pregnant with an idea big enough to kill us. Don't you think?"

Without any of his usual glib remarks, I hadn't noticed Mace sitting there. He was in the corner for a reason and it was obvious that he was seeing himself in the same dark mirror I had moments before.

"I understand your concern. That's pretty philosophic coming from an abject pragmatist like you Mace." I replied hoping to pull him out of himself a little.

"Guess I haven't found all seven pennies yet." Mace continued introspectively. "Fosters…Restores…Sustains the harmonious interconnectedness…." Mace mulled, thinking aloud about the mission statement. "Sounds ok, but we should say we're, The Consonance Commission: We tune the music of the spheres," he concluded with his customarily droll skew.

With Mason's sense of humor back, the group seemed to be returning to normal but his dissuasion about the task ahead reflected the validity of Hahn's insights; we needed to "clean house" and prepare for a heavy load. Of course, Andrea suggested we consider a fitness training protocol that would improve our mind-body connection. Predictably Mason objected to anything that would get too "touchy feely," but Jake, who had a black belt in Aikido was enthusiastic. Hahn we discovered was also proficient in Tai Chi a martial art with a similar philosophy and both could instruct us. We committed to each other, no matter how heavy the load, that we would vent feelings immediately, before they became irrationally charged.

An effective way for this group with different spiritual backgrounds was to stay "dogma free" and reiterate the story of A God Named Joe. Predominantly, our backgrounds were Christian. It turned out Hahn became interested in Tibetan Buddhism from other migrant settlers on the Silk Road and had raised Ch'ien Li in that tradition. Janell was reserved, volunteering nothing about her heritage.

"I was born in Haiti." Janell began wearily after some delay and Andrea coaxing her. "My mother was a beautiful, unusually fair skinned, Haitian woman who worked in the sugarcane fields. Papa was a sugar buyer, a Castilian Spaniard who lived in Tobago and traveled the plantations across the Caribbean and northern South America to conduct business. One day he saw her in the fields and won her attention but his infatuation came with no intention of a relationship. Still, Mama loved him deeply even though he provided very little for us. Unfortunately, to him it was only a brief tryst." Janell suddenly stopped sitting very quietly as if she hadn't wanted to say anything at all.

"Go on," Andrea coaxed again. "We've become closer than family here. You need to tell your story to really put it behind you." Andrea reassured as if she knew more of Janell's experience than she let on.

"We were so wretchedly poor living in a one-room house with Grandpapa." Janell continued hesitantly. "A powerful and fearsome man, Grandpapa was a "bokor," a Voodoo sorcerer. Voodoo frightened me but, it was everywhere in Haiti and I couldn't escape its influence...there were always strange goings on. Then, when I was eight years old, our life changed completely. The despotic Haitian President, 'Baby Doc' Duvalier, designated grandfather as his personal bokor. Duvalier, who engaged in Voodoo himself, was very rich and equally corrupt; though Grandpapa didn't like him, you couldn't say no to 'Baby Doc' and live. Duvalier was very impressed with Grandpapa's prowess putting him to work immediately casting spells against his enemies and performing rituals at his palace. As part of his payment, Grandpapa demanded that I be educated at a private boarding school in the US Virgin Islands and that he provide for my college education. Grandpapa tried to send Mama with me but Duvalier wanted her in the country to maintain his threat of retaliation and control over his strident bokor so...I went alone." Janell paused looking at Hahn as if appreciating his protection of Ch'ien Li, then silently leaned apprehensively against the arm of her chair. "My Grandpapa never imagined...," she faltered, emotions welling in her throat as she resolutely resumed. "He never imagined the awful price I would pay before I left.

"Duvalier sent his strong arms to collect me saying they were transporting me to school. Instead, they brought me to a prison-like cabin on the north coast far away from Port-Au-Prince and home. For the next few days, they did whatever they wished to me... I was only eight... there were several men who... I thought it was finally over, that they... that they had stopped... but there was one last hideous.... The brutes branded a large "D" on my thigh as if I was a calf... livestock. They said, 'Now you will never forget and everyone will know who owns you.' I don't know if that was Duvalier's order, or if they were drunk with the power that he gave them. I felt owned and never forgot, the brand insured that...until only a few days ago. I thank James for releasing me from everything that scar meant.

"Despite that horrid beginning, the school provided me the very best education in the Caribbean." She continued steadfastly intent on finishing. "The school was for the children of means; under the circumstances, I was raised and treated there as if I was a member of the Duvalier family.

Children from all over the Caribbean and South America became my surrogate family and I learned about their religions like *Candomble, Santeria, Umbanda*, and Catholicism. *Umbanda*, which blended many religions together, interested me most and I became a trance medium. Sometimes I worked at the local temple doing healings when I got older. Still, I could not heal myself. Of course, you can understand why I don't talk about my past; most people find it too disconcerting. My path may have been different, but the *Aché* sustained me thanks to *Oxala's* intercession."

No one said a word at first trying to wrestle with thoughts of the abuse Janell had endured. I understood that she felt her strength had come from the *Orishas*, beliefs I knew from Brazil, and that they had sustained her through these many years. Almost in unison, we softly thanked her for trusting us with her story and I for allowing me to be part of her healing.

"During my senior year at college in Florida, *car le destin l'aurait*, or as fate would have it, Duvalier was overthrown." She continued seemingly relieved to have shed the secret she had carried for so long. "I left Haiti under his personal protection, and because of that, I became a person without a country having only the money placed in trust for my education. Fundamentalist Protestants took power putting Grandpapa, and many Voodoo practitioners, to death during the rebellion and though I haven't given up hope, sadly I don't know what happened to Mama. I have no country, or family, to call home. Well, that's my story, and my strength. Maybe I've said more than you expected?"

Janell was much far more mysterious than her "take care of business" persona suggested. She had clearly learned to organize and control her world after all she had endured. Haiti, Voodoo, the trauma, her life in school, and her spiritual experiences were so different from our own. With such diversity in our backgrounds, the lesson Malchizadec taught us quickly became clear; we needed to focus on the heart of all the traditions rather than get lost in the dogma of their descriptions. At the core of all our experiences was a meaningful encounter with the Creator; sharing that with each other would hold our work together.

The morning was slipping away but not without surprises and I started mentioning Remington Parks when we heard a car enter the drive. I excused myself and told everyone I would see if Mr. Parks were credible, available, and affordable as they dispersed to allow us privacy. If he was the right person, he could properly set up the organization and deal with the various legal issues we suddenly faced.

"Are you James?" the robust stranger asked, stepping out of a ten year old Subaru wagon wearing a pair of Levi's, his short silver-gray hair almost reflected the bright morning sunlight.

"Yes," I called back, still conjecturing whether he was the barrister in question as I strolled across the porch trying to shift my attention from Janell's emotional account.

"I'm Remington Parks." He said, reaching out to shake my hand with a well-mannered smile as he surveyed the farm. "Maybe I caught you at a bad time. You must be hosting a farm auction or swap meet to draw all these people," he continued.

"It's a long, unbelievable story," I said, "much of which is why I need your services. Who would have expected this from posting a single message on the Internet?" I said intending to leave it there.

"You have me curious now. Please, let's get started." Remington said inquisitively. "I'm a good listener and at sixty, I've have had some inexplicable experiences myself."

"Let's go in the house and talk over a cup of coffee," I suggested, uncomfortable about saying anything more. "A former Senator should be considered company," I joked, extending a more formal invitation as we walked around the porch to enter through the front door.

As we passed the frosted swan, it reminded me of our entry into this altered reality, the hidden birds, and our current need for legal counsel. I ushered him into my office where he took a seat on the sofa while I went to the kitchen to complete my duties as a host. Like a lawyer spending much of his career in the upper echelons, he was meticulously polite with impeccable timing, I thought as I poured the coffee. Carefully juggling the brimming mugs of Java, I came back to find Lorenzo in the room pleasingly plopped on Remington's lap. Mostly he'd been scarce since the barrage of people showed up, occasionally peaking out from under the porch where he still felt he ruled the kingdom. In fact, I had seen him there as we entered. Nevertheless, he was flaunting his aristocratic ambience here whether my guest cared to be one of his subjects, or not.

"I'm sorry Mr. Parks," I said, apologizing for Lorenzo's conduct as I set our coffee down to free my hands and eject the uninvited lollygagger.

"No, it's fine and please, call me Remy," he said. "I like cats, and he seems to be quite a character." Lorenzo looked me in the eye with an excruciatingly satisfied stare as if he had just won a grand prize.

"That's right James, I'm quite a character." I heard an unfamiliar voice say in my mind and realized it seemed to come from the feline interloper. What, was Lorenzo talking now too?

"Why so surprised, you've been listening to bugs, birds, and butterflies for weeks now. Did you think I was a mute?" It continued with a lofty air. "Besides, I'm checking him out for you," the baronial voice advised in a cat-like brogue.

Taking a long sip of coffee to avoid gawking and mask my complete shock at the covert creature, I tried to act normal, not as if I was hearing voices in my head. Remington I noticed, when I set down my cup, was already inspecting the corner behind my desk.

"I like your 'feathers and floss' arrangement, those replicas are very well done," he said, focusing on the dominating enigmatic plumes. "So James, tell me what intrigued so many people to draw them here." He inquired.

"Do you know the word synchronicity?" I replied, wishing I had hidden the arrangement and that he hadn't asked that question. It appeared I wasn't going to avoid any subject as I fumbled for a plausible theory.

"Do you mean 'meaningful coincidence' as Carl Jung described it?" Remington inquired.

"Yes." I replied, "I'm glad you've heard of it as there seems to be many 'meaningful coincidences' taking place here, including my being referred to you. I made an Internet posting about a dream. It seems all the people here had the exact same dream. It wasn't collective symbolism, in this dream everyone witnessed a real event. I never imagined when discussing it that other people had the dream and would show up here," I concluded feeling some relief at having said it clearly.

Lorenzo's repose caught my eye. He seemed completely relaxed on Remington's lap as if to say, I could trust him and everything was A-OK. "Cats know people." The voice interjected again, "Spill it."

That communicated, Lorenzo hopped down from Remington's lap, casually stretching one leg out behind him at a time, and strolled out of the room maintaining his unruffled eminence. A little odd getting advice from a cat, I thought, but whether it was Lorenzo, or my subconscious, the message felt right in my gut. I gave him all the details about the dream, the people coming to our ground, and then I mentioned the tanker's name showing in big white letters as it callously sailed away.

"*Hitam Emas?*" he interrupted with surprise. "I helped put the *Hitam Emas* on the sea. I feel partly responsible if this actually happened. Maybe I'd better tell you more about me since we seem to have another 'meaningful coincidence' on our hands."

"Please do, it's my turn to be curious." I responded without admitting what I already knew.

"I used to have a rather prestigious law firm in San Francisco," he started. "For several years, Luther Mallory Inc. was one of my personal clients. I handled all the big actions with a staff to deal with the lesser responsibilities but in the many years I worked with that company, I never once met, or talked with Mallory directly. There were many rumors about his whereabouts; they almost reached the level of a myth by the end of my time there. Everything LMI requested me to do was ethical, legal, and on the 'up and up,' for the first many years but that began to change in my opinion. I think Luther Mallory's continued absence allowed lesser executives in the management structure to gain too much power. A mean-spirited mid-level administrator named R. Harry Nash was the most aggressive. He was formerly an ill-defined government legate with an undisclosed past."

"So he took over LMI?" I questioned, wondering if Remington had clashed with him and anxious to probe for any further information. I was more than happy to have him talk and avoid further explanations.

"No, but within a few years, Nash and those under him gained control of several corporations within the holding company engaging in ruthless takeovers and very questionable activities." He continued. "Unfortunately, I could never substantiate their criminal activities. Many of the subsidiaries they controlled operated outside the United States where they bribed officials, eliminated witnesses, and did whatever they needed to make exceeding profits. Greed was their only standard. I'm sure they engage in the same practices here when they think they can get away with it. What happened in your dream sounds like the kind of events I suspected."

Whether he knew it or not, Remington had keyed in on Nash, the very person who concerned me when I had traced the ship to ORTI. Though he was unaware of my knowledge, he voiced my feelings about the operation, and its leader. That precipitated an uncanny, thought-filled, hush as Nash's probable acts distracted us simultaneously.

"I became very uneasy doing business with them and subsequently sold my partnership in the law firm after I had a life changing awakening." He expressed with an unexpected candor. "Normally I wouldn't mention this, but it feels like you might appreciate yet another synchronistic event.... Well, for a few moments one evening, I felt as if I had merged with all of creation. It seemed like the violet glimmer on the horizon during sunset expanded outward and surrounded me."

"Yes, that is a synchronicity I can appreciate," I responded amazed that he, with this experiences, had happened to be referred to me.

"After such a transformation, I could no longer tolerate an association with those that cruelly advanced their interests at the expense of others. I couldn't 'talk the talk' unless I 'walked the walk' you know. I moved to Kansas City, changed the focus of my practice to charitable organizations and I sleep much better at night.

"Back to your situation," he continued, regaining his professional persona. "ORTI, the company that owns and operates *Hitam Emas,* is part of the group of companies that Nash controls; I believe the dream could portend some danger. I don't know what connection a company operating in the South China Sea has to you in Kansas, but obviously, the dream has already had jarring effects, look at the crowd. Do you know a connection?"

Remington's story struck so close to the mark that I wondered if he was some well-informed despot's designee here gathering more information about us. There were connections, lots of them, and what he said made startling sense. I didn't know how to answer his question when perhaps his very presence here conveyed another threat. His past connection to the company that was indeed upsetting our lives, his expedient relocation, and the flawless timing of his appearance, were troubling. The errant corporation and individuals he described had already reached from the dream world and snared Andrea's business in their wanton greed. Perfect Form was the first casualty; did Remington's visit foreshadow more? Still, as strange as it seemed, my gut said he was trustworthy and his similar sunset experience bolstered my confidence in him.

I answered his inquiries, unfurling the long series of events from the fire at Perfect Form through ORTI's Consolidated Chemical division that seemed to be engaging in the land grab for it and the surrounding properties. I also described the mysterious appearance of Hahn and Ch'ien Li, and the beginning that first morning on the hill. During my cathartic diatribe, Andrea had joined us in the room lending credibility to the events I described including every detail about JOE and our sunset experiences stopping short only of revealing the Avans. A knock at the kitchen door finally interrupted my train of thought. Knocks at the door hadn't brought much good news lately, I thought.

"I'll get it," Andrea said springing up to answer the door.

"It sounds like you could use a good lawyer," Remington intervened as Andrea left the room. "It just so happens that I know one." He added wryly. "Would you like me to represent you?"

"Well yes, but I'm not sure we can afford you." I said, when I noticed Andrea motioning me to join her. Politely I excused myself and walked towards her slightly bewildered by her expression.

"Is something wrong?" I whispered, when we were well down the hall-way.

"I don't know. Take a look at these," she said pointing apprehensively into the kitchen.

Like cubic manila orphans, two large cartons sat commandingly in the middle of the floor. I cautiously inspected them as I approached, neither had a return address. The boxes were very heavy, wrapped in plain brown paper, and addressed to *Just Our Earth* c/o Andrea and James Davidson. Who would know that?

"Who sent them? I didn't order anything did you?" I asked. My first thought was – it's a bomb.

"No, that's why I interrupted you," she replied. "The delivery driver didn't know either."

Paranoid maybe, but we both feared that this might be some further repri-sal for Andrea's resistance to sell; the memory of the explosion at Perfect Form was still fresh in our minds. On second thought, we decided that a bomber probably wouldn't send two packages and any parcel these days, would likely have gone through detection equipment sometime during transport, especially with no return address listed. Therefore, Andrea cau-tiously opened one, while I unwrapped the other.

"W h a t..." Andrea shrieked, her voice trailing off uncertainly; in her hand, she held up an improbable bundle of $1,000 bills. "It is full of these," she continued with astonishment while I quickly returned to my package and tore into its contents discovering more bundled bills. "Do you think these are real?" she asked. "Why are we getting...I mean who...?" Andrea couldn't even finish a sentence she was so exasperated. Neither could I!

Lorenzo walked in to the kitchen and promptly jumped up on the boxes to sniff at the bills followed by Remington who undoubtedly heard our commotion.

"Is there a problem? Oh..." Remington said and paused almost as stunned as we were before circling around the boxes with fastidious curiosity.

"Do you know anything about this?" I asked apprehensively, noticing the coincidence of his visit.

"Not a thing!" He replied emphatically tossing his hands up in the air. "I have speculated about this kind of dealing though. I suspected Nash and his group used unbelievable displays of cash like this to buy off crooked politicians, silence witnesses, and sometimes even frame people with dirty money.

"This could be millions...so... speaking as your attorney, here's what I advise." Remington continued, immediately adopting his professional role.

With a questioning glance, he elicited my approval. I gladly nodded acceptance of his services and waited to hear what his advice might be.

"Reach into the middle of each package and pull out a couple of these bundles." He added. "Since the money's a bit suspicious, I'll have it checked out to make sure it's not counterfeit, or marked bills from some robbery. Before you do anything, we need to know this money is clean and legal. Now, wrap the cartons back up and put them where absolutely no one will see them." he emphasized as he put the bundled bills in his coat pocket and assured us he'd get back with what he found out.

Remington would set up *Just Our Earth* as a nonprofit corporation, check on the insurance to expedite settlement and call an old friend at the Bureau of Immigration and Naturalization to ask a few general questions about resident alien status. Whether it was a bond formed through meaningful coincidences, or the relief that paying his fees wouldn't be a problem, we had a lawyer. I looked down at the receipt he had hand-written for $400,000.00, which tallied only four of the bundles, as Remington picked up his coat and I followed him out. Upon hearing the door, Lorenzo emerged from hiding under the porch and sauntered to the door. That's odd I thought, noticing that Remington's stare suggested he felt the same.

"Wasn't that cat inside scrutinizing our morning's business?" he asked starting his car as I reflected... maybe this cat's antics were the workings of another surreptitious shapeshifter.

Andrea and I moved the boxes of cash to the safest hiding place we could find in the house, the attic above our bedroom. Should anyone mention the money, Remington instructed us to direct him or her to our attorney. It would be safe there only as long as we could keep another secret. I didn't dare dream of how we'd use it lest we discover that its arrival was a curse and not a blessing. There was obviously a ridiculous amount of money in these boxes if it was real and there was no sensible explanation. No matter whether these packages were a bribe, a frame up, or what I could least imagine, a benevolent gift, I dreaded hearing one more knock at the door.

Meeting Remington was far different then I expected. His foresights, and acuity, were dazzling, but the synchronicity of our experiences fostered confidence. This morning was like no other, once again the line between dreams and reality had blurred, but this time the money seemed to fit in neither. "Tell no one;" he repeated, "no one, not friends, not family – nobody!" his words came back to me. "When it comes to money, especially this much in cash, people leave behind all sense of reason." His last words warned us. We would keep the lid on this clandestine cash in the attic and wait to hear from him. The startling sum was to alter our course and

Remy, as he requested we call him, was a meticulous ally, not a despot's designee here to implement our wreck and ruin; but, what impeccable timing!

CHAPTER 14
THE EYE OF THE STORM

What happens when dreams comes true? A dream happens in your mind, without a palpable odor, taste, or touch, doesn't it? Characters and events don't jump out of your dreams into real life; or, do they? Then there were the visions. Were they dreams, or reality, or maybe something altogether different? When you think your cat talks to you, and it makes sense, dreams and reality merge. When hordes of bugs discuss your relevance to their existence and you can hear them, the boundaries between dreams, visions, and reality fade. It tests you. My life had become something altogether different, it included all of these without boundaries and I was getting strangely comfortable with that. Things had subsided some from the relentless squalls of change, as if we had entered the calm at the eye of a storm; but the cached cash in the attic was unsettling as was keeping it secret from those whose lives it would most affect. Nonetheless, I had to do it.

Fortunately, there were no more knocks at the door to worry about. More days passed than Remington indicated since the money arrived and I was so anxious for a resolution that I was screening every call to avoid any questions.

"James, you better sit down," he said through the answering machine. I didn't! I leapt up and ran over to pick up the receiver. It was a great relief to hear his voice on the phone but how was this news going to affect our lives, for good or bad?

"Here," I answered. "I've been hiding behind the machine until I know who is calling. What have you found out?"

"Like I said, you might want to sit down." Remington began again and this time I did. "Sorry it took so long, but I wanted to be careful, and certain of what I found. It's real, no counterfeits. The money is not marked, and the serial numbers don't match any money under criminal investigation; I know because I checked the entire country through the FBI. It's good clean cash."

"Are you sure it's clean, with no expectations?" I questioned. "Maybe it's a bribe, or hush money. Do we have any idea where it came from?" I rattled off questions considerably more anxious than I cared to be.

"No we don't, and we probably won't know, but it's too much money to reasonably be a bribe." Remington calmly explained, adopting his professional tone. "Besides, there is no contract concerning the money nor is any implied. You didn't offer services or solicit money in any way. You can accept this as an anonymous donation to *Just Our Earth*, which is now a nonprofit corporation with all the paperwork filed. You can use the money with no strings attached."

"OK," I replied too stunned to say more.

"It's about 9 *A.M.* now, and I'm currently leaving Kansas City for your place." Remy continued. "Once I'm there, we'll discuss how to invest these funds over the long term so they will do the most good. This is a lot of money, so I've arranged an armored courier to transport the funds to the bank. Before I arrive, you better gather your group and prepare them for the good fortune. You've now become a very well financed operation. Do some dreaming!" He summed up on a cheerful note and ended the conversation.

I've never seen five more fully flummoxed folks in a room before, nobody said one word for at least two minutes after I told them about our sudden prosperity. Even Andrea, who had been keeping the secret with me, was speechless. You'd think we had not been in the presence of unfathomable occurrences and this was the first. Somehow money, lots of money, brings a kind of awe that apparently is unparalleled even by fantastic phenomena. Perhaps it's because money is tangible; unlike experiencing numinous events, you can't argue with yourself long about whether it's real or not. Finally, the group began to stir and then the murmur erupted into laughter.

"So how much money are we really talking about here Chief – a million bucks?" Mason asked, thinking he'd highball it with feigned nonchalance.

"We haven't counted but taking a guess, I'd say it is more like 50 to 100 million bucks." I answered. Boy did the silence roar back again!

"Well, that's enough to make a silk purse out of a sow's ear," Mason replied in astonishment. "Even if we weren't in Kansas, that'll put wind in the windfall."

"The birds don't know about this, do they?" Jake asked, almost as if he were thinking aloud. "Before we plan how to use it, shouldn't we hear Malchizadec's thoughts?"

"Well then… let's jack up this dirt-track daisy … hit the barn and overhaul for the big-time!" Mason expounded, deliberately adding his hayseed color while we adjourned to the loft.

Continuing to cloak the Avan asylum inside the old structure, we went one by one out to the barn as if doing routine farm operations. Malchizadec and Sorrano were huddled down to the hayloft floor intently working on lichens, and some small moss like plants with their characteristic luminous energy; Bashira was quiet in her nest.

"So, what will you do?" Malchizadec asked once we had all gathered. "Money can be as much a problem as it is a solution you know. Don't lose your seven pennies of trust." He didn't seem surprised, or even excited about the extent of the windfall.

"We need some direction about how to use this for the tasks you've alluded to?" I expressed, hopeful this would fit into their furtive grand design. Malchizadec stood up without response. The loft dimmed as the revitalized flora faded from view and he took a few moments in thought and said:

But ask now the beasts, and they shall teach thee; and the fowls of the air, and they shall tell thee: Or speak to the earth, and it shall teach thee: and the fishes of the sea shall declare unto thee.

"What have they taught you James?" He asked after quoting from the Book of Job. "Haven't they already answered your question? Do what you know, learn all you can, and the rest will be provided." He repeated. "Every creature wants to live and everything is connected – everything! Take every action. Think every thought without fault -- like it matters. Remember, money is not the measure of merit. True worth counts success in the lives it serves but there is still more to teach you. We'll meet in the grove when all the pieces are in place." Malchizadec concluded.

He turned and began to illuminate some unusually green lichens that appeared beside him. Dismissing the group to continue his work, we had just started down the loft steps when he redirected, Janell and I to wait for a moment. We found a seat away from where they were working on the last remaining straw bale not used in Bashira's nest.

"You fear the power within you Janell for good reason," Malchizadec resumed as the barn door closed on his captive audience. "Still… it is yours to master." His words brought alarm to Janell's eyes. "You have questioned it all your life haven't you? You have suffered from people who wanted to diminish your potency," he asked and then waited for her response.

"Yes, My Grandfather said I would continue his linage because *aché* was highly concentrated in me," Janell said in a grave tone rubbing the palms of her hands on her knees, "but I was afraid and refused to let him teach me to be a *bokor*. Knowing all this money has mysteriously appeared, reminds me of Grandfather's work with Duvalier. Money has flowed into my life since then and never stopped. I worry that I'm directing the *aché* without realizing it and fear the repercussions of tainting the money." "Your Grandfather was right about you, but not about your work." Malchizadec replied, settling on the dusty loft floor beneath Bashira's nest as she peered over at us with reassurance. "*Aché*, as you call the life force, is very strong in you. You have always known that, and tried to hide from it. Your Grandfather was a prisoner of his time and culture; your questions about the purity of his work are valid. He sold his services as a *bokor* and sometimes his magical intent was for selfish purposes. That is not the case with you. It's time for you to embrace your gift, focus your intent, and learn to direct it positively.

"A Seventh Ray soul like me, you are a magician, meant to manifest what your imagination can see in the physical world. You must always take care that you align with your soul and allow it to guide your work, rather than self-centered ambition. *Aché* is nether good, nor bad, it is the force of life. Your intention directs it and determines whether magic is white or black. Intention precedes every act. Be certain you know what guides you." he emphasized standing to his full height as if to punctuate his comments. "Your task until now was to purify your physical, emotional, and mental faculties by visualizing and directing the aché through them. You withheld the healing from yourself, not because your body bore the brand, but because your spirit did. You feared selfish intentions until James brought your final release. Your purpose now is to visualize the Divine plan and help manifest it. Guard your intention carefully and the rest will be provided.

"James, I asked you to remain simply to support Janell, you know what lies ahead. We'll meet again in the grove when all the pieces are in place." Malchizadec repeated and directed his attention back to the lichen as we made our way from the illumed loft down into the shadows on the barn steps.

I was a little frustrated that Malchizadec hadn't given a specific answer to our question about the money. Janell's load lifted from her shoulders but the yoke remained on mine. What did he mean, "When all the pieces are in place?" The influx of funds made immediate action possible, I needed his advice now, wasn't building the physical facilities getting the pieces in place? It seemed as though he was focused on a "big picture" and unconcerned with mundane matters like the organization, or money. On the other hand, maybe he was trying to make us stand on our own, but I didn't feel capable.

Like a diligent student, I reviewed the experiences since my extraordinary encounter with Coyoté, Owl, the Shaman, and Little Oak. I appraised the lessons from Sorrano and Navu, remembered the cold wet darkness of the dream, my conversations with plants, animals, and the compassionate sorrow of the "Soul of the Earth." I saw the Tempest Light, heard the Great Chord, and oh yes, denied myself deification by boisterous bugs. All the encounters were quite different. If a common thread ran through them, it was that humankind was not separate. The lives I encountered all desired respect; everything had individual purpose and everything mattered. Humankind was not the Crown of Creation; Creation was the Crown. Nature was more than a natural world; the ecosphere was spirit too – everything mattered! I was a part of nature, but nature was every part of me. If "one part cannot change without changing the whole of them" as Malchizadec had said, then if I change, the whole changes. One person matters. One person makes a difference. I make a difference.

Sketching an organizational diagram before Remington returned, we began to paint the "big picture" as best we could for the ordinary world. We were the Board of Directors and as such, we all had ideas in our heads but it was time for a practical plan. We started with the physical facilities. If possible, we would purchase the land surrounding the farm, which would allow open areas for animals, treatment pens, and a refuge. It would also allow research on a rapidly disappearing environment, the prairie ecosystem. Energy was available from wind and solar generation; our structures would mindfully blend with the habitat complementing what surrounded us. It seemed logical to include traditional medicine, as we knew it, along with the healing skills Malchizadec and Navu continued to teach us. A veterinary clinic would serve the community and help shield the mystical aspect of the healing work; we could work effectively while hiding in plain site.

The educational component faced challenges. Most people can't believe a global ecological crisis is possible; it's too big, with too many areas of blame. We had to reach the people who weren't normally interested.

Environmental groups were working thanklessly to evoke change, but other special interest groups had become very successful at marginalizing their message. Most of us resist change. It is human nature. Too many humans are creatures of comfort and if someone suggests that change isn't necessary, they comply. In contrast, I had seen visions and had remarkable encounters that made it easy for me to believe. What, short of a global catastrophe, could awaken people and tune them in, not out? What would elicit individual responsibility for a worldwide solution? This was going to take imagination. The Seven Penny Trust would provide experiential education for children allowing them to form a deep appreciation for the Earth at an early age and perhaps become better inhabitants of the planet. Spending more time with living things rather than computer games could change how they experience the Earth. They need time in the environment, not just learning from a distance. A campground for children's retreats could help accomplish this.

The most difficult part of informing anyone about anything, is overcoming his or her denial. The overpopulation of humankind and the associated use of resources is the greatest threat to the survival of life on the planet. That's a fact no human wants to grasp personally and it's a lesson needed worldwide. It's easiest to think the problem exists somewhere else. The world population increases by nearly 75 million people every year. True, population growth in underdeveloped countries is far greater than it is in the heavily developed countries of the Northern hemisphere; however, energy and resource consumption are disproportionately vast in our developed nations. As underdeveloped nations advance, they will adopt lifestyles that consume more energy and resources similar to the countries they view as wealthy. As Malchizadec put it, "in the Great Chord, humankind is playing too loudly."

"We're all idiots on this bus!" Mason brashly declared. "We ride along like happy fools assuming the driver knows where to take us. We don't question or worry about where we're going, playing with our gadgets and gizmos as we get the latest fix. What's worse, there isn't any driver! We're dependent with all the symptoms of being hooked and we need more and more." Mason persisted.

While I agreed that Mason's insights were right, many in the group appeared unsure about his meaning. How can we convey a problem this big when we have trouble communicating it with each other? I thought.

"We obsessively consume," Mason resumed from his chair in the corner of the living room. "We desperately search for more, and even when we know it is killing us, we can't live without it. We're energy junkies buying our buzz from ghost pushers."

"What mean ghost pushers?" Hahn queried, trying to clarify Mason's intense remarks.

"Corporations…" Mason retorted. "A bunch of stockholders invest for the sole purpose of making money. The companies are like ghosts with no soul; they're an artificial intelligence focused on making profits for stockholders and the more the better. They're hooked on making money and their customers are hooked on their product. Cigarettes to cyberspace, ecstasy to energy; a junkie can't stop until he hits bottom. Been there, I know! We're even expecting the pushers to solve the problem." Mason concluded, his personal experience fueling the emotion in his words.

"Wait a minute," Janell interrupted sitting forward on the sofa and clearly irritated by Mason's comments. "I grew up with no electricity, little heat, and no running water. We cooked outdoors on an open fire using dried up sugarcane pulp brought home from the sugar factories. The sickening sweet smell of the sugar residue hung over the yard every mealtime. I had to wait for two weeks until we had enough extra wood, pulp, and trash saved up to heat water for a bath. Having modern conveniences is not all bad!" She concluded pointing to the stain glass lamp.

We all took a breath surprised at our intensity. If it brought up this reaction amongst us, how could anyone else get the message? Trying to paint a "big picture" was going to be difficult.

"When I went to school in the Virgin Islands, I could be clean everyday, eat hot food, and be warm when I slept at night." Janell continued calmly, realizing the outbursts had startled everyone. "When I didn't smell burning sugar anymore, I felt like I had gone to heaven. All I'm saying is that if energy use is a problem, the worst part of the problem is that people don't share it equitably. Grandpapa taught me that everything - people, plants, and animals - belongs to the Earth. That seems most true of natural resources, the Earth's body itself. It's more than a 'junkie's' problem -- it's avarice." She concluded trying to synthesize Mason's thoughts with her own.

Energy dependence is like an eating disorder, I thought. You have to eat to live, but if it's your total focus, it can kill you. Using our resources requires the same kind of care and discipline. How do we overcome the dissent of energy-abusing nations, and at the same time, convince impoverished nations to avoid such dependence when they clearly see the benefit others derive from it?

"Greatest denial is idea always find more." Hahn said, with certainty. "Greatest mistake is fear not find any. Nature not play favorites, always have enough. Greed cause scarcity, extremes - that the problem. Must teach the middle way. Then everything balance, find rhythm."

Everything has a beginning -- everything has an end. We cannot avoid that. Hitting bottom, an ending with repercussions on a global scale, seems inevitable unless as Hahn says we find the middle way. One extreme to the other, that's the calamity. The antique Seth Thomas mantle clock in the living room chimed eleven, as if to remind us that even with the passage of time, things continue at their own rhythm. Lions' heads adorned each side of the old timepiece keeping an eternal watch as the relentless pendulum played a tic-tock counterpoint to the steady progression of the chimes. I wound this chronometer each week realizing it was from a different age when life's implements connected directly to those who used them, a lesson easily overlooked in this digital era. If we were to help move humanity from this era to the next without a calamitous turning back of the hands of time, we had to re-entrain the world with the relentless pulse that had sustained creation since inception; like the lions' everlasting vigilance, it was no small task.

Informing people about energy abuse, the "pushers" who keep us dependent on it, and the greed that inflates markets to elicit the highest price, would be difficult. Education was the weapon to counter the problem. To accomplish this, we would use the media developing spot announcements that highlighted the problem and named names; the logical place to start was in our own town where the Consolidated Chemical Corporation was exerting its power. It felt right but unnerving since they had already demonstrated a willingness to win at any cost and we suspected their acrid embrace in our loss. Just as we were wrapping up the discussion, Remi strode across the front porch where I had first ushered him into the house.

"Have you counted it yet?" Remington asked, poking his head in the opened door. "We better have an idea before we go to the bank."

"Feel like playing with a little money everyone?" I responded with exuberance. Mason and I retrieved the two boxes from the attic and dumped the bundles into a green heap on the front room floor. Our eyes widened, our breath held, and we all vaulted into every kid's Monopoly fantasy as we spread the real money out and started counting. Calculated and counted, it was an awful lot of bills that when finished, formed a large contiguous square like mahjong tiles aligned for play.

"There, that makes it an even $105,000,000.00, that's quite a way to open an account." Remington said throwing his four bundles into the pile as we heard a heavy vehicle slow and turn into the driveway. "That must be the armored courier."

I went out surprised to meet our usual parcel service driver on his way up the walk and signed for two more large packages that were identical to the first.

"I think there's more," I said, holding back my laughter as I called into the living room, "I guess a $105 million wasn't enough."

It struck me, as the sound of the second vehicle rumbled down the driveway, that both deliveries came while Remington was here; when he noticed my curious glance, he shrugged his shoulders to acknowledge the coincidence. This time opening the door, it was the armored courier.

There was no more time for questions or counting but I don't know who was more baffled, the armored car driver pulling into a small farm for a pickup, or me seeing the heavily armed driver walk up to take a deposit from me.

"Have you decided where to deposit this?" Remington asked.

"We'll open our account at The Meadowlark State Bank, the oldest, and smallest, bank in town," I said. "It's a locally owned with only one branch. That should help some of our neighbors and maybe prevent the extinction of a few family farms."

"I better call and tell them to prepare for us," Remington suggested. "This won't be an average day at the teller window for any bank, let alone a tiny bank like this one."

The Bank President met us at the curb outside the historic bank's front entrance. That had never happened to me before. Armored cars normally come and go during bank hours, but this was a private deposit and curious bank employees lined the windows to witness our arrival. The President ushered us in, leading the armed guard across the old marble floors, past the teller windows with their wrought iron cages, and into a secure room inside the vault. Once again, we opened the boxes and spread their contents, this time over a long maple table. Two tellers joined us at the table where they agilely counted the crisp green cash and did the appropriate paper work. *Just Our Earth's* opening balance was $207, 005, 116.00, and of course .07 cents. Understandably, the huge cash deposit raised a fair amount of suspicion in the little bank who reasonably could be concerned that we were laundering drug money or some other illegal funds. Fortunately, Remington knew exactly how to address any concerns and insure the legality of our transaction. We set up the Seven Penny Trust with $20,000,000.07, put $10,000,000.00 in a checking account, and put the rest in savings to move into longer-term investments over the coming weeks. *Just Our Earth* was now official, and we were loaded.

Our good fortune spread rapidly over the summer months. This was "small town Kansas" and in no time, we had more people talking about us than a gussied up pig. It was amazing how many different stories, and subplots, we heard about how we received the money, who had contributed it, and what we planned to do. I hadn't seen so many folks twitter with hushed conversations since a country music star's tour bus broke down in town and she spent two days in a local motel. We divulged nothing and didn't comment on any stories when people asked us about the money; but everybody knew, and everyone had an opinion. Our focus was on bringing the big picture into reality.

Building the facilities had progressed with astonishing speed for three hot summer months. It's surprising how quickly ideas become real with enthusiastic help, and ample finances. With Remington's skillful negotiation, we purchased the entire square mile of land surrounding the farm. Janell and Mason used the demographic sheets collected earlier from our campers, matched the professional skills we needed at the facility, and hired people. Jake arranged a volunteer program for anyone else who wished to be involved. Within a few short weeks, and with the help of dozens of barn raising volunteers, we had erected a large building with room for a veterinary clinic, stalls, and pens, under the direction of Gabardine Armano, a local design/build contractor.

Gabardine's buildings were as unique as her name. She used the natural setting to shelter her designs placing the structures partially, or sometimes completely, underground while allowing abundant light to enter from many directions. Similar to an Earth Home, the barn-clinic gracefully merged into the adjacent hill with minimal visual impact on the landscape. Several comparable structures were under construction around the land, scattered about to diminish environmental impact. Two apartment buildings in town replaced our tent encampments. Once we had housing for the volunteers and staff, we reconstructed the campgrounds turning them into day areas set off by the beauty of the vineyard, pond, and orchard, where visitors could have weekend picnics and enjoy the prairie's grand panorama.

The bustle of construction, delivery trucks, and new faces on the farm had perplexed Lorenzo all summer. The striped sentinel held firm to his post under the porch coming out only for meals and at night when the hubbub died down. Peering out from his cavern, I saw his disgruntled acceptance that it was better to be safely restricted, than flattened under a tire of those humongous trucks. Seeing Lorenzo cornered again, I sat down on the steps so he could find the safety of my lap without having to venture far from his comfort zone. He wasted no time expressing his inconvenience, looking me in the eye with great deliberation; I could almost hear him paraphrasing Malchizadec. "The mice are playing too loudly," I thought I heard him say, concerned that his absence was allowing the barn's mouse population to explode. I assured the displaced mouser that he would have free range of the place again soon. To which, I'm certain I heard Lorenzo retort, "There are too many people here since you had that stupid dream," and with that communicated, he hopped determinedly down from my lap, wagging his banded tail in discontent as he slipped back into the shade beneath the porch.

One of the people gathered by that "stupid dream" was Stephanie Solaris, a retired creative director from a publicity agency in Chicago. A powerhouse in her early sixties, with salt and pepper hair she didn't look a day over forty-five. She had spent years as a journalist before working in television, magazine, and billboard advertising. Retired with considerable wealth at the top of her game, Stephanie didn't need a job, but we offered, and she accepted the public relations position. We gratefully gave her carte blanch and after hearing about the situation surrounding Andrea's business fire, she wrote the first investigative piece on Consolidated Chemical Corporation. Within the first few days with her media connections, our new PR person had human-interest stories in print.

Stephanie suggested we bring in Mateo Ghirardelli, a filmmaker and colleague from previous projects. Mateo hit the ground running with *Davidson and Goliath*, a documentary film, which paralleled Stephanie's investigation of Consolidated Chemical, the fires, and the other businesses concerned. The film quickly found its way onto several national cable channels. Network news shows picked up excerpts and soon the story was nationwide. In one short piece, Mateo fired a shot across the bow that started the public asking questions and demanding answers.

The filmmaker's vision was to put a human face on the cause so people could relate to it. The next project, now underway, was *Strands of Sorrow, Strands of Light: A life's tapestry woven on the Silk Road.* The film portrayed Hahn's story showing the consequences of corporate corruption on innocent individuals, the cultural struggles between ethnic groups in the central reaches of Asia, and the arduous decision to escape tyranny in one's home at any cost. Hahn and Ch'ien Li, being very modest, took some convincing before they agreed. Remington had secured green cards for them but since they had refugee status, they were unable to go to China for any of the filming. Mateo retraced Hahn's journey out along the Silk Road and would return from location shooting to begin editing this week.

The media center for JOE was nearly functional now. Gabardine designed an underground building in the slope above the pond with a sunroof that swept across a sunken courtyard and opened out to the view. A small video and recording studio, digital editing facilities, art room, and office space for Stephanie, Mateo, and Janell, surrounded the central atrium. All these rooms were underground receiving light from the atrium, skylights, and window wells on their outer walls. Even though the entire structure nested into the earth, you could see the sky everywhere in the building.

Even my refuge, the workshop, underwent Gabardine's alchemy getting a face-lift though Mason insisted that the old couch remain. I complied. Perfect Form's rebirth was on newly acquired property at the far end of the pond where, like the Jade Dragon rising from the ruble of the burned out building, a large gazebo flowed from Andrea's earth structure almost as if it were a waterfall. Classes could take place at the gazebo in favorable weather with lots of fresh air and an inspiring view of the pond. Other times, activities could move indoors to the structure's large exercise gym. The facility was state of the art in every aspect and even utilized Jake and Hahn who taught Aikido and Tai Chi respectively. Perfect Form had undergone a perfect transformation; it was as charming as the old building but with the panache and planning to serve a swelling clientele.

Trucks ebbed and surged through the gate filled with construction materials, equipment for the clinic and the production studio; workers and volunteers flowed across the grounds. Liatris, Black Eyed Susan, Sunflowers, and Snow on the Mountain replaced the delicate carpet of spring flowers painting the hillside anew with the bold colors of summer's heat. Like nature's palette, the farm was transforming too. At times, the activity seemed as frenetic as the horde of insects that once clambered up my legs in the barn but through all the commotion, calm remained on the farm; purpose infused every task no matter how commonplace. Lorenzo even adapted, finding a shady overhang on the roof from which he performed reconnaissance on renegade rodent loudening.

A padlock on the old barn prevented any stray workers from happening upon our inexplicable Avan guests as they moved about. The upper hay doors remained open so they could come and go as they wished but Bashira was nest bound and couldn't evade any intruder without harm. Malchizadec and Sorrano on the other hand, moved with instantaneous speed without any hint of detection; they circled the summer sky high above the hill on airborne lookout diligently watching the progress below. From the ground they looked like two eagles, lazily riding eddies rising in the summer wind. In reality, they were the master architect, who instilled the ideas and impetus, and his understudy mapping out the fulfillment of his genius.

The clinic construction went quickly; the search for someone to staff it took longer. As Navu said, the patient has to believe in the method of healing for it to work. We needed a clinician who could adapt their methods to many beliefs. Finally, after dozens of interviews, we met Dr. Breanne Rainer who seemed open to every aspect of our work as a complement to her scientific background. Dr. Rainer had an extensive resume, working with several zoos and wildlife refuges around the world. Her interest was saving animals that were near extinction in the developed world. She felt that the sprawl of highways and cities, aggressive agricultural practices, and clear-cut forestry, had done so much damage, that the general populous had more or less adopted a "what's one less ferret" attitude. It was easier to rally defense for exotic animals like great whales, pandas, and gorillas than to demonstrate the need for the habitat of a butterfly, a bird, or even a mouse. Restoring the balance of life, for the less popular as well as the photogenic species, was the deep spiritual perspective we shared about the value of all life. Fortunately, JOE recruited her to head the clinic.

Dr. Rainer suggested an ecologist from Uppsala, Sweden, who might fit with our mission. Dr. Ingmar Johansson's published work had a "living systems" approach that frequently referred to the Earth as a living sentient being, a standpoint that often drew contention from his scientific colleagues. Many Swedish homesteaders came to Kansas in the past. Would he be willing to make such a huge change in his lifestyle?

"Well that's it. All the pieces are in place now. I can't wait get to work." Breanne said, concluding her phone conversation with Uppsala.

What happens when dreams come true? Summer had been that. We had done some dreaming, as Remington suggested, but received far more than we ever could have imagined. JOE emerged from a dream; the professional talents of Stephanie, Mateo, Breanne, and now Ingmar, would assist its transition from that world of imaginings into physical reality. Remington and Gabardine grounded its fledgling steps on terra firma. Between the dreamtimes, and because of those dreams, a great deal had changed on the farm but in the tall grass prairie, Coyoté still called, and Antelopes played. It was a respite and realization, a consolidation of strength and finding bearings. Months ago, Malchizadec said, "We'll meet when all the pieces are in place" and when Breanne unwittingly repeated his words, I knew it was no coincidence. It was a call to return to center, to gather again around the circle in the grove. Much had begun; more would surely follow and though turbulence may lie ahead, through the summer's sweltering heat, we had lingered undisturbed in the beautiful calm at the eye of the storm.

CHAPTER 15
STARING DOWN THE MOON

The determined chime of the mantle clock sounded in the living room, breaking the still calm of first light as I slipped quietly out of bed. Without getting dressed, I went to the kitchen to make coffee. The house was ours again. Hahn, Ch'ien Li and Janell all had quarters of their own around the compound as did Dr. Rainer, Stephanie, and Mateo. I had quite a day ahead of me. It was time to gather the group together with Malchizadec, which I would facilitate tonight if possible. As strongly as I sensed it was time to meet, I felt our new members should be included; still, I had promised not to reveal the birds' presence without their agreement. If acceptable to Malchizadec, I would try to explain what they might expect and what transpires in the grove. I supposed that if I could surmount Mason's cynicism, I would find words at least to engage the curiosity of our more empirical participants. My coffee ready and dressed, I would have my first cup this morning with the sunrise atop the hill.

The accustomed blue-silver ribbon of light greeted me on the horizon like an old friend awaiting my return. The hustle of activity through these past months had all too often prevented me from spending time in contemplation and quiet, at least that's the reason I had given myself. The timeless luminous band didn't care about my excuses; it simply beckoned me to return, to continue the journey that had led me to this point. I sat down, relaxed, and focused on my breath as I awaited the ascending sun. So often at sunset, I allowed myself to sink into the Earth and feel the motion of the planet but I had not been as successful at the sunrise, perhaps because the energy was increasing rather than waning, and it was harder to become calm. Maybe this morning would be different.

The sun was slightly below the horizon and its golden colors washed the sky as I moved my consciousness downward into the planet imagining I were a pair of eyes looking out from it. Suddenly I felt an abrupt change of direction, instead of merging into Mother Earth; I was steadily rising above her. The higher I ascended, the further I could see beyond the horizon until I burst into the first rays of morning. I had risen to meet the sun. A sense memory swept through me of that first vision watching the sunrise on the Tall Wood and I felt the sensations I had imagined in the trees as the sun washed down their aged trunks. The memory instantly passed through my mind until I recollected gliding down a pathway right on the edge between sunlight and shadow. Stretching out my arms, I began to soar.

Above the hill, circling higher on the updrafts, I glided over the compound inspecting the work we had done and the dreams still in progress; I was riding the sky like Malchizadec and Sorrano. I saw several round cottages for staff and guests nestled in small clusters around the hills. The dwellings looked enchanted from here, even like mushrooms sprouting from the middle of the earth and I almost expected an elf would answer if I were to knock on their doors. I floated above the grounds where a new aurora glimmered from the farmyard, the light shining up through the sunroof of the media center. The sunrise on my back, the earthly glimmer below me, the compound was barely beginning to stir in the poignant peace of early light. Breaking the silence of the dawn, feathers swooshed by me, a sound I often heard Night Hawks make when they pull out of a steep dive. It was the sound of joy, of their exuberant freedom, and of the pleasant hours I spent watching them. Swoosh! I looked around to see Malchizadec soaring beside me with precisely that exuberance. Different in flight, he seemed lighter, more naturally himself and playing like a soundtrack to the experience, my mind kept singing, "*As we sail into the mystic....*"

"James, as you begin to surrender to the qualities of your soul, you will notice some unusual abilities." I could hear Malchizadec's voice clearly in my mind as we circled skyward on the wind. "Hindu Yogis call these '*Siddhas*'," he continued, "the flowering of the spirit. They are the powers latent in your being that become active as your consciousness expands. Pay them no attention! Simply acknowledge the gift but don't try to practice or increase your ability. Seek only to develop the stillness of wisdom. Keep your attention on the voice inside you, the one that precedes your thought. Your soul knows how, and when, to use these gifts. So, be sure you can trust your instincts. Your task is fervently to align your personality with your indwelling soul. Learn to serve its purpose," the projected monologue concluded.

Malchizadec flew directly beside me, never taking the lead, as if equalizing our status but I was far from his equal and felt honored that he granted me such respect. Though I was ready to ask him about bringing our new guests, there was no need, I could feel his trust that I would choose correctly. He had pushed me out of the nest and it was time to build the strength in my wings, literally and figuratively. We soared!

The coffee in my thermos had grown lukewarm when I came gently to the ground again. More time had elapsed than I expected; it was nearing 8:00 A.M. and Andrea would already be teaching her morning class so I would need to hurry to catch her between classes. Making my way quickly down the prairie path, Malchizadec swooshed past me again.

"It's imperative that you be at the grove no later then 9:00 P.M.!" I heard a clear, final direction.

Before I could give him a second glance, he was gone. My task now was to explain the unexplainable to a hard news journalist, a lawyer, two scientists, a contractor and a cop. Maybe I wouldn't try to explain it; I'd trust my fledgling wings and sail into the events knowing they would unfold as intended.

"Did you see the two birds flying around this morning?" Andrea asked, coming out to the gazebo before I could say anything. "It must have been Malchizadec and Sorrano but my morning yoga class thought they saw a pair of eagles. We were mesmerized for several minutes watching them silhouetted against the dawn sky; it was beautiful. They zoomed and soared all over our property. Did you see them?"

"No, I missed that. I was flying around with Malchizadec." I replied, waving my arms like wings and thinking here's my first explanation for the day.

"You?" Andrea asked, pointing her finger upwards and looking struck by the bolt from the blue. "Here then," she said pulling me close to her for a serious kiss. "I understand it's the tradition when a pilot gets his wings, even if yours do have feathers."

"We're meeting tonight…." I said, slowly withdrawing from my amorous award. "Tell Hahn and Jake to meet us at the media center promptly at 8:30 P.M. I'll find the others."

Walking around the pond to the media center, the contrast of the views from ground level, as compared to sailing high above it, struck me. From both perspectives, the structure melded earth and sky in a near hallowed embrace. Inside the media center, I explained to Mateo and Stephanie that we were having a gathering tonight as Janell poked her head in the doorway. Mateo had returned from China during the night and had been enthusiastically editing film for several hours. I found Ch'ien Li with Bre-anne in the clinic engrossed in new equipment only a scientist could love. Both were completely enthralled opening crates and boxes in the research lab like two kids on Christmas morning ripping ribbons from potential treasure. I interrupted the two "Magi" at work and without explanation told them of the evening meeting.

Most likely, Gabardine and her crew were working on the far side of the property, a site I'd flown over this morning but it would require my truck this time. Around the other side of the section on the county roads, about a half mile from the cottages, I noticed Sheriff Blackwell in my rearview mirror following in the dusty plume behind me. Well that's convenient I thought.

Inspecting Gabardine's design from the ground, I noticed the arrangement of the clusters, as if built around a sacred common space, their mushroom-like roofs overhung to form a central *Kiva* amongst them. Surrounding the elfin edifices, an engaging arrangement of native perennials accented the walkways. I bent over to smell the Beard's Tongue when Jake stood up from behind a newly planted Viburnum bush, brushing the moist dirt from his hands. He was landscaping as they completed the new structures and his design work harmonized perfectly with Gabardine's, adding to their ambiance. Hearing the cars arrive, Gabardine emerged through an arched doorway her long dark strands blowing in the south wind, which she whisked from her face as she approached.

"Good Morning," Dan said, getting out of his patrol car and strolling towards us. "I have to serve you with these. In my office we call these harassment papers," he apologetically continued, handing me five documents.

Petty complaints filled the documents, filed in the court and stretched into various code violations with a summons to appear, their sole purpose was to put us on the defense and tie-up our attention. They were harassment as aptly described.

"Every permit, license and tax record you've ever submitted to this county has been gone thru," he said, "and I mean gone thru. Three high priced 'Suits' spent the last week looking for anything that could cause you trouble. Sorry, but I thought I'd bring them to you myself. Your article on Consolidated stirred up a hornet's nest so I hope you took my advice and retained a lawyer. Unfortunately, you're in this too." Dan continued, handing a packet to Gabardine.

"Yes, I took it seriously and retained Remington Parks," I said, noticing that my response evoked a slight smile on his face. "He'll be here in a few hours and he can take care of ALL of this."

While both of them were together, I invited them to the 8:30 P.M. gathering and told Dan it might explain more about the light he saw that night on the hill. The plainspoken peace officer was surprisingly interested. He agreed to come before disappearing down the road into a cloud of dust, and curiosity I'm sure.

"I saw the strangest thing early this morning," Gabardine said, as she looked skyward. "There were two eagles flying around over the prop-

erty almost… inspecting it. I've had the feeling that there was something
different about your place. It's as if Spirit is bringing the place to life, I
just put the pieces where they belong. Maybe it sounds crazy, but tonight
seems like it has to do with that." She concluded, as Jake and I squelched
our catbird smiles, not the least bit taken aback by her insight.

Gabardine was active in the community and we knew her from previous
functions at Perfect Form. She grew up in southern Kansas from French/
Cherokee ancestry and her Native background showed in her designs;
her feelings about the land didn't surprise me. It also seemed natural
that she would notice the eagles, what shocked me was that she saw two
eagles. My awareness was of being myself during the flight; I didn't think
I became a bird, let alone an eagle. Yet somehow, others perceived two
eagles. My messenger duties completed, saying goodbye I headed back to
work with Mason.

The afternoon went quickly and with the workday done, Mason and I sat
on the back porch waiting for Remington and Dr. Johansson to arrive.
The sun had gone down and a thin sliver of the moon was chasing after
it towards the horizon. We were staring down the moon. Over the summer, Mason had been invaluable; he had essentially become the Chief
Operating Officer for the farm and, along with Janell, for *Just Our Earth*.
Perhaps it was the disciplined side of his Army training that enabled him
to hone in on the most necessary task on any given day and organize the
resources to complete it. Since Malchizadec had essentially released him
from the demons in his past, Mason's energy, focus, and will had been
unbounded. He was my friend and I was proud to see him feeling capable,
confident, and connected. In addition, there was a new contentment in
Jake's eyes concerning his dad. Mason's healing had touched us all.

Dusk had changed into darkness and the tip of the moon had dipped beyond the horizon when Remington's car turned into the driveway. There
was no time to greet Dr. Johansson before we needed to be at the grove, let
alone to prepare him and Remington for the meeting. Everyone including
Dan was already waiting for us in the atrium of the media center. Malchizadec said it was imperative that we be prompt so we apologetically
said our quick hellos, asked them to come with us, and entered the atrium

to hear conversations filled with expectations about the evening.

Our rag tag band once again trekked through the vineyard towards the grove, this time with new comrades in tow. Andrea led the parade walking with Mateo who seemed more than ready for an adventure. Ch'ien Li and Jake walked together hand in hand. Their now public relationship had deepened steadily through the summer and both Hahn, and Mason, seemed quite pleased. I held up the rear walking beside Remington with Breanne and Dr. Johansson immediately ahead of us.

"Extraterrestrials, I'm sure there must be some other rational explanation." I heard Breanne say, her disbelief infusing the intonation and only a "hum" in response from Ingmar.

Mason and Hahn were speaking a conspicuous mixture of Mandarin Chinese and Vietnamese in the middle of our processional. Now that he had someone to practice with Mason was regaining his Asian language skills. The two of them would often sit cracking inside jokes and conversing for hours. Perhaps Jake and Ch'ien Li's relationship accelerated it, but an inimitable bond had formed between the Kansas veteran and the Mandarin farmer. It was hard to know just who was teaching whom.

Nearing the humble cluster of trees, I sensed the shift into magical time again. My senses became acute, my awareness more inclusive until I could distinguish the mummers of life behind the explicit. Apparently, the others could as well for a calm reverence replaced conversation as each attendee entered the trees. Watching from my position at the rear of the procession, one by one, I saw their mouths drop open; their heads turn upward as they witnessed the modest limbs of hedge ascending to form the vaulted boughs and cathedral ceiling.

"Remington, you better get ready for another one of those inexplicable experiences," I advised him as his eyes widened to observe the transfiguring trees.

The fire was already burning in the pit, lighting our pathway to the stone circle. Malchizadec, Sorrano, and to our disbelief, Bashira were all standing on the far side of the swirling flames, their shadows dancing across the gnarled tree trunks behind them. Our new guests were dumbfounded and slightly hesitant; you could feel the mixture of fear and wonder, and practically hear paradigms shifting in the balmy night air. Andrea immediately went over to Bashira, which helped relieve their tension. We were delighted to see her out of the nest but it was obvious why they were worried about the pregnancy. Bashira was huge. I couldn't see how she could incubate the egg much longer and live.

"How was Bashira even able to get here?" I asked when Sorrano came over.

"Malchizadec insisted we both come tonight, even knowing the difficulty for her," he answered. "Bashira glided down from the hay door like a rock, and we walked to the grove after dark. It was a real struggle but I trust he had a good reason for it," Sorrano supposed.

The Avans graciously mingled with our understandably curious new guests, as if we were at a cocktail party, one dialogue following the next. Breanne and Ingmar were most precise in their investigations, asking every detail about their species and habitat. Dan and *Remi*, in contrast, conducted inquiries through observation, quietly, meticulously, watching the interactions. Malchizadec tried to explain briefly their metamorphoses on Earth without diverting from his intentions for the evening, intentions that remained a mystery to all of us. When Malchizadec was satisfied that everyone's curiosity had been satiated, he moved to the center of the grove stretching his wings out their full 25-foot span. With one dramatic flap, he signaled a resounding drum from the outer edge of the grove. Driving the rapid beat, Navu stepped resolutely out of the night almost as if his towering black form were the dark corners come to life. The thundering pulsation continued until, discerning that he had sufficiently charged the atmosphere, Navu stopped abruptly with a bow pointing his drumstick towards the fire.

"Each one of you has faced a moment in your life," Malchizadec began, statuesquely backlit by the firelight, "when the truth you believed, failed to explain the reality you encountered. Whether joyous or fearful, the experience radically challenged your worldview, and precipitated a struggle through which new truth grew to replace your outdated knowledge. You can look back on those quandaries and see that they were turning points, moments when through the quaking ground on which you stood, everything changed. This situation, with all it suggests, is probably another of those moments.

"Like children shattering their belief in Santa Clause and reforming it into personal altruism, such transformations repeat many times in the course of a life." He continued. "It is a developmental process through which more and more of your whole being is integrated. Such development is a cumulative process; your vital energy, or light body, integrates with your physical form first at birth, then emotions arise to express your needs when you are very young. Eventually, your mental facilities integrated with all those and you became a coordinated personality. You experienced a developmental crisis as each transition took place and now, you face a greater ordeal that will test your worldview again. Resolving it will lead you through even greater dilemmas as your body, mind, and emotions begin to assimilate your spirit's direction.

"Scientists prefer to study what they can measure, a useful perspective which I encourage you to keep," he said, drawing his attention close to Ingmar and Breanne. "Nevertheless, anomalous phenomena, whether corporal appearance, or transcendent experiences, neither fit easily into any known box, nor readily connect to existing knowledge though they merit your attention. They are glitches scientists have yet to measure and explain. For most researchers, it is generally best not to study them too seriously if they want to keep their grant money coming in. However, you needn't worry about grant money here."

The new members, upon instruction, then circumnavigated around the Spartan stones directed as before, circling until the sonorous melody rang out as each person neared their particular stone. Malchizadec, satisfied that each inductee had identified their individual resonance, directed the original group to join those who shared their mutual frequency. We all sat coupled by our soul's inherent quality: Mason with Remington, Hahn with Dan, Jake alongside Ingmar, Ch'ien Li joined Breanne. Andrea sat with Mateo, Janell beside Gabardine, and Stephanie with me.

"Your integrated personality has guided you before today," Malchizadec continued, particularly keying in on the new members. "That is, the interactive sum of your physical body, the vital energy that surrounds it, your mind, and your emotions. The stone that sings for you here is resonating with the quality of your soul! It intones its core frequency."

"What do you define as the soul?" Breanne asked timidly raising her hand as she requested an empirical explanation.

"The awareness within you that asks that question now Breanne." Malchizadec replied seemingly expecting her inquisitive nature. "It is the window of consciousness upon which the breath of Spirit appears. Your indwelling soul is an individualized spark of Spirit conscious within you, whose quality causes this resonance. It now seeks to guide you directly. Be mindful that at every point of integration, when a higher element seeks control, the lower element of your nature will resist and a crisis ensues. The experiences to come hereafter are no longer of your personality's doing; they are the calling your soul has chosen. It is time to seek your soul's direction.

"Close your eyes for a moment." Malchizadec guided, turning our attention inward with a hypnotic softness.

"Imagine yourself seated comfortably alone in an auditorium." He continued in a clear calming voice that deepened as he spoke. "As the lights go dark, and the curtain opens before you, your thoughts parade across the stage one after another; simply watch them. Let them pass knowing you are the observer and not the parade of thoughts.

"In your active imagination, as that observer, imagine gently floating upward until you can see your surroundings, the thoughts upon the stage, and yourself seated below. Your soul is the observer. Your integrated personality with body, mind, and feelings, is the observed. Take time to notice the character of both of them, their similarities, and the ways in which they differ.

"Now imagine that as the soul, you are a tiny star floating the short distance above your body. As you have heard it tonight, sound your tone in your mind, while extending a line of silver white light downward to right in front of your physical heart.

"Feel your heart warm as if it were a rosebud opening to the warm morning sun.

"Feeling the warmth of your open heart in blossom, extend the soothing beam of light down further to your solar plexus, the symbolic seat of your lower mind or ego. Visualize this line from your soul star, through the heart, to the solar plexus and vivify it with your emotions.

"Now imagine that your soul is transferring its intention to the ego. They need no words; they have their own language.

"Let your ego accept this intention and in return send gratitude. Visualize a ray of golden white light carrying your thankfulness upward, through your heart, through your throat, illuminating your head, and back to the observing self, the soul star floating above the crown of your head. Hold that image, see the circulation of light and with all your devotion, express your cooperation.

"Believe that change has happened.

"You may open your eyes now." Malchizadec conveyed in his normal voice.

The image remained clear in my mind and I could feel the light circulate as if I had been reacquainted with a part of me as familiar as my own hands. Even more, with my eyes open or closed, there was a vivid, sustained, light inside my head as if the soul star's radiance penetrated my cranium illuminating it from within.

"Set aside a little time each morning," he continued, "before you start your day, for this exercise and watch the changes in your life. Your conscious personality must learn to resonate with your soul, to follow its wisdom, and evoke its power to succeed, indeed perhaps even to survive, the mission of *Just Our Earth*."

Realizing our sobered alarm, he stopped. Sorrano, Bashira, Navu and Malchizadec moved to their stations in the circle, each by a different stone. Navu directed us each to create our tone in our inner ear. Once we focused our intention, Navu asked the Creator to guide us safe in Spirit, and bless our work as his slow steady beat rose again in the grove.

"We stand together three times seven;
Lift our hearts, our spirit leaven.
Our minds set right, oh Soul of Life,
Fill us with your Hallowed Light."

Navu reverently chanted, his voice resounding above the drum. As he repeated the lines, the tone I heard in my mind became audible. The low-pitched sound also started again, filling in with harmonics until I heard the Great Chord. Navu continued his incantation as the chord intensified with colored beams swirling upwards from the center of the circle and blending into a bright gold, silver, and white column of light. The sound and light continued to intensify until out of the radiant shaft stepped the Soul of the Earth, the woman we saw in the jungle.

"JÖrd, JÖrd," Ingmar exclaimed bending over in respect as the gentle presence became visible.

"Yes Ingmar," the Lady said in recognition, "you know me, but I am known by many names and my name is not important; your response to my need is. My wish is that all the lives that exist within me might progress as the Creator intended. I cannot bring balance alone. Carry this message out to every people, every nation: *Life will not continue much longer unless every species respects and holds all others in equal regard*." She stressed, her words lingering as if reverberating in the stars and every branch in the grove's verdant canopy was repeating them.

"The eagle respects the mouse, the Coyoté the rabbit; each knows their existence ties to the other," she continued. "Only humankind has removed itself from the wheel of life. Am I to destroy one life that I may save another? Am I to die, or let them all perish because I cannot love one above another? The time of domination is over. The time of domination must be over."

Fading gradually back into the light, her message complete, the Great Chord and the radiant beam slowly diminished with her until the fourteen of us were around the fire with the Avans listening to the droning beat of Navu's drum. Malchizadec bowed respectfully as her shimmering form vanished, bending to the ground and spreading his wings forward like a cape. Once she had departed, he slowly stood straight up and silently waited for our attention.

"It is not my desire to frighten," he continued with gentle understanding, "but you must realize how dire the situation is. There is little time left, and the Creator has given us the task to be stewards of the Earth. It is imperative you understand.... realize that there are many who remain ignorant of its true nature. They know not the sweet Soul you have seen with your own eyes, the Lady who has joined us. In their zeal, they will do anything to advance their interests including, label, defame, and attempt to destroy you. Throughout this, you must remember they are not your enemy; they do not understand. Unfortunately, their folly makes them tools of dark forces beyond your power to foil. Do not allow evil to seduce you into the glamour of battle."

Echoing in my mind were words from the Gospel of St. Luke, "For whomsoever much is given, of him shall be much required." Enveloped by a stifling, somber stillness, we all began to comprehend what was before us. Much had been given us and it appeared that much would be required. I could not help but consider whether the new aspirants, whether any of us around the circle, had bargained for this.

"Navu said 'three times seven' means there ought to be three of us at each of the stones." Mason questioned finally breaking the sober trance. "Where were the other three?"

"The three you did not see are here in spirit," Malchizadec responded.

"Spirit is more vital than either mind or body. The three at each stone symbolically represent the body, mind, and spirit of this work. If they wish to, they will reveal themselves to you in time but tonight there won't be an opportunity to inform you more." Malchizadec concluded.

As he stopped, a loud explosion rang out followed by a concussive shock wave that knocked most of us to the ground with the sudden force of an earthquake. Mason reacted immediately as if he were still in combat, scampering with cat-like agility across the ground over to the edge of the grove to see. Dan, Jake, Remington and I followed behind him. At the other end of the vineyard, above the orange tips of flames, a large mushroom plume of smoke rose steadily over the farmyard. I felt an eerily gnawing collapse in the pit of my stomach accented by the hair on the back of my neck rising as quickly as the flames.

Like a small infantry charging a hill, Dan and Mason bolted for the yard while I ran back for the others in the grove. "Fire, fire," I yelled expecting they would come along to fight the blaze. Instead, I found everyone huddled over Bashira; like the rest of us, the violent blast had knocked her to the ground. She landed hard on her side and the shock seemed to have induced the equivalent of labor, but her body was unable to lay the enormous egg. Malchizadec and Sorrano were surrounding her with the violet light but this was a physical problem; the light would help sustain her, but it could not free the egg from her womb.

"Easy Bashira...someone fetch my bag quickly." Breanne commanded, moving in next to her with a surgeon's precision. "I think I can remove her egg safely without harming it or Bashira. I've done it before but we have to hurry."

"I'll bring it," someone yelled, disappearing into the rows of vines and trellises before I knew who it was.

The flames were large, clearly visible, and growing. Bashira's critical condition exponentially added to the panic as Breanne urged her to hold on; she was dwindling in the glimmer of the inferno as surely as the old barn's roof was sagging and weak in the conflagration. Even though the barn contained nothing to generate the first blast, once on fire, the dry wood and straw burned furiously, I hoped Bashira's circumstances would be more manageable. Then I realized the explosion and fire would have killed Bashira had she stayed there. It was no coincidence; Malchizadec had deliberately drawn us out of danger, which emphasized his warning that we would need wisdom "perhaps even to survive this work." I was not prepared for that tonight.

Torn between two emergencies, Malchizadec motioned me to go tend to the farmyard while he focused on Bashira. Andrea and I took off towards our besieged farmstead. Near the end of the vineyard, we met Ch'ien Li who was going full throttle back to the grove with Breanne's medical bag. One fire was infuriating but this second fire left us emotionless. Yet somehow the flash of red lights approaching, an unusual spectacle on our bucolic byway, seemed all too fitting amid our panting dash towards the fire. The heat was searing as we ran into the yard where Dan was spraying the house, and Mason the media center, with garden hoses already in place for the vines. Flames completely engulfed the barn and even though Dan had radioed for help immediately, no amount of water was going to save it. A fire truck rolled in, followed by a second, and a captain who jumped out of his truck fully focused, gauging the damage and efficiently deploying his resources.

"We'll take over now," he said, "but I'm afraid there is nothing to do for the barn except let it burn down safely." As if he new his enemy well, he confidently signaled his crew to use their hoses on the house, and media center.

"I'm growing weary of fire, how about you?" I asked rhetorically, in stunned exasperation. We clumped together instinctively like startled elk, unable to flee but roused and ready, poised to persevere against attack, even if from a pack of unseen wolves.

"Do you smell that?" Mace asked quietly, leaning over towards me as I confessed that I didn't. "It smells like C4," he said. "This was no accident; someone blew up your barn."

"It smells like explosives to me too." Dan agreed, the perilous red-orange flicker reflecting from his face. "Well, at least this investigation will be under my jurisdiction and I'm practically an eye witness."

The next hours we wearily probed for inspiration amongst our crumbled embers of hope. Before us stood another monument fashioned in debris, the melted memories of Perfect Form's demise melding into the bonfire before us. Our passion to contribute, the feeling we could make a difference, simmered in the heat petulant and dispossessed. "The Creator exists beyond duality," Malchizadec had said; clearly, we did not. We subsisted, simultaneously lashed between opposing poles, light and dark, mercy and severity, dynamic revelation and stern structure, having time neither to, assimilate knowledge, nor surmount despair. What was to come of this? There was Bashira and our deep concern for her wellbeing; I could do little to help, but pray that all would be OK. A few hours ago, things were calm and promise flourished on the front porch. Now, hope had waned and progress felt a jagged season. Instead of gazing into the barn's sullen coals, I wished we were still sitting on the porch in our reverie, staring down the moon.

CHAPTER 16
MIDWIVES OF THE BURNING GROUND

In the windless night, the air drooped over the waterlogged ground, heavy with the smell of wet ash and charred aspirations. The barn, the hub of the farmstead for generations and the repository of its memories, was now but a memory itself. If we were a Phoenix set to rise from the pyre to live again, then this second fire ended a life shortened by hundreds of years. Long fingers of smoke stretched out in layers across the vineyard, orchard, and hillside as if the last vestige of the barn were struggling to keep its grip in this world before dissipating into a nostalgic void. It was 1:00 A.M.; the fire engines and crews had gone. One lone officer remained to watch the cinders through the night, when I heard Malchizadec's voice calling in my mind. It seemed all of us did, so our crumbled cadre forsook the clustered farmyard outpost and despairingly rushed back to the grove.

We entered the grove to see a large crescent illuminated by the campfire that looked as if Mason and I had brought down the moon. It was the egg reflecting the amber light with Bashira standing upright and seeming to feel much stronger.

"I've never seen anything like it." Breanne said as she came over to me. "I performed a Caesarian to remove the egg, but when I was done and ready to suture the incision, Malchizadec bent down, covered her with lavender light, and passed his wing along the wound. I saw the skin close and heal; her condition restored right before my eyes. How did that happen?" Knowing I couldn't explain it, I suggested Malchizadec would explain later.

The egg was a neon palette of multicolored speckles spread across a blend of pastel swirls. The hard leathery shell had a bumpy texture more like a pineapple than a bird's egg. It was about three feet in diameter and five feet long; no wonder Bashira was suffering. The egg lay on a wide canvas halter the clinic used to hoist large animals with Malchizadec standing over, maintaining a steady light on it, which highlighted the speckles and swirls in varying patterns. Sorrano informed me that they were keeping the temperature constant so incubation would continue.

"We have to move the egg back to the clinic," Breanne directed. "It's very heavy but I think if all the men grab hold it can be done safely."

We all found the best grip we could on the halter and began to lift together. Remington, Ingmar, Dan, and Mateo on one side, Hahn, Jake, and Mason lined up with me on the other. Even with all of us, this was going to be a long, slow, and grueling endeavor. The egg must have weighed near 500 pounds. We moved carefully, able to go only a few yards at a time before we needed rest. Malchizadec stayed to the rear, moving in rhythm between the bearer lines and steadying the egg in the light as we toiled. Walking through strands of smoke under a moonless sky, it felt as though we were medics, carrying our wounded back through a war zone with the red embers of destruction still glowing in the distance. It was going to take some time, a good deal of fortitude, and we would have to soldier up to cover the half mile back to the clinic.

Breanne ran ahead to fashion some sort of nest for the egg but since Avans normally incubated their eggs internally, roosting alone wouldn't keep the egg warm enough to gestate. The doctor planned to supplement the surrogate womb with heating pads and electric blankets wrapped around the egg as Bashira brooded over the nest. We were moving so slowly they would have a couple of hours to prepare and we were stumblingly stupid with fatigue when we finally arrived about 3:30 A.M. The hastily constructed nest, fashioned from Styrofoam packing peanuts, sofa cushions, empty feed sacks, and straw all held together inside an empty stock tank was complete with adjustable heat. Moving carefully into the make shift brooding chamber, located in one of the quarantine areas in the back, we beleaguered bearers situated the egg gently in the provisional incubator while Malchizadec and Sorrano helped Bashira into position and continued warming the egg with lavender light.

"That's weird!" Breanne exclaimed, as she leaned into her office to turn off the light before we left the clinic and allowed Bashira some rest, "I didn't make this mess."

To our dismay, her office was a shockingly thorough debacle. We plodded through the door to see her file cabinets open, drawers, files, and papers scattered about the room while her ransacked desk teetered on three remaining legs. Remington pointed to jimmy marks on the doorjamb that affirmed someone had calculated the incursion. Instantly, the putrid aura of our vulnerability overpowered the enduring smell of smoke and cinder. The fire, it seemed, may have only distracted us while they searched for something more. Andrea and Dan promptly left to check the gym in case someone was still on the property while Stephanie, Janell, and Mateo scoured through the media center. The rest of us investigated the cottages and access roads. In a half an hour, everyone was back at the house and it was clear the elusive intruder had gone through the entire compound. The invasion was total.

"For now, lock it down and go get some rest." Dan suggested, jotting down a few notes as he paced around. "It's been a full evening and we're all too tired to do anything now but mess up the crime scene. I'll have a few deputies patrol the area throughout the night and be back with a full investigative team first thing in the morning," he assured and with that, everyone dispersed.

Remington and Ingmar took our guest bedrooms in the house while Dan waited resolutely for his Deputies on our porch steps with Andrea and me. "James," Mason said, uncharacteristically using my name as he pulled me off to the side of the porch. "We're chest deep in a hog wallow here and the situation ain't going away." He continued, speaking in a hushed voice. "This wasn't local boys, it was military precision that covered the whole place, and that smell.... Creeper Dogs Man, it seems like a Special Ops team to me."

"You know, I doubt we will find anything," Dan said leaning forward to put his forearms on his knees still flipping through his notes. "With this incident added to the two fires, I have a few ideas. The real question is, 'What are they looking for?' You don't suppose somebody knows about your Avan guests do you? Well, I won't speculate before the investigation," he concluded, as he stared out at the cinders and seemingly considering different possibilities in his mind.

It wasn't long before the deputies arrived and we said goodnight. I was tired from the inside out and couldn't wait for sleep to end this day. My body ached and being horizontal in bed felt great even though the night would be far too short. As I lay there, my mind was flooded with images of forest and flame, Perfect Form, and the barn. Dots were connecting. Images that personally confirmed Malchizadec's statements about integration and crises floated to the fore of my thought. With my eyes closed, the flames reminded me of watching the national news earlier in the week as another raging blaze destroyed part of my past. A forest fire had consumed a small mountain village where I lived years ago, while there, my worldview shattered, and I began to transform.

During the months of my mountain retreat, I had my first glimpses of the interconnectedness of all life, the permeability of physical form, and the awareness that I was something more than my body, mind, or personality. In that place, I became acquainted with what Malchizadec called the soul, or perhaps more accurately, my soul made its purpose known and began to guide me. In a way, it was my birthplace, my sacred ground that I saw burning. Now another home burned and we were in the throws of transformation again, was this meaningful coincidence? Yes. It had meaning to me. It reinforced the purpose that found me so many years ago, and validated that those early insights were all grown up. Ironic how when the body needs rest the most, the mind won't cooperate, but finally a deeper voice reassured, let tomorrow take care of its self, and I drifted off.

It was well before daylight when a weight on my chest with a low-pitched rumble awakened me. Unable to rouse me, Lorenzo was escalating his command that I open the door for him by persistently kneading my chest with his paws while batting his tail across my face. I submitted. Trying to get my bearings, I went quietly to the kitchen door hoping not to stumble in the darkness and wake everyone in the house. I couldn't have slept more than an hour. There was an unusual snoring noise coming from outside so I turned on the porch light as I cautiously peered out to investigate. There, asleep in the wicker chair was Jake and securely adhered to one of the columns that suspend the roof, was a stranger dressed in black clothing, gloves, and a hood. Black grease paint covered his face and except for his unseemly snoring, he looked like he had stepped right out of a spy novel. Jake assumedly had restrained the man, tied his hands behind his back with duct tape, bound his feet with an electric cord, and affixed him to our column.

"I found him going through my apartment," Jake announced, waking up after Lorenzo shot across the porch, disturbed that more commotion from the "stupid dream" had invaded his nighttime haunt. "I couldn't find Dan's officers when I arrived so I secured him up here to wait in case he's part of all this." He concluded, seemingly satisfied with his citizen's arrest.

In the glimmer of porch light, the Deputies came running up out of the darkness with pistols drawn and took charge of the suspect asking the camouflaged intruder his name. He remained silent. They informed him of his rights, and told him he was required to identify himself. Still the man said nothing; he acted like a soldier captured on a mission behind enemy lines. This masked marauder was no local heister trying to bag a few treasures to hock. He was definitely a hard case and I couldn't believe Jake had taken him down, subdued him, and then nonchalantly slept securely on the porch.

"How…. Did you…? Good job Jake!" I asked in amazement.

"Guess I've learned something in all these years of practice." Jake replied looking somewhat mystified by my admiration.

"I guess so." I answered, unable to hold back my dumbfounded laughter.

"Can I use your phone?" one Deputy asked. "Sheriff Blackwell told us not to use the radio, and to call him personally if anything happened," he concluded.

Anxious to listen to the phone conversation, I took him inside while the other deputy filled out a field report gleaning the key information from Jake. I surmised that Dan wanted a set of fingerprints on this guy immediately and my impression, from the little I overheard, was that he was coming back right away. Something seemed urgent, that justified departing from the standard arrest and booking process because the Sheriff arrived in about ten minutes, no small achievement considering he had driven into town and back. When he got out of his car, he looked like I felt, sapped. Dan strode officiously towards the suspect in the predawn shadows seemingly determined to bring resolution, and opened the squad car door to see his potential link to evidence.

"Well birds, bombs, and behemoths, I've seen it all tonight and now this! This man is a ghost," he said stepping back. "So Mr. Allworth," he continued, this time speaking to the suspect, "you live again, or do you have another name in this lifetime?" he questioned, clearly intrigued by this new twist.

"This is Officer John Allworth, yes I said officer," he proclaimed stridently to us mystified onlookers. "He's formerly with our city's Police Department. The problem is he died eight years ago when the sports fishing boat he was vacationing on blew up in the Gulf of Mexico."

"Yeah, yeah, yeah," the suspect muttered breaking his silent resistance.

"Investigators found little of the wreckage and never recovered a body -- I guess he was still using it." Dan resumed, ignoring Allworth's mutterings. "Suspecting murder, the death triggered quite an investigation. Turns out, and listen to this, the fingerprints, and the previous employment records in his personnel file, all belonged to the real John Allworth, a soldier who died in training over at Ft. Riley, a year before this man joined the Department. You see, this man doesn't exist at all, that is until now.

"Mr. Ghost," Dan continued, leaning down toward the man cuffed in the back seat, "you committed the unforgivable in your line of work I suspect, you got caught. I don't imagine anyone will admit knowing you or that any high priced lawyer is coming to bail you out. You're alive now and investigators will have hours of questions about that fishing boat. They may even implicate you in the murders so I suggest you help yourself out here. Let's start with who you really are and your connection to the fire on this farm last night?"

"What the hell, they're going to kill me anyway." The ghost began, through the open door realizing the Sheriff had "made him." "We came here last night to capture Luther Mallory. I don't know him or these people; I just follow orders and do what they tell me. We've been watching this place for weeks! All the money and the precautions around the barn made my client believe Mallory was probably hiding out there. It's all about finding Mallory. That's all I know, period. As for my name, it doesn't really matter after twenty years. Think I'm a ghost now, wait till you run my real prints."

"Does this make any sense to you?" Dan asked, focusing his questions on me. "Do you know this Luther Mallory?"

"No…. We'd never even heard of him until all this started… much less know him. I do know he's one of the wealthiest men on the planet. Why would he be here?" I replied, baffled by Allworth's revelations.

"I can make a little sense of it Sheriff," Remington jumped in, clearly awakened by all the commotion and keenly observing Dan's interchange with the suspect. "I WAS the head attorney for Luther Mallory Inc. He solely owns the corporation and nobody really knows how much it's all worth. Mallory though, is even more elusive than his money; in fact, he's a ghost too. Nobody has seen him in decades. If someone where to kidnap him, the ransom could be staggering."

"What about his family? Where are they? We need to contact them right away." Dan continued, trying to unravel some lead that would bring things into perspective.

"There is no family," Remington replied, "so the target would probably be LMI; but, it would be hard for a kidnapper to convince an invisible corporation that they had the invisible man. On the other hand," he added, "Mallory was an eccentric investor. He never owned more than 50% of any company's stock, never exercised any control in the companies or took any profits, and he immediately reinvested every dime of dividends. LMI was exclusively a holding company acquiring lots, and lots, of stock."

"What would happen to all that if Mallory wasn't around?" Jake inquired flabbergasted upon hearing about Mallory for the first time.

"If the man were conclusively dead, it would set off a power struggle throughout the corporate world likened to a civil war. I severed my relationship with LMI because I didn't want to be in the middle of the power grabs, or be the mouthpiece for their unsavory covenants. Let me make some calls, maybe I can still find out who is moving in the shadows." Remington concluded with cell phone in hand.

"Who is 'your client' in this equation?" Dan resumed, questioning Allworth again, or whoever he was sitting in the backseat of the patrol car. "Who sent you for Mallory?"

"My job is to do, not ask questions." Allworth finally answered, leaning back in his seat with contempt, as if he was above the law and bored with Dan's inquiry. "Five of us were brought in for this operation. We were to bring what we found to a meeting point near Aeolian Woods later tonight. The barn fire was a diversion so we could search the other buildings when we didn't find him. It worked. Listen! That's... that's all, period!" Allworth, his hands cuffed behind his back, punctuated the end of his statement with an indignant kick against the steel mesh separating the front of the cruiser.

Allworth was done talking. Slamming the door shut, the Sheriff pulled us out of earshot towards the house behind a large Lilac bush. Speculating quietly about corporate mercenaries, he apparently suspected that Allworth was one. He explained how big interest groups hired them to advance company plans covertly, or even change the power structure in governments unfriendly to their cause.

"I think he knows a lot more than he's letting on," Dan concluded, "and one thing is certain, if their drop-off point is Aeolian Woods, you can bet there are some big players behind it, very big!"

All of us looked at Dan confounded that our local sheriff, our friend, knew so much about corporate mercenaries and the elitist doings at Aeolian Woods.

"What? I have connections beyond these boondocks too you know." Dan said, rebuffing our astonishment and then briskly walked the fifteen paces back to open the suspect's car door.

"Mr. Allworth," he said. "I've changed my mind. I'll bet they probably know we captured you and don't want you around talking with any of us. There probably is a high-priced lawyer on his way to bail you out as soon I book you. Your problem is, rather than a 'Get out of Jail Free' card, it's most likely a 'Get out of Jail Dead.' You tell me everything else, all that you say you 'don't know,' then maybe I can keep you breathing. If that's not acceptable, you can take your chances."

The sheriff instructed his deputies to forget this took place as they moved and secured Allworth into his car. He emphasized that they not file any reports yet. If he was willing to talk, Dan would put Allworth in what he called his "Boondocks Protection Program" until he testified, moving him around from one "Podunk" jail to another for a few months. Ultimately, no one but the Sheriff would know exactly where he was, thus keeping him alive and off the radar screen.

Jake and I watched the patrol car come to the road, start towards town, then stop, turn the other direction and accelerate down the dirt road. We assumed Allworth wised-up, accepted the Sheriff's offer and they were off to the first stop in the Boondocks. Feeling pleased with the outcome, Jake and I hastened towards the house for a few more hours of sleep before the long night's final stars turned into tomorrow. He crashed on the couch and about midmorning, I reawakened anything but refreshed. Andrea had slept through the nocturnal negotiations and gratefully, with a few hours of rest, had awakened in time to tend to our guest, Ingmar. I could hardly conceive of the mixed feelings those must have who had just met the Avans and served as the midwives of the burning ground.

Last night's extremes in mind, I headed out the door ready to assuage feelings after the mayhem and to check on Bashira in the clinic. Crossing the yard, I noticed a large group of volunteers surrounding Mason, many were very angry and a few looked beaten up. Mason was right; we had quite a situation here and it seems the attack on the farm wasn't all of it. According to the uneasy covey, last night, several hooligans accosted them at various places around town deliberately trying to provoke violent exchanges; they slashed dozens of tires, smashed bricks through windows of our apartment buildings and sprayed the words "Tree Huggers" in green paint on several of them. I was fine with being a tree hugger, but I didn't want to expose others to danger. No matter what the bedlam, neither fight nor flight would work.

"Have you seen Jake?" Mason asked, yanking me off to the side by my sleeve as if he was bristling with an idea.

"He's in the house sleeping on the couch." I replied, realizing he knew nothing about the overnight Allworth affair.

"These people feel like clay pigeons at a skeet shoot." Mason implored, sweeping his arm towards the crowd. "It's too much to let them take the flack without cover, don't you think?" He argued and continued suggesting that Jake and his Aikido association could avert more havoc if they handled security.

I agreed; we needed to think of protection but I didn't want to be "seduced into battle with evil" as Malchizadec had warned. Aikido was a completely defensive marshal art and it might work. Its prime code of belief was to protect yourself while protecting your opponent from harming himself. Jake had already shown its effectiveness so I left it to Mace to arrange and I went on to check on Bashira.

The contrast struck me between the former barn, a building designed to protect against the forces of nature, and the clinic, which was to protect both nature and its inhabitants, as I turned past my workshop and leaned into the gentle incline that led to the graceful new structure. The long sweeping lines of the new construction invitingly melted into the slope of the hill as if to say, "It is safe within." The new building could not replace the history of the steeped shelter, nor could it remove the sorrowful memory of its blazing demise, but its eco-centric ambiance was our connection to the future, a future that was arriving with sharp edges.

Inside, Bashira was sitting atop the new nest, appearing physically rested and strong. The incubation system within the nest was working fine which I hoped meant the egg would hatch soon without problems. Bashira and Sorrano both had that parental glow of anticipation but there was an unusual disquiet in the room. The Avans must feel even more vulnerable than before and they were noticeably protective of their egg. Malchizadec was curiously gone and my thoughts churned over the escalating violence. Glancing around the room, I felt a trancelike detachment as if I were free of my body, expanded, and my senses felt heightened. Then my glance came to rest on a single feather, Bashira's feather fallen by her nest.

I could feel Sorrano's worry as palpably as if his thoughts were my own. I looked at Bashira and the makeshift mound where she perched and upon which her egg's very survival depended; it all seemed so fragile. Her offspring was in terrible danger, even their purpose here was in jeopardy. There was no way I could truly understand their plight nor could I comprehend what it must feel like to confront giving birth on a distant world. I couldn't even assure Bashira or Sorrano that everything would be all right. What must these great beings be experiencing? My thoughts turned entirely to them; I looked at Sorrano first and then stood beside the nest only aware of intense compassion.

As if instinctually directed from inside, my hands became very warm. It felt like an electrical current was flowing through from the top of my head to my heart, and out the core of my palms. I put my hands on Bashira's back, visualizing her wellbeing, and imagining that I was a vessel for healing energy to flow. A soft golden glow began to extend from my hands that merged into the emerald radiance shining around Bashira, and the egg. The jeweled emanation was sticky, glutinous, like a thick liquid that surged tenderly through my body outward to engulf Bashira and adhering as it flowed around us. Still unsure of any healing ability, I simply allowed the Creator's life to pass through me. As it was before when I stepped into that middle world, the place between spirit and form, time was of no consequence. Whether we sat for a moment, or a day, we were only souls, together in the Creator's grace.

"Thank you for your kindness James. All things are possible when given with a pure heart." She said softly returning my gaze.

"James has learned to tune the Tempest Light." Sorrano said proudly to the small group who stood frozen studying the bright emerald dome. Looking over from a few feet away, Sorrano gave me an interesting smile, like a big brother watching his sibling ride a bike for the first time without training wheels. Since I first met him in the rain by the barn, he always found the kernel of joy in every situation, even now when they needed our compassion.

"I came to check your egg," Breanne said moving hesitantly towards us. "Is that OK now?" Bashira nodded, and motioned her forward. "There's a lot you haven't told me about, isn't there James," She added as we exchanged places beside the nest and I moved to the back of the room.

"The heartbeat is different than other animals," she said with her stethoscope placed on the rough leathery shell, and listening intently. "It's very slow and steady for such a young creature. It almost seems as though there are two heartbeats. No X-rays though, I am completely unfamiliar with your Avan physiology so I don't want to expose your offspring to any more risk. We'll just have to wait to find out," she said concluding her examination.

"You're putting on quite a show Chief." Mason whispered, almost respectfully as I joined the group.

"The light changes everything doesn't it." Remington said next to me with calm deliberation and looking at me directly. "The look on your face reminded me of my experience in San Francisco. The light changed everything."

"Say Ingmar, what does '*JÖrd, JÖrd*' mean anyway? I was going to ask last night but it got crazy around here." Mason questioned.

Ingmar dropping his usual methodical deportment became excited. In the hurried greetings, and the onslaught of events the last night, I hadn't noticed how young Ingmar appeared. Despite his academic pedigree and long list of research publications, beneath his straw blond hair, his glacier blue eyes flashed with youthful exuberance.

"In my study of ecosystems," Ingmar began in his heavy Swedish accent. "I examined cultures with closer ties to nature; ones that haven't separated themselves from the environment with technology. During my research, I spent countless hours with the Lapp people living in the far north of Scandinavia and met several of their Shamans who graciously allowed me to observe their ceremonies. *JÖrd* is their name for the Earth Spirit that sometimes appears."

"You mean people have seen this in other parts of the world? Well this I gotta know." Mason uttered, with unusual reverence.

"Yes Mason." Ingmar responded, clearly enlivened to talk about his favorite subject. "Many cultures have seen the Great Mother, perhaps appearing as the Virgin Mary, White Buffalo Woman, *Gaia*, or *Jemanjá*. Norse mythology refers to her as *JÖrd*, the mother of Thor. Every society seeks its place in the scheme of things. I saw her several times and the understanding that granted me, that the planet is a living being with purpose of its own, changed the focus of my work. I learned that she is not a Goddess we should worship, but a mortal entity, a living system in which we have our being, one that needs our cooperation as much as we need her to survive. *JÖrd*, my old friend, directed us together," he concluded, "I will be a part of this work."

"Glad to have ya," Mason replied, "and welcome aboard, or should I say welcome 'aJÖrd.'"

"Malchizadec's meeting with the Counsel of Elders." Sorrano answered, before I had asked the question. "He is very concerned by the violence and we hope the Counsel can help keep matters from getting any worse."

Thoughts swirled about the Tempest Light, and the incredible surge of energy that flowed through me as we left the Avans to their privacy. Malchizadec's words came to mind: "Pay them no attention! When they appear, simply acknowledge them but don't try to practice to increase your ability. Seek only to develop the stillness of wisdom. Keep your attention on the voice inside you that precedes your thought. Your soul knows how and when to use these gifts. When you need them, you will use them instinctively, so be sure you can trust your instincts." I got it. I acknowledged to myself the gift of Spirit, and we walked out into the bright sunlight where it was already late in the afternoon. An unknown SUV was loaded down in the drive so we briskly trotted to the house where we discovered Dan sitting comfortably at the table with a room full of women.

"I don't know how I slept through all that," Andrea said to me. "He's been filling us in on the last night's excitement and it sounds like you're not going to get much sleep tonight either from what Dan's been saying."

"Raise your right hands." Dan said standing up and looking expectantly at our perplexed hesitation. "No really, raise your right hand and repeat after me." He reasserted.

Whatever the oath was, we repeated it and in about 30 seconds, we were his Deputies. Then he opened his bag and tossed us each a black jumpsuit.

"You better have another one of those for me." Gabardine piped up to which the Sheriff, somewhat taken back, took a breath and started to dissuade her.

"Look, my crew built several of the buildings at Aeolian Woods," she rebutted undeterred. "I know the system of caves and quarries under the whole place. We refurbished the Main Lodge. The wine cellar is in one of the caves and there are several openings to it on the bluffs above the Missouri River. I can take you right into the whole complex undetected if we disarm a few sensors in the cavern."

The Sheriff paced a few steps, took a commanding stance and sternly emphasized at least a couple of times that there would be no fancy stuff, we would stay outside the resort tonight and use a few of their tactics to find out what's going on. Satisfied that we all understood our task, Dan tossed Gabardine a jumpsuit and swore her in.

"I was Allworth's tunnel to daylight," Dan continued. "Back from the underground, he voluntarily revealed the specific meeting location, a small cabin on the outer edge of the Aeolian compound. According to him, my department is full of informants. I need people I can trust to help set up surveillance equipment before they meet. We're going to go to the cabin where they are supposed to deliver Mallory tonight. We'll listen in on a few of their conversations but we have quite a drive, and a bit of back-packing, ahead of us. Remember, no fancy stuff, this operation is strictly 'listen and learn.'"

"Listen," Remington interrupted, sighing in a deep serious tone. "I have to warn you… if this rendezvous is at Aeolian Woods, Harry Nash is probably involved. He's as wicked as he is wily. His boys play for keeps so don't be heroes because if they catch you, they will kill you and think nothing of it. I'll be at my office in KC, call if you need me and be very, I mean very careful!"

A veil of heartrending concern blanketed the room. We heard the warnings but no one knew what we might face or what to say about it. The metallic ping of the teakettle heating over the steady gush of propane in the burner beneath it, dominated the kitchen until a rhythmic sound, a tapping, became loud enough to draw our attention. Janell was inexplicably rocking forth and back in her chair. Her head drooped forward, her chin resting on her chest as if she had fallen into a deep trance. Then her head jerked back brusquely and with a faraway glaze in her eyes, she got up and stuffed something into each of our pockets

"Great deception lurks beneath the Woods and you will find no safety in trickery." Janell said suddenly from her daze, still shaking by her chair.

"You can not remain untouched when you look upon evil and there is no time left to protect you." She continued in a deep, disquieting tone. "Without great caution we will remain the midwives of the burning ground.'"

CHAPTER 17
DUNGEONS & DRAGONS IN THE AEOLIAN WOODS

If places could speak of what they've seen, Aeolian Woods had stories most authors couldn't dream up. Lewis and Clark allegedly camped in the caves along the river on their expedition and many say that John Brown used the same caves to hide his marauders during the Abolitionist raids of the Civil War. A big place, Aeolian Woods stretched twenty miles along the bluffs of the Missouri River and extended over 10 miles from the river's bank. Gangland figures from Chicago, Kansas City, and the East Coast purchased the area and built the resort in the 1920's. It was a favorite rendezvous where underworld royals took their flapper girlfriends on trysts, their business partners to negotiate, drink and carouse, and their enemies to disappear. The grounds included a large lake, a golf course, mineral springs, lodges and dozens of bungalows with all the amenities. Beneath the expanse of hills covered by pristine black oak woodland, were miles of tunnels and caverns carved by man and nature into the limestone substrate. Rumor had it that during prohibition, as much as one half of all the liquor and beer supply in the United States was either made, or stored, in the maze of limestone caverns and quarries that honeycombed the property.

The property fell into disrepair during the war torn forties and, in an attempt to save it, opened to the public in the fifties as a resort. Unfortunately, it never gained acceptance because of its sordid past and finally closed in shambles. It sat vacant and lonely for decades like an aged beauty queen haunted by past glory, it ruled a kingdom of mice and memories like fading footprints spread across serene dust. Then in 1980, a private investment group purchased the grounds and redeveloped it as an exclusive retreat for members only, a very <u>private</u>, private club. For the past years, it has served as a haven where the world's most influential individuals and corporations connect, protected behind a veil of heavily guarded discretion. They say the hidden decision makers of the world, those behind the news but rarely in it, come to the Woods for two weeks each year, to decide where wars will break out, how economies will fare, and who wins favor in world elections. If the commandos that raided our place were to deliver their target, Mallory, here, it meant they were working for very elite clients with dreadful power.

The abandoned quarries that lie beneath Aeolian Woods once produced the limestone block used to build many of the early buildings in Kansas, the very building blocks of the state. Chillingly for enemies of its constituents, the deep passageways left behind also provided expedient tombs far from scrutiny or an interloper's chance discovery. Remington had filled me in on the history of our destination to emphasize that those behind the raid on *Just Our Earth* may have intended exactly such a fate for Mallory; I hoped it wouldn't also be ours. Aeolian Woods was a dark enigma shrouded in years of obscurity and 128,000 acres of seclusion.

What do you do if you stare into the darkness and it calls your name? The drive to Aeolian Woods sped by quickly, like the qualms in my mind. Dan had placed his removable flasher on top the unmarked SUV; for much of the trip along the interstate he exceeded 100 miles an hour as we rushed into the unknown. Mostly, we rode in silence considering the gravity of what we were about to undertake and echoing Janell's enigmatic warning. We approached from the north side of the massive resort to avoid its main gate several miles to the south. Arriving in the area slightly before dark, looking like an ordinary family wagon, we leisurely drove like sightseers past the targeted cabin.

The cabin sat cloaked in trees well back from the corner of two deserted county roads. About a mile from it, a small fire road led back into the woods that provided a place to unload undetected. We put on our dark clothing, rolled the SUV behind a clump of brush, grabbed our gear, and started hiking behind the ridgeline up towards the hill above the cabin. That would be our observation post. The woods wore a deep darkness as we moved softly beneath the hickories and oaks in single file. With cautious intent, we slipped past greenbrier vines and poison ivy smelling the musky perfume of mushrooms freshly crushed beneath our night-blind steps. I hoped that from the darkness, we would hear what we needed. Either way, the match was afoot.

As we walked across the ground strewn with the fallen products of a summer's growth, a strange shift happened. Almost as if playing "Dungeons and Dragons," with each crackling step upon the acorns, twigs, and leaves, we assumed our task more fully. Our roles were real though and this game had genuine consequences. Gabardine glided naturally across the forest floor like a Native, placing each step gently on the fore of her foot and barely making a sound. Mason noticeably, wasn't role-playing; he had moved to the head of our line and was walking point as if back on patrol in a Southeast Asian jungle. Vigilant of every shadow's sway, attune to the slightest rustle in the trees, he was aware and analyzing every fluctuation in our panoply of night. He was skilled at this, moving us flawlessly up onto a rock outcropping above the cabin, he then asked Dan if this spot would work for him; Dan agreed and we began to set up the equipment.

The gaggle of gadgets unfurled from the bags intrigued me. He had night-vision goggles for all of us, still and video cameras equipped with dark light, listening apparatuses for both in and outside the cabin, headphones, and a multi-track digital recorder. We blanketed the area so we could hear the conversations from cars to the cabin including a laser device that would essentially hear right through the cabin's rough cedar walls, everything connected to the recorder and the headphones. The video camera with a zoom lens went on a short tripod to keep it stable, which Gabardine would run while I operated the recorder. With much forethought from our commander, he decided that Mason and he would furtively move about focusing the instruments on the unfolding action. We were ready. We had only to wait until midnight when the covert coven planned to arrive.

It was the new moon and the stars blazed against an obsidian sky. From our hovering perch, we could see out across the hills glimpsing the shadowy silhouettes of trees on the slopes that rolled down to the river's edge. Night sounds rang through the forest; Owls' wings whispered their swift presence from the dim lit sky accompanied by the hoots and howls of creatures I didn't recognize. It felt primal as I listened to the voices of the animals like I had in the jungle and for a few minutes I escaped our purpose on the rocks. The animals knew we were here and waited to ascertain our motives. In my mind, I voiced that we had not come to harm them, but to curtail a greater danger. "To do so, you need to pay attention to your task." I heard one retort. Realizing the voice was right; I returned my focus to the cabin, feeling the prickle of anticipation slither up my spine.

At three minutes to midnight, they came like spiders. Four black Hummers shot out of the darkness without headlights and encircled the cabin as if they were darting to their prey at the center of a great web. The vehicle doors opened, one individual got out brandishing an automatic weapon as he swept the area with a flashlight, investigated the perimeter, and then motioned for the others to follow. We were safely above the focus of his search. Two darkly clad men then emerged from each Hummer gathering like eight forsaken shadows near the walk leading to the cabin. I turned on the recorder, the cameras focused; it was time to listen, and learn in silence.

"What the hell do you mean you found nothing?" a voice yelled so loudly we didn't need our equipment to hear.

"We went through the entire place sir, no Mallory, no indication that he's ever been there." Another voice answered subserviently.

Through the night-vision goggles, the figure yelling looked like Harry Nash from the picture I'd seen on the ORTI website and behaving as cantankerously as Remington described. Clearly, everyone there was subordinate to him and no one challenged his aggressive style. Four of them were dressed in dark militia style fatigues filled out by the turgid angles of highly conditioned bodies. The business attire on three of the others looked custom tailored but Nash looked like a corporate sovereign, lording over them in his felt fedora and long cashmere overcoat, his hands in pocket except when waving them in angry animation.

"Those damn do-gooders are becoming a pain in my ass." Nash barked, flaying his arms wildly. "First, the little blonde bitch won't sell her property. Then they suddenly have tons of money and nothing better to do than stick their noses in our business. Mallory has to be bankrolling them. The loony bastard has lost it completely, he's been hiding all over the world for years. We have to control him, or get rid of him before he ruins all of us. If he wants to hide, he can hole up with the fishes permanently! You agree?" He asked in a rhetorical rant, looking at the other business types who nodded in tacit agreement.

"Mr. Nash, sir," one of the fatigues began, more timidly then his militant guise would suggest. "What about our payment, we…"

"Payment?" Nash interrupted angrily, "You've brought me nothing. You lost one of your men and probably put us all at risk. I've made payments where it counts, politicians who smile and lie for me; I've bought police and sheriff officers to enforce my law. You are the pros who are supposed to get results!"

"But sir, w…" the mercenary started again but before he could finish his head flew backward and he collapsed, a torrent of blood flowing from a hole in his forehead.

"Is there anyone else who wants to renegotiate?" Nash bellowed up the hill, waving the pistol he had pulled from his pocket. "Find Allworth and silence him, NOW! Is there anybody who doesn't understand his job, NOW? Davidson and his tree-hugging bastards connect to Mallory somehow; I know it. They even have that turncoat, son of a bitch attorney Parks working for them. Find Mallory and I do mean IMMEDIATELY!" he said, kicking the body of the fallen man repeatedly. "Take this piece of crap away and get rid of it." Nash screamed as he and his associate retired with confident disdain to their all terrain transport and callously sped away.

What do you do when darkness looks you in the eyes and it knows your name? Unknowingly, Nash looked directly at me when he screamed up at the hill and I looked directly into his eyes through the night scope. A dark malevolence seethed in his core and I couldn't get that look out of my head; it startled me so much that I instinctively jerked away from the edge dislodging a stone as I moved. Reflexively, Mason pulled down our upright microphones and dove on top of me covering my mouth. Following his lead, I could hear Gabardine and Dan flatten to the rock.

"Hear that? Who's up there?" voices called from below.

I saw the two remaining "suits" flee immediately as I peeked carefully back over the edge. Lights swept the hillside again, coming up the slope in a methodical search for the source of the disturbance. Lying prostrate on the crag, I could feel my heart pounding fast against the rock. I heard Gabardine gulp undoubtedly trying to swallow the same lump that had risen in my throat and hoped the thunderous roar inside my chest wasn't as audible. The beacon was splashing the edge of our outcrop and creeping insidiously close when a large buck leapt from the brush behind us, burst over the rock ledge into their searchlights and ran down the hill. The lights followed the deer away from us, as we lay motionless, silent, and relieved.

"Just a deer," a voice declared, "let's get out of here."

Without speaking another word, they picked up their murdered comrade in unison, threw him in the back of the Hummer like crumbled rubbish and disappeared into the dour shadows as hastily as they had arrived. We waited for several painfully long, anxiety driven minutes to be sure the ruffians had gone before peering over the edge with our goggles to see if anyone remained. It looked clear.

"Thanks Mason," I said gathering our equipment and packing for the walk to the car. "Looking in Nash's eyes, I felt like I was being sucked into some demonic void. I freaked when I should have frozen and couldn't help but jerk away."

"Been there, done that." Mason quipped, "Besides, you should be thanking that deer. I mean, where did that big boy come from? He saved our asses."

The deer did have perfect timing, almost as if it intentionally sprang out to distract our attackers. With the mention of the graceful buck, I simplistically whispered, "Thank you," and no one was completely surprised when we all heard "You're welcome," resonate back from the woods.

"Nature takes care of her own," Gabardine whispered, reverently pulling a small pouch of tobacco from her pocket and sprinkling an offering to Spirit in the four directions.

If anxiety and trepidation dominated the hike into the woods, terror pervaded walking out because we knew Nash was behind the fires, knew he intended to harm Mallory if he could, and that he killed without hesitation or remorse. What we didn't know was why he focused all that rage on us. Yes, our article and film criticized the chemical plant in town, but the first fire preceded that. It was getting hard to think of him and his associates as merely "those who did not yet understand" when they certainly considered *Just Our Earth*, and me, their enemy. Nash understood exactly what he wanted and without conscience, he would do anything to get it. I didn't have a clue how to prevent that from seducing us into battle especially, when this evil was already stalking us.

Without the kindness of an unforeseen deer, we already would have lost; a fact present in our minds as we maneuvered the brushwood. Mason walked point as before, listening carefully on the way out and leading cautiously towards safety, the freedom waiting when we reached the car. We marched in silence, sobered by what we'd seen and wanting only to escape, to be somewhere we could think and make sense of what we'd witnessed, or more desirably for me, stop the canker that was boring through my conviction. Well away from the cabin, we moved doggedly through the night until Dan suggested we rest and recollect ourselves on a fallen hickory trunk that stretched like a chase lounge beneath a canopy of redbuds, and papaws laden with banana-like fruit. Our venture had born a crop too but its savor wasn't sweet.

"Is there anything to Nash's allegations about the money?" Dan asked turning directly to me.

"No," I answered with exasperation. "Remington is trying to trace the money because it arrived with no indication of where it's from. Maybe Nash is right and Mallory is behind the donation, but not to our knowledge. Sometimes I feel like this money is more of a curse than a blessing."

"It's my job to check all the angles." Dan added, apologetically. "The good news is, all the evidence we gathered tonight is legal, and it's damning. A judge signed off on this surveillance based on Allworth's confession and the two fires. More warrants will follow based on tonight's work; that will put a stop to it.

"The question is," the Sheriff continued, scratching his chin as he leaned forward on the log, "what officials can I trust? I don't want one of Nash's stooges to make this evidence mysteriously disappear. Since this crosses state lines, other authorities will have to be involved to arrest Nash, and sometime soon, before his 'Show Me State' performance becomes an 'I'll show you' vanishing act."

Remembering Janell's cryptic warning and concern for our safety, we all agreed to get going and out of potential danger. Mason headed out resuming his vigilant hunkered gait as he moved across the fallen forest debris, mindful that a bonifed boogeyman inhabited these woods. The danger moderated with a sense of accomplishment and we slipped through the trees feeling better after Dan's comments. It was empowering to know we had pulled it off. I supposed this would put an end to the problems, hoped it would bring closure, and expected Dan would be able to use the law as intended. Approaching a tall cottonwood on the trail, I recalled that it stood on the creek bank where we had started up the ridgeline and that we were nearing the last bend before the fire road and the SUV when Mason stopped abruptly.

"Hear that?" He whispered, waving us all down to the ground.

There were voices ahead in the stillness and that couldn't be a good sign. Crouching close to the ground, we watched as headlights turned from the county road onto the fire road. If they drove in all the way… if they looked around very much… they would spot the vehicle and if they found it… well, we wouldn't be having a Teddy Bear picnic in these woods today. Flat to the ground, my heart pounding again, we waited anxiously as the headlights slowly moved up the fire road with searchlights scouring the brush on either side. They were looking, and looking hard.

The vehicle came to a stop. Somehow, the lights hadn't revealed the SUV concealed in the brush. Doors swung open on both sides and boots to the ground; it was the spiders, the private militia in their black Hummer. The headlights soon revealed the three men in fatigues. We could hear them discussing their predicament, where to bury the body. Mason, doing reconnaissance, continued to sneak along the trail until, about 50 yards ahead of us I noticed him slip off his jumpsuit, stash it in the underbrush and remain motionless. One of the fatigues started walking over towards our cloaked vehicle when, Mason pulled down his pants and started yelling.

"Hello, hey over here," he hollered. The lights instantly directed on him, as did their weapons. Holding his skivvies with one hand and raising the other, Mason continued. "Didn't mean to alarm anyone, I guess a bear can't shit in the woods around here without calling out the militia?"

There was silence. Without lowering their weapons, they whispered amongst themselves and then one yelled back, "On your knees and keep your hands in the air, both of them." His voice penetrated the forest night recoiling up our trail like the scream of a cougar prowling too close for comfort. From our position, hidden on top a bolder beside the trail, we could see Mason comply, his skivvies falling on the ground as he released them to raise his hands. The men quickly moved up, surrounded him, and after searching him, commanded him to stand up slowly and put on his pants. At gunpoint, they led him back to the Hummer.

"This is private property for members only. What are you doing on the grounds?" The interrogators began. Their inquiry was forceful and polite but their suspicion was palpable, after all, we knew the truth behind their good cop personas.

"It was kind of an emergency; I got tired and needed a place to sleep."

Mason said, quickly fabricating a story to tell. "I'm driving to Chicago. I was just relieving myself, when you showed up, before I stretched out and caught a few winks; you can't argue with Mother Nature you know. Sorry, I thought I was past the resort."

"You can't sleep here. You'll have to leave." One sniped back in a scolding tone. "Where's your car?"

"Back there, out of the way," Mason said pointing to the brush. "The last thing I figured was anybody would care out in the heart of nowhere." Mason grumbled as they took him over to the hidden SUV.

"All right Buddy, it's time for you to get out of here." Their leader said maintaining his suspicious stance, but it seemed like he was buying the story. "Get in, and be on your way."

"I must have dropped my keys when I had my drawers down," Mason said reaching for the locked door and then fumbling through his pockets.

Dan, on cue, scurried down and over to the place where Mason had just been standing, dropped the keys, and returned to cover. The fatigues marched their detainee back to where they had captured him and started searching the ground with their flashlights for the metallic reflection as they spread out through the buck brush and gooseberry undergrowth.

"Here they are," one of them yelled, as he bent over to pick up the keys. "You're a lucky cuss; they could have disappeared forever in this underbrush," he concluded sternly handing the keys to Mason.

Mace's quick thinking and clever ruse was impressive, but he was lucky, the last guy got shot. The fatigues beamed their flashlights into the vehicle, remaining very cautious as Mason unlocked the door, swung one leg in, and started to settle in to the treasured escape.

"Hold it!" one of them said. Wrenching Mason forcefully out of the doorway, he reached in, pulled out Dan's red emergency light, and shoved it in Mace's face. "What's this, an all terrain cop car?"

"Are you a cop? What are you looking for around here? Why are you really here?" The questions flew as two of Nash's hired henchman slammed Mason up against the vehicle while the third jumped into the front seat ripping through everything in sight. After finding the police flasher, they were jerking Mason around violently though they hadn't thrown any punches.

"You better have a good reason for being here Buddy and you better tell it this minute." The mercenary threatened.

"Yes, I'm a reserve officer back home," Mason replied staying with the same story, "but, I'm on my way to Chicago, and I had to stop. That's all!" He concluded emphatically knowing that this time his captors weren't buying it.

"It's clean, too clean, like it's an unmarked car," the second fatigue yelled after rummaging through the glove box, the consol, and under the seats in earnest.

With calculated precision, Mason kicked the gun from the assailant's hands following with a surprise sweep kick that knocked the stunned henchman to the ground. Grabbing the freed weapon, he ran for cover in the woods, and ten yards away from the SUV, Mason was about to vanish into the trees when the snapping hiss of lead flying, ricocheted from the forest wall. Helplessness descended over me like a heavy frost, wilting the hope of our accomplishment as all three fatigues advanced military style, their spotlights and weapons aimed into the trees, into the darkness, towards Mason's position. Instinctively, I started to jump up, to attempt to help him, but a vice-like grip commandeered my shoulder hard and arrested my futile charge.

"There's nothing we can do at this time, nothing!" Dan whispered as he dragged me back to the ground. "If they find all this, they'll kill everyone for the evidence and there will be no one to do anything about it."

The wanton warriors moved forward advancing one at a time, each covering the others as if capturing a position in battle. Wherever Mason was, he had captured one of their weapons but he wasn't firing it. I couldn't see him in the darkness but he had either, disappeared in the thicket of under brush, or he couldn't fire.

"Got him!" a voice called. It was over.

Mason lay sprawled across a gooseberry bush in their spotlights, his head smashed against a fallen log and he wasn't moving. Still, they approached cautiously. I could see from our position, still slightly above the road, there was a lot of blood running down his face from where he smacked against the log, but most of it looked like it was coming from his leg; his entire pant leg was soaking wet and glistening red in the light. The errant guard, who had lost the gun, grabbed it out of Mason's unconscious grip while another checked his pulse.

"He's alive, but we really nailed his leg, must be near an artery," one reported.

"Wait a minute, he's no cop." His comrade announced, his beacon shining directly on Mason's face. "Nash will want this guy; he's one of those damn tree huggers. I thought he looked familiar. You better stop the bleeding and keep him alive or we'll be in more trouble. Well Buddy, looks like you found a place to sleep for the night."

They tied Mason's hands, roused him enough to be sure he was going to come around, carried him off, and placed him in the back seat of the Hummer with one fatigue. Both vehicles started and drove off. That was it; they had our way home and worst of all, they had my friend. We stood up in disbelief watching the taillights disappear into the night around a wooded curve. The spiders had Mason. Now what? Stunned, speechless, and fresh out of cheeks to turn, I would have killed them if I had the opportunity. Mason saved our lives and he was probably going to lose his, as a result. Hollow and heartbroken, I was completely powerless.

"We may be stranded, but we're not stuck," Dan said, reaching into his pocket for his cell phone. "Remington can pick us up. We'll find a way to get Mason. One of my 'Boondocks Protection Plan' sheriffs is a few counties over." Dan added, continuing to dial after receiving no answer from Remington and leaving a message.

I didn't like that we couldn't reach Remington after hearing Nash's comments but in a few minutes, our ride was on the way. The other sheriff suggested a meeting point about a mile away, safely off the Aeolian Woods property and well away from any of their patrols. We gathered our things, went down to and crossed the county road, and started a cross-country hike into the hills and woods to the north. It wasn't going to be an easy mile. It required going over a good-sized knoll and maneuvering through the vines and underbrush that we had battled all evening. On this leg of the expedition, we were all pumping adrenaline, driven by fear, worry, and outright rage. In what seemed like no time we came down into a small clearing that was to be the meeting point, dropped our gear, and waited safely out of sight until breaking our silent vigil, the cell phone in Dan's pocket beeped; at last, it was Remington. I heard Dan explain our predicament and arrange for Remington to meet us. Then he handed the phone to me.

"Hell of a mess, huh," was the first thing I heard as I put the cell to my ear. Remington was a good listener and like when we first met, I started rambling. As if he was debriefing me after a combat mission, I spelled out what had transpired over the past hours in graphic detail. When I had finished he assured me that he would tell everyone else and then informed me that his research on the source of the money had revealed a mystery regarding Andrea's family that might change everything.

"I'm confident Mason's courage will keep him going," he concluded. "I'll be there about daybreak and we'll find a way to get you ALL back safely."

Yes! The lights flashed twice. We watched the signal Dan had arranged with his friend as a car slowly turned into the area by the clearing. I don't think I've ever been so glad to see a pair of blinking headlights, or to end a forest foray. At least some of us were on our way to safety. Mason remained in peril and maybe for the first time, I understood a little of what he felt in Vietnam, an unexpected insight learned from Dungeons and Dragons in the Aeolian Woods. The consequences were already staggering and our security felt far too tenuous after touching Darkness, the Darkness that lurks beyond the shadows outside the reach of civil imagination. These woods derived their name for the musical sound heard when the wind blew through them, like an Aeolian harp. This night they had played a dark and dreadful dirge. I know this; the next time that Darkness stares me in the eye, I'm turning on the Light, before it calls my name.

CHAPTER 18
BROKEN WISDOM

"The Devil came down to Georgia," the rockabilly radio played as we rode safely along in our rescuer's patrol car. We were on our way to sanctuary, yet I knew we would be back to this dark place, back to hear another mysterious refrain played by wind and woods. Duty bound us to return, and I was certain the Devil wasn't fiddling around in Georgia alone. Sorrano's warning about the seduction of evil kept repeating in my mind and for the life of me, I couldn't understand it. If good is more powerful than evil, don't some causes justify a fight? What's the point of all these spiritual insights if we are only going to be victims? Where are the Siddhas, the flowers of the Spirit, when you need them? I wished I could just blip in at light speed, get Mason, and blip out without a fight. It's best I don't have such powers, if I had been able to throw lightning bolts from my fingers earlier, I would have destroyed half the country. At the very least, there would be four fewer Hummers in the world and maybe the Devil wouldn't get down to Georgia ever again. Sorrano was right, thinking of them as the enemy justified all sorts of hideous acts. If my job was to help repair the world, I couldn't destroy parts of it to serve my needs.

The dim yellow street lamps of a small rural town were visible ahead. It was one of those few towns where you can still measure the crime rate by how many of those bulbs had to be replaced after a midsummer Saturday night. Much like Dan, his friend Volley enforced justice by following the ledgers of his heart as much as the letter of the law. There were towns like this everywhere once, but they were fading into the past like the family farm. The adrenaline flight was now over and I was in a state of exhaustion; it was comforting to know we were coming into a place where right and wrong were still discernable by incandescent light. The sheriff's office was a storefront found beneath the lights on Main Street. It rested amid feed stores, the mercantile, and the town's only diner where life histories were recounted daily over coffee, a short stack of pancakes, and a side order of compassion.

Sheriff Volley parked in front of the diner instead of his office. The storefront looked like it hadn't tasted paint in several decades. In its window, an unlighted neon sign read "Betty's" by the door and a hand painted picture depicting a stack of steaming pancakes was in the far corner. We followed Volley up to the darkened window where he taped a coin repeatedly on the glass until an elderly woman appeared from the kitchen wearing a white apron already soiled by hours of work. She recognized him and quickly unlocked the door.

"Not open quite yet Sheriff," she said wiping her hands on a towel. "But that never keeps you from getting your breakfast does it." Clearly, they had known each other a long time and this was a familiar routine.

"Betty, these folks have had a troubled night in the woods," the sheriff explained. "They need a little nourishment. Show them what a Betty's breakfast is all about."

"Sit down; sit down." Betty said flipping on the lights with a curmudgeonly grumble. "May as well open these old doors now, lots of hungry folk will be along now," she complained, disappearing into the kitchen.

Within a few minutes, characters wearing coveralls and denim beneath short-billed caps bearing the names of seed, feed, and farm implements filled the frugal diner. The room was alive with conversations, expected yields, and hungry anticipation, when Betty's breakfast began to arrive in waves. The first breaker on the beach was a basket of buttermilk biscuits with homemade butter and wild plum preserves. I swear there was as much magic in her plum preserves as in Malchizadec's healing luminations and we all needed it. The texture of the biscuits, the complex of flavors in the butter and plums, evoked a near religious experience with each bite. Maybe I was hungrier than I thought, but the combination was like a drug. You had to have more. I could see why the place filled within minutes of opening; the locals knew about Betty's potions. The next wave brought pancakes and eggs to suit every palate. This was no short stack; served family style there was a mountain of cakes on our table, and every checkered tabletop in the restaurant. Finally, platters of sausages, ham, breakfast steaks, and bacon completed the hedonic feast. The indulgent aromas alone were a meal. From biscuit to bacon, every morsel was beyond delicious.

Betty never seemed to hurry in her work. Though it seemed there must be an army of elves at her disposal, she toiled by herself moving back and forth from kitchen to table increasing the mouth-watering mass in front of her customers each time she passed. A single plaque adorned the plain, worn white, walls that read, *Hope for tomorrow, strength for today.* That was Betty's mission, and the charmed flavor of her cuisine. She gave the town a place to dream each morning. Preparing her food with love and attention, she nourished people with hope and strength for their lives. She was a surreptitious sage that gave much to the small town's soul. Her elixir had worked just as Sheriff Volley intended; our hope restored, we had strength to face the day when Remington pulled up outside. We thanked Betty and Volley, said our goodbyes, and loaded ourselves into the car for what remained the beginning of an unknown journey.

Remington had arranged a rental for us to drive back to the farm. We were going home, but we couldn't stay there. Despite our desire to charge immediately back into Aeolian Woods and rescue Mason, Remington argued that it would serve Mason better if we went back to the farm, consolidated our power, and allowed Dan to employ proper law enforcement. He would contact Nash, demand Mason's safe return, and leverage our position by revealing that there were three eyewitnesses to his abduction. I had soared like an eagle, and been a luminant conduit for healing but I couldn't think of any better course than to follow his advice.

"The evidence you collected will implicate him in the fires, assault, kidnapping, and a murder," Remington extrapolated, as the incandescent yellow street lamps faded from the rear window. "We'll save those nuggets for you Dan, to swing as the final hammer; but to be safe, let's duplicate everything you gathered and keep copies in my vault." He suggested, smoothly accelerating onto the two-lane highway as we relaxed into safety and the quiet grounding of tires on secluded blacktop.

Kansas City was 50 miles, and a whole world away. As Remington drove the winding byways, the three of us grappled with the shift from one reality back into another. We had lived through the experience and there would be many times coming to retell it, but few words would ever explain all of it. When the copies were completed and safely stashed in the document vault at Remington's office, the three of us loaded the rental car and prepared for the longer drive home. Out in the parking lot in our last exchange before leaving, Remington handed me a packet labeled "James and Andrea."

"I'm not sure yet what all the connections are, but I think you'll find it out of the ordinary," Remington explained, pleased with the product of his investigation. "I did a complete search of both your family histories because profiles of the past often yield accurate patterns that may lead to the source of the money. Look at this with Andrea, there's some information left with a stipulated release 'to an heir of' Andrea's great grandmother. That may be Andrea. Go home and stay calm, we need to use our heads. I'll take on Nash," he concluded with reassuring resolve.

The drive through the Flint Hills marked familiar territory, the home-stretch of the trip from Kansas City and the fall landscape across these hills was always a favorite with the prairie grasses often standing six feet tall and colorful. The Big Bluestem grass, and its smaller cousin Little Bluestem, both turned a beautiful burnt sienna hue with blue purple highlights at this time of year. These early tones of autumn covered the hills as we passed through, but throughout the drive, thoughts of Mason were foremost in my mind. The solitude of the hills could not replace them.

Once I was down the off ramp and back on home turf, we drove the last few blocks into the center of town to the courthouse. The Sheriff would advise the Judge directly about Mason's capture, the surveillance, the probability and extent of corruption in local officials, and express his utmost concern for protecting the integrity of the evidence. Dan and

Remington were methodical; a much-needed approach in this situation that now seemed governed by pandemonium. We arrived to near anarchy at the farm, a huge gathering of people who were ready to invade Missouri and "storm the Bastille," Jake and his compatriots included. They all had degenerated into a primal mob thirsting for retribution and it wasn't going to be easy to turn aside.

I knew Andrea had been up worried all night, which evoked an enormously comforting hug as I walked through the door. The women were with her in the house lending support and the rest of our group came quickly when they saw us arrive. I chose not to go into the evil we had witnessed, or the depraved performance of Mason's captor, but apparently, more assaults had occurred here last night even with Jake's security patrols accompanying the workers. They were brazen. Obviously, there were more involved in these dealings than the combatants seen at Aeolian Woods. I tried to assure everyone that, even considering Mason's situation, our operation was successful and would bring resolution if we let the law take its course. The immediate problem was how to soothe the fuming throng in the yard that wanted vigilante justice.

Facing the crowd was inevitable, though I wanted to consult with Malchizadec first. Remington was correct, we needed to stay calm, so I listened to their concerns more than I talked, understanding that my vision had led them to this state of distress. Finally, I suggested they could come to the farm, camp, and sleep in the various buildings around the place. Together, we would have safety in numbers, a place for us to vet the problem, and we could work towards a solution rather than continue settling scores. The idea seemed to satisfy everyone for the time being and may have quelled their fears, but it didn't provide redress. Mason, who had worked closely with many of them, had become a symbol; only his freedom and the complete cessation of danger would end the uproar.

If revenge is sweet, it is only because we sugarcoat it with self-deception. Beneath the thin veneer of justice deemed as righteous, one unbridles their darkest fantasies. In such a clouded state, one seeks not an eye for an eye, but instead to return the act in greater measure. One pays back an insult with a fist and reimburses a blow with a bullet. Each side acts, convinced the other's contrition can be extracted by inflicting the appropriate amount of pain. Anger congeals into hatred until war begets war and as it has for millennia, evil multiplies easily masked beneath the cloak of moral rectitude. We tottered at the zenith of just such a treacherous grade; we must choose actions carefully to avoid falling to its abyss.

"Now that you've seen Darkness... really seen it... what will you do?" Malchizadec said, waiting in the clinic. "Your instincts tell you to fight or flee, yet neither of these options will dispel Sentient Darkness. First, it tries to draw you into a fight through your anger. If that doesn't work, it tries to scare you away. Fear, is the second seduction of evil. Unspeakable fear becomes silence and denial. You must stand your ground without engaging and turn evil back upon itself. Let neither anger nor fear guide your actions. You can not vanquish evil to dispel it; that is the Creator's task."

"Hold on, I need real solutions, people are being hurt." I retorted, not here for philosophy. "I thought we were supposed to help restore the life on Earth. How did this become a struggle between good and evil? How am I supposed to protect everyone, let alone deal with evil forces? How are we to save Mason?" I asked, stunned at the level of my frustration with his gobbledygook and the powerful feelings I'd kept in all night.

I wanted someone to rescue us but Malchizadec wasn't going there. Folding his wings with the tips joined behind him, almost as humans clasp their hands behind their back, he began to pace forth and back across the room. His violet crested head bowed in contemplation, his talons tapping against the tile floor as he paced for several minutes muttering as if he were having a conversation with himself, or some unseen visitor in his head. Abruptly the mammoth Avan stopped; ruffled his feathers as if concluding his reflection, unfolded his wings as if to gesture in response to me and re-approached.

"Forgive me James; I forgot how difficult a Spiritual Gauntlet like this is to endure," he said, slightly upset by his oversight. "It has been centuries since I faced these particular challenges. I have focused so intently on our task that I failed to help you grow into yours and for that, I am sorry.

The truth is, I can't tell you specifically how to proceed because we are different, and each of us has to find our own way through. However, I do need to tell you more because at the deepest level, the level where you can effect the greatest change, what's transpiring... is spiritual. Even though events are playing out in the physical world, they are only the visible symptoms of a spiritual problem. Please indulge my 'gobbledygook' a bit longer.

"Our creation story, much like those found in traditions here on Earth, tells how the worlds we see, and the creatures that exist, came to be. It describes the world of vibration, dualities, right and left, wrong and right, good and evil. The Creator, on the other hand, exists beyond duality. Unfortunately, from our perspective living in duality, we perceive the Creator as the Supreme Good; we assume with our limited acuity that there also must be an equal and opposite force of supreme evil.

"The Dark One, or Prince of Darkness as your traditions call it, is a constituted being that was once a beloved part of the Creator's Realm. The problem arose when that entity became jealous of the rest of creation. It so loved the Creator that it wanted all the light and love emanating by grace, for itself. In its greed, the Dark One began to lust for everything it could take, degrading any part of creation that received the Divine's attention. Because of these actions, the Creator cast the covetous entity out of the Celestial Realm to exist in the world of duality where it continues to horde the Creator's work. It is called the Dark One because its greed is absolute; like a 'black hole,' it swallows all that it influences, gluttonously devouring any reflection of Divine Light.

"Whether you believe in the existence of sentient evil, or not, is immaterial. You will never see a being that completely hides in darkness. However, you need only to look around you to see that there are those who do believe, who cultivate its dark influence, and engage its purpose. They extend this entity's greed and threaten creation. Greed is the original sin that stains the hearts of humankind. Many people succumb to its deception, believing they must further their fortune for self-protection, or for their family's. Others totally commit to the darkness because it justifies their misdeeds. Greed is a rationalization for every imaginable vise, including war. No matter how the creature snares its prey, or promotes its minions, its only motivation is to possess more of the Creator's light. In its twisted jealousy, it seeks to destroy all that it cannot possess.

"This universe, and all those beyond it, exists in constant flux, constant vibrations. The whole is a free oscillation of energy - to matter - to energy, and all the states we may discover between them. Hording what the Creator gives equally to all under the guise of protecting one's kind, literally stops the vibration that sustains creation. That is the result of greed. Unchecked, it will bring about the ultimate demise. Thus, it is imperative to center yourself always within the Divine's light, love, and protection."

Malchizadec paused as if he were waiting for me to assimilate his discourse. I was struggling with it. It was much more comfortable to think of Sentient Darkness as a subject for myths, Sunday school stories, and scary movies; still, I had stared into the black hole. Denial and intellectualization wouldn't maintain my worldview anymore. Things had changed; I had changed.

"So, you have looked into the Darkness, you can't fight and you can't escape." Malchizadec continued in a reassuring tone, satisfied that I had sufficiently absorbed his thoughts. "I've told you to use what you know, learn all you can, and the rest will be provided. You know more than you think. However, you've not yet come to trust that the rest is provided. There is no way to learn trust. It is faith reinforced by observation and experience so for now, it is a decision that your undeveloped faith will guide you. Mason needs your help but you must respond without anger or crippling fear to succeed. If you do that, the rest will come. To start, bring those who are troubled outside this building to trust what you already know. Attend your friends with kindness, for their fortitude, when wisely directed, protects your way." He concluded, retreating again from my desire to have him find a solution.

I was out of the nest and trusted to fly on my own. Faith leaves no room for doubt but I was human with more doubts than Lorenzo peeking out at the construction traffic from under the porch. We both could be squashed. Nonetheless, everything Malchizadec had taught me had proven true. The light I had seen, and the wings that carved the wind beneath my flight, Spirit provided both and I had to trust it. If I remained convinced perhaps, I could persuade those around me to forego their anger and fear, even though I knew we were about to walk deep into the halls of darkness. The key person to changing the crowd's mindset was Jake; no doubt, they all identified with his pain and by avenging his loss, they felt more control over their own. All of us had to be spiritual warriors now, calm, collected, and able to rise above the difficulties that the next few hours, or days, would surely bring. I pulled Jake aside and into the house to discuss Malchizadec's suggestions.

"It's Remington," Andrea said, rousing my attention inside the door and handing me the phone.

"James, Nash was not cooperative." Remington uttered carefully. "He believes we're bluffing and will only return Mason in trade for Luther Mallory. Nash is still convinced you're hiding Mallory. Anyway, I'm just coming to the bridge over Deep Creek."

"You're coming here?" I asked, very concerned by the urgency in his voice.

"Yes. I have the packet; it contains important documents, you must have dropped it in the parking lot loading up," he answered. "You can bet Nash is going to try something…. Hold on…there is…a big truck is trying to pass…he is WAY too close." He stammered dropping the conversation as I heard the screech of colliding metal and the muffled ping of shattering safety glass. "IT IS CONSOLIDATED CHE…" he shouted over a series of smashes, crunches, and metallic groans.

"Remington," I screamed as I heard a loud bang and the line went to a static hiss. No answer; the line was dead and my reason was disconnecting.

"A car accident…Deep Creek bridge…an ambulance…. Help!" I said after frantically dialing 911, barely aware of my words over the muddled soundtrack replaying in my head.

Fifteen miles away, Deep Creek flowed through a chiseled dell in the Flint Hills. Normally an idyllic vista, this time I sensed the hand of darkness toying with us there. The bridge came at the bottom of a long slope where cars normally built considerable speed and the span across the creek was one of the few places in Kansas where a vehicle could fall some distance. The eleven of us at the farm fretfully piled into whatever transportation we could find and hoped that Dan had also monitored the emergency dispatch. We arrived at the unremarkable concrete bridge fearing Remington was badly hurt but fighting to believe he wasn't. Red lights flickered at least a mile up the highway as Highway Patrolmen slowed the traffic safely around the area. Carefully, we pulled into the center meridian by Dan's patrol car, amid the chaos and questions; we prayed the ambulance on the scene would answer them soon.

Cautiously, we crossed the multiple lanes of congested travelers, approaching the empty ambulance that stood with back doors open waiting for its charge. Dan and the Emergency Medical crew were making their way up the embankment carrying a stretcher past a wheel, a bumper, and debris severed from the vehicle. Remington's car was a crumpled heap of twisted metal, shattered glass, and broken wisdom left forsaken at the creeks edge. There was no Consolidated Chemical Truck anywhere. Time decelerated like the circumspect rubberneckers navigating warily through the flash of emergency lights and the relief that it hadn't happened to them. The restrained squeal of tires, braking as much to shun danger, as to bequeath a voyeuristic first hand glimpse of the evening news, harmonized with the slamming doors of onlookers.

I felt encased, peering out from a dreamlike bubble that was about to burst. I saw us running to meet the EMTs and the cloth-draped stretcher approaching the road as if it was all happening in slow motion. The sheet, pulled all the way up, covered the face of the person lying there. Blood drained from my face, my emotions paralyzed between expectation and anguish; the sound of my heart drowned out the din of highway noise and dulled the only words I heard. "I'm sorry."

Remington was dead.

The bottom of my stomach was in free fall like I had hurdled off the bridge with nothing to grasp, nothing to restore my equilibrium. Remington had been our rock, our compass who always knew the steady course through the cascading events of the past months. As the Avans inspired our spirits, Remington had showed us how to ground those inspirations in the physical world. To make matters worse, I knew who was responsible. I wanted to lash out, to mine my vengeance from his callous flesh. Fear had turned into fury and my molten anger had hardened like steel. I was far from denial and equidistant from reason when I realized Dan was shaking my shoulders.

"It was an accident, a terrible accident!" He exclaimed.

"No it was Nash," I screamed back, swallowing hard as the feelings welled in my throat. "Remington's last words were 'It's Consolidated Chemical.' It's a murder, Dan. It was Nash, and it was murder. I was on the phone with him; I heard the whole thing."

Dan's face grew ashen; his practiced impartiality was waylaid and faltering. We both knew things were out of control and it must stop. Remington had warned about the danger concerned for our safety; but instead, Nash's retribution came against him.

"Let's see if we can find Remington's cell phone, maybe its still works," Dan said dialing his number as we started down the grade towards the crushed wreckage and in a moment, we heard a ring from inside the Subaru's mangled carcass. "That will help prove your testimony," he continued, reaching into a protected nook beneath the front seat to retrieve the auto's last service to its owner.

"This is yours," Dan said handing me a manila envelope he had retrieved on the slope where the car flew from the road. It was the documents Remington was on his way to deliver. Remington wouldn't be dead I thought if only I hadn't lost this plain brown packet in KC, this would not have happened.

"If only" is a powerless place. There is no way to act there, only everlasting questions. It's where defeat feels like relief and it's easier to blame yourself than seek resolve. Remington deserved more and I wasn't going to become a prisoner of an everlasting chain of self-doubt. Mason deserved more. I had to make a choice, a hard choice. It felt like evil was nibbling away at us life by life and I had to decide if I believed that "the rest would be provided," as Malchizadec said, or not. I chose to believe.

"Dan, we have to get Mason out right now. I don't think he'll be alive if we wait," I said calling up my last resolve. "We can't let them kill Mason too." I concluded, feeling my heartbreak and the horror emanating from our group as they looked down at Remington's crumpled car.

"I'm not sure if we can." Dan said gravely. "It requires a lot more officers, officers we can trust, and who have jurisdiction in Missouri."

Jurisdiction in Missouri - I wasn't about to let the body count double because of that and suggested he call Volly who could make the arrest. Dan acknowledged that we needed to act immediately but remained diligent about doing it properly and dissuaded me from a rushing down the road this minute. He finally consented that if he dotted every 'I' and had all the 'Ts' crossed, we could go tonight. Allworth had revealed that Nash was residing at the Aeolian Main Lodge with a small Army surrounding the place. Mason was likely beneath it, somewhere in the miles of tunnels. It could get very ugly, and we wanted no more killing. Slightly annoyed that I was formulating a plan without him, upon explanation, Dan finally agreed that it might work. I wasn't taking the law into my own hands and it could help spin the wheels of justice a little faster. I promised to go home and rest, while he considered its execution until this evening.

Numbed and empty, rest would definitely not come easy…nor would the road home. I had traveled these miles many times; twice this day, but never had I driven these hills and felt so hollow, so helpless. Maybe helplessness was the only doorway through the sorrow and the hollowness makes room for something more. This day had started beneath the words "Hope for tomorrow, strength for today," and collapsed into nothing like I had ever experienced. Grudgingly, I had strength to meet it, but hope…. Tonight, and tomorrow, I would travel this road again with the hope that this time it would be the road to resolution. Resolution must transcend the painful experiences of the past hours, days, and weeks, which required that, we turn our esoteric conjecture into practical certainty. If wisdom is knowledge peened by experience, the events of today had done their job; they hammered everything out of me. With my last ounce of strength, all that remained was hope mauled in the presence of shadows. I was a vessel shattered and empty, but the void made room for wisdom. Hammered, hollow, and open to hope, I could carry broken wisdom.

CHAPTER 19
MEMOS FROM THE EDGE

If the last journey into Aeolian Woods was unsettling, this adventure was a staid sortie. It compelled us to shift from hoping for the best, to absolute faith. Hope bubbles to the surface from some nameless wellspring of our psyche. It comes like a memo from the edge, just when we can suffer adversity no longer. At our lowest point, it enables us to find another perspective, to discern the silver lining in a gloomy sky. Faith is a choice, a total commitment without reservation, whether the skies are gloomy or fair. We made a silent passage through the hills this night with faith, our hearts still heavy with remembrance of Remington and duty to Mason, but we harbored no doubt.

Jake had organized the volunteers who wished to help; there were a staggering number of them. Word of the unjust acts Consolidated Chemical Corporation had carried out against JOE, and other townspeople, had galvanized the community. They wanted it to stop, and they showed up in force to help make that a certainty. Now, a caravan of about five hundred cars, trucks, and vans filled with conviction was about to cross the state line and drive into harms way to underscore their point. It was a convoy to reckon with. Dan insisted that a few Deputies accompany the caravan. Armed with a search warrant, they had a large truck equipped with a battering ram on the bumper to lead them, in case they needed to "knock firmly" at the front gate. My plan, subsequently approved by Dan, was to get all the people into Aeolian Woods quickly in a swarm, surround the Main Lodge, and hold a peaceful, but very noisy, demonstration.

Our incursion force was a small cluster of cars that turned off from the main caravan heading north along the Kansas side of the river. We were heading for a rendezvous point with Sheriff Volley five miles north of Aeolian Woods on the river where several deputies would join Dan and an FBI agent since Nash's crimes crossed state lines. Guiding us through the underground caverns into the resort was Gabardine's duty while Hahn and I well, we would do whatever needed doing. Though everyone wanted to come, Andrea, Janell, Breanne, and Ingmar remained behind at the farm to protect things while Jake and Ch'ien Li accompanied the protestors, intending to keep things peaceful. Stephanie and Mateo were the final safety clause having coordinated full media coverage for the demonstration. Whatever happened would be in plain sight and seen by millions.

"I hope it was OK leaving the girls and Ingmar home." Dan said as we rode along, sounding too much like the macho cowboy that he was, "I wouldn't want anything to happen to them," he drawled genuinely concerned at their vulnerability.

"Are you kidding," I replied laughing before he added to his inadvertent chauvinism. "Andrea is stronger than most men I know; she's tiny, and tornadic, but Janell! Janell's a refugee Enchanted Priestess of Haiti; she'd give them a zap to remember. That's why she gave us that blessing putting the red and white beads in our pockets as we left. She evoked Xango, one of her Orishas, to give us strength and protection. Anyone would be a fool to tangle with them."

When we arrived at the river well after dusk, Volley and his deputies already had three inflatable boats in the water. The fifteen of us would float quietly through the darkness downriver to the bluffs, and then hike along the shore below the embankment until we came to the caverns; from there, we would go underground. Five in each boat, pushed off into the slow steady current of the placid river flowing along with its unhurried pace. Dwarfed beneath the Great Plains' sky, it was possible for a moment, to forget the danger waiting a few river bends ahead.

The tranquility of the water's surface belied the grief I sensed in the vast waterway. Water once filled the Missouri filtered through thousands of square miles of tall grass and forest. Great herds of buffalo, elk, and antelope once drank from its tributaries and grazed along its banks. Coyotés crooned and wolves wailed songs that proclaimed the diversity of its life from shore to swale and summit. Black bears and cougars nurtured their young here, and countless generations of indigenous tribes lived in balance with the cycle of life maintained by this grand artery. The river we floated on was different.

The voices of life that swam in these waters and drank from its shores were silent, all of them silent. The Earth's own flesh muddied the waters that carried us. The land, once held in place by vegetation, now eroded beneath the plow and turned the river into a suffocating murk. Where great wild herds had roamed, sewage treatment facilities, fertilizer plants, scrap yards, and cattle pens now lined the river's banks dumping the residues of progress onto the river's careworn creatures. The spectral sheen of petroleum swirled atop the water in the dim starlight and the chemical perfume of nameless distillates drifted from the ripples. Humankind was quashing the notes of the river and its animals in the Great Chord; we played with loud abandon, they were dying. I recognized the flowing giant's sorrow, it was that same felt by the Soul of the Earth for living beings it could no longer support. Quietly I vowed to help.

My melancholy reverie, shared with the river, came amidst our effort to rescue Mason and arrest Nash. In those moments, I saw why Malchizadec said this was a spiritual problem. From far away jungles, to the great rivers on our continent, both were losing their ability to support life, the problem was everywhere. I realized the "black hole" was everywhere; greed and apathy are so pervasive that their effects literally ooze from every pore of creation, mingle in every waterway, and waft in the mélange of our atmosphere. It is insidious and it all stems from our failure to "do unto others, as we would have them do unto us," the simplest spiritual value. Whether people or species, kingdoms of nature or nations of men, if we treat them with the respect we desire, these problems would not exist. It is our most basic spiritual task and we are failing. The solution is knowing that the Creator's Spirit lives in all of these, and giving all of them the Creator's rightful esteem. That is all that is required.

Malchizadec's words came back to me, "Your instincts tell you to fight or flee, yet neither of these options will dispel the darkness." My first reaction to these insidious effects was rage. I wanted to fight furiously; but fight against what, against whom. It was all of us. "Fear, is the second seduction of evil. Unspeakable fear becomes silence and denial," his words continued in my memory. Denial was how most of us deal with this. We believe, it really isn't a problem; or that government will protect us, science will save us, and technology can overcome it. Denial is commonplace and it's granting us all a slow squalid demise. "You must turn evil back upon its self. Stand your ground without engaging. Let neither anger, nor fear, guide your actions," Malchizadec's counsel continued. That would be my challenge for this journey.

The boats were floating to the shoreline beneath the bluff and as I crawled out of the small vessel, my foot stepped in the shallow water by the river's edge verifying the waterway's feelings I had experienced. There are no words to describe communion. It is a union of spirit. The river had carried our spirits safely along; now I would carry its spirit forever with gratitude. I turned from its banks and began hiking behind Gabardine towards the yawning opening in the side of the bluff. Once inside the quarry, she said there were about a dozen shafts that extended from the large opening where we stood. The one we needed followed the river about 50 yards inside the edge of the hill, then the shaft turned inward and eventually opened into a natural cave that would take us right beneath the Main Lodge. Slowly, we trailed behind Gabardine with our red filtered, low intensity flashlights.

The red glow from the lights provided enough lumination to see without making us blind in the dim shadows outside the beam. We edged quietly along, step by precision step, where the ruby radiance revealed safe footing. One of Dan's deputies constantly swept the path ahead for laser and sonically triggered detection devices prepared to disarm them as required. There was no other light in the tunnel yet Gabardine moved us with swift caution, knowing the terrain and pausing periodically to listen into the darkness that lay ahead. Cut into the vein of limestone that ran beneath this hill, the floor, walls, and ceiling of the tunnel through which we passed were smooth from the quarrymen's blades. Side tunnels branched out every few yards where the stonecutters extracted more rock from the stratum. The honeycomb continued for about a half mile through these manicured burrows until the main passage ended and to the left, a side tunnel extended beyond the reach of our lights, but not my imagination. I envisioned a dozen dangers lying in shadowy wait as we carefully advanced into the darkness where the smooth floor turned rough and the ceiling, and walls, vanished completely.

Revealed beneath my feet in the dim red glow was cave popcorn, a cave formation made by dripping water. We had reached the point where the quarry opened into the natural caverns. Gabardine pulled us all together directing a more powerful flashlight upward towards the ceiling. Hanging in front of us were stalactites, and curtains of flowstone that joined the ceiling and floor of the cave. Stalagmites towered upwards out in the center of the grotto. Reds, oranges, and occasional stripes of blue and green colored the unworldly panorama of calcite sculptures dangling in the vast cavern. Thousands of years hung displayed for our vetting. Since the grounds above the grottos were privately owned; the caves were sealed and remained unspoiled. The grotto dropped off to a still pool of water a few feet in front of us where hundreds of calcite rafts floated undisturbed, suspended in time, until they became too heavy and settled beneath the surface. We tread softly through treasured halls with care not to disturb the mineral dreamscape; a subterranean frozen flow sculpted by hoary waters forever to adorn this portal and, as if on custodial watch from the ceiling high above, a colony of bats noted our civil passage.

We passed through several similar grottos each with unique coloration and formations until, the grottos became smaller; the domed ceilings began to lower and sound seemed to amplify in the tight surroundings. The drip, drip, drip of water keeping an eternal rhythm as it fell from stalactite to mirror pool, shifted my awareness and an ancient insight began to flow into my consciousness. We were living a shamanic journey; a journey usually made in a trance state driven by the rhythm of a drum. The dripping water had been my drum. A Shaman's spirit finds a hole in the Earth to travel into the Lower World and retrieve information, visit animal and plant allies, or search out the lost soul of their patron. Where Shamans ventured in the realm of spirit, we traversed in physical form, slipping through this cavern into a Lower World to retrieve Mason. It seemed we had walked more than a mile into the hill stooped in single file; we plunged ever deeper through the caves, searching for the edge of our Midgärd.

"This wasn't here before," Gabardine said stopping abruptly and grasping the wrought-iron gate that barred our passageway, "it's locked from the inside."

"Is there any other way?" Dan asked pushing against the unyielding iron.

"This is the only way I know; they must have installed this sometime recently. I was here just six months ago," Gabardine said disheartened as if she had jeopardized our goal.

Beside the gate was a control box with a security key pad. Beyond, we could see a grid of laser beams crisscrossing the passageway. With an electronic decoder, Dan's deputy disengaged the alarm system in about a minute but the iron bars were about six inches apart with a steel wire mesh welded to the backside preventing anything from passing through. Two inches gaps above and below the gate were the unobstructed courses to frame our disappointment.

Malchizadec's words came to my fore thoughts, "use what you know, learn all you can, and the rest will be provided." I remembered flying for some reason, and that others had perceived me as an eagle, maybe I had become an eagle. My thoughts became still, I felt tingling in my arms, my sight dimmed slightly but as it did, my hearing was intensifying exponentially and then, I suddenly felt myself rising from the floor. I could hear the lights waving around and hands swatting at me. Gabardine was swishing me away, but her hands seemed huge, larger than I did. I began an erratic flight to the top of the tunnel, out of reach, and headed for the gate. I was a bat, the perfect form for a cave and small enough to dart through the gap at the top of the gate. I seemed guided by radar so I took a brief flight through the dark tunnel ahead exploring the benefits of my navigation system until I came to another gate.

Exactly like the first barrier but, this one led into the wine cellar, or I assumed it was the wine cellar beneath the Main Lodge. Darting through the opening above the gate, I fluttered around in darkness to sense if anyone was there. It was empty. Another tunnel led from the opposite side that I could vaguely see behind a tall wine rack on the wall. Banking sideways, I sailed between two bottles of Château LaTour Burgundy and approached a doorway a few yards down the passageway. My emotions welled with excitement and started changing me back into human form as easily as my instincts had transformed me into a flying mammal. Through the door's window, I saw Mason sitting tied to a chair in a dimly lit room. He was alone in the room, barely conscious, and still bleeding slightly from his leg, which had a tourniquet tied around it. Relieved to find Mason alive, I was now standing by the door. Certainly, I didn't know what I had done, so I guess, "the rest had been provided."

"Mace! Mason! Are you all right?" I said with cautious relief, bursting through the old wooden door to the chamber that imprisoned him and untying the ropes that bound him while I tried to rouse him.

"Jake, is that you?" Mason muttered, still barely conscious.

"Mace, it's James; Jake is outside the lodge." I said. "We've come for you, you're going to be safe now," and with that, his eyes opened a little to recognize me. "I've got to let the cavalry through the gates," I concluded realizing the group was stalled in the tunnel with no idea where I'd gone.

My two legs carried me as fast as they could down the passage, pushing open the wine rack. I ran across the cellar, opened the wrought-iron barrier leaving a bottle in the gateway to prevent the gate from latching and then pushed my way back into the dark cavern. It was a lot easier navigating by radar. At last, I came to the gate where the rest of our party was still plotting a means to surmount the impediment.

"Where did you come from?" Gabardine asked seeing me on the other side of the iron barrier. "We were worried you got lost."

"I found another way and found Mason up ahead," I responded motioning them through the gate and not wanting to attempt an explanation of having gone "batty."

Dan took a small radio from his pocket and signaled the caravan with Jake and the crew to go through the gates and surround the Main Lodge. The diversion in play, we moved quickly up the passageway, through the gate, across the wine cellar, and into the action.

"Glad you made it Chief." He greeted me, a little more alert. "I wasn't sure if I was going to."

"Can you walk a little ways?" I asked seeing the wince on his face as he put pressure on the injured leg when Dan and I threw Mason's arms over our shoulders and lifted him up.

"Nope, I feel hamstrung and hard liquored, but I can hobble. Now get me out of this musty crypt." Mason responded with a dim glint of his usual wit.

"We'll be back soon and walk you out the front door this time," I said, resting him safely in a nook outside the first gate with Gabardine and well away from the uproar that was about to start.

"OK, now it's law enforcement's show," Dan said pulling his pistol from its holster and striding deliberately back towards the wine cellar. "You have been deputized, but this is an insurgency into an armed camp, they are trained better than us, and they don't have any rules. Our only advantage is surprise and the diversion out front. Follow us and stay safely out of the way! This will get ugly fast." He emphasized.

The rumbling scramble of footsteps running in the lodge above us became frantic in response to the sound of the gathered crowd outside. The deputies took cover, pushing us out of the way as they aimed for the stairway. Within seconds, the cellar door opened as two mercenaries started down the steps with rifles ready. Hahn, Volley, and two of his men, clustered stealthfully beneath the steps waiting for the four flailing camouflaged legs to descend. Then, without making a sound, Hahn stepped out unassumingly, did a flip that a man half his age wouldn't dream of, kicked both of their weapons out of their hands, and moved nimbly out of the way. In shake or shine, Hahn was as unflappable as the clear sky was blue.

Completely dumbfounded at how easily the unexpected warrior had disarmed his opponents, Volley, and his deputies, stepped in as backup with pistols cocked and aimed at point blank range. The two mercenaries, realizing they had no chance to fight, surrendered chagrined that a seventy-year-old Chinaman had subdued them before they could even put up a fight. Sheriff Volley arrested and cuffed, the two mercenaries confining them to plead their case in the dusky light before a magisterial millipede and a jury of encrusted carafes in the wine cellar.

"Maybe Hahn's is more invincible than the rest of us, but here, put these on." Dan said before we made our way up the steps at the rear of the ascending insurgency.

A bulletproof Kevlar vest over my chest brought home the reality of what was waiting at the top of the steps. The two men we captured had military style automatic weapons so I'm sure there were many more like them waiting above, or as we hoped, distracted by the demonstrating crowd. Two by two, our guerrilla force advanced up the stairs disappearing through the doorway onto the first floor of the lodge. When the area was secure, Dan waved Hahn and me into a room nearby since we were unarmed. From that viewpoint, we could see and hear the crowd outside rumbling louder and louder, as they drummed, and chanted, "Two, four, six, eight, no poison from Consolidate." Not a very catchy phrase, a clichéd basketball cheer, but it focused the attention away from Mason and our furtive intentions.

I peered out the window to see more than a hundred of Nash's private army in front of the Lodge with weapons pointed at the crowd and clearly agitated. Standing front and center on the first row of the undulating mass were Stephanie and Mateo with cameras rolling, aimed with complementary precision at the armed militia while Jake and Ch'ien Li were marching before the gathering with placards. There were more people demonstrating than had traveled down in our caravan, many more. I wondered how that could be. Equally bewildering, was an extremely tall man drumming who looked like Malchizadec in Shaman's garb the way I first met him with Little Oak. At the front of the multitude, driving his drum, I spotted Navu leading the chant. People seemed to appear out of nowhere steadily increasing the throng and causing the mercenaries perplexed discomfort that they couldn't control.

That's strange I thought; the very stars I had watched floating down the river were gone but I could see them lower on the horizons as if something was blocking their light above us. As if a great canvass covered the Lodge and the crowd surrounding it, absolute darkness shrouded the entire area. The guards seemed fearful of the shadowy presence above them and many of our demonstrators were looking up with equal concern. Replacing the depth of the ebony sky was flat impenetrable charcoal blackness. My hands felt clammy, my stomach sank, and the hair on the back of my neck began to bristle, was some soulless being in league with Nash? Had Hell's Fiddler come to play at our demise? The shroud was ominous, but it didn't emanate the utter malevolence I would expect or perhaps that was its seduction. I remembered Malchizadec's admonition "Let neither anger nor fear guide your actions." Navu and Malchizadec were still drumming. Hahn too, had an unusually serene look, almost like quiet recognition, as he stared at the coal gray sector of missing sky above us. They weren't afraid, so I didn't need to be "dirty the drawers" scared either and fear wouldn't guide my actions.

"Fire a few rounds over their heads and see if that doesn't scare the bastards off." We heard Nash shout over the walky-talky on the floor above us.

Dan pointed upstairs; he had heard it too. Apparently, the full force distraction on the front lawn had worked and we encountered no resistance as we cautiously mounted the flight of stairs to the next floor where Nash was bellowing orders. Dan, Volley, four deputies, Hahn and I made our way carefully along the upstairs hallway and we were outside his suite of rooms when a burst of bullets sprayed out over the demonstrators with the ear-piercing impersonal snarl of automatic weapons fire. We ducked into a window bay along the hall uneasily watching the activities outside. The pack of protestors had grown to several thousand people, how it was happening I didn't know, but I was sure Malchizadec and Navu were behind it.

"Shoot a couple of the Sons of Bitches," he yelled becoming louder, angrier, and throwing things around in rage, "that'll rout them! If that doesn't teach them not to fuck with me, fire into the crowd. There's room to bury the lot of them." He railed against the mass, which hadn't even flinched at the warning shots as the color of his cowardice began to show.

Nash was losing it. The mercenaries responded to his commands with a strange, silent, and stunning stillness. The orders were maniacal; these soldiers may have killed in far off jungles, and murdered on command without remorse, but this was too much, their were too many people and it was far too close to home. It seemed the mercenaries weren't going to be party to this mass murder and to my astonishment; like a ripple spreading across the regiment, they started standing down, dropping their weapons to their sides as gunshots pealed from Nash's command post.

"That's insubordination!" Nash shrieked. "That's failure to follow a direct order in battle. No one, not Mallory, not these tree-huggers, and certainly not you little piss ants, will stand in my way."

A few of the men careened backwards as the bullets hit. Through our window, we could see many fatigues react, immediately returning fire on the arched window where Nash stood watching his dreams of conquest scatter like a nest of cockroaches exposed to the light. Nash showed that he could not brook what he so easily dished out and ducked from the window being the true coward with character utterly devoid of content like the blackened chasm I had seen looking in his eyes. We could hear him thrashing across the floor as he scrambled for shelter. Nash's elite guard would no longer stand beside a raging lunatic; they ran. Their battle was over.

That was the signal. Dan, Volley, and the deputies quickly overtook the doorway to Nash's room. I heard one more shot fire from Nash's lair and saw it knock Volley backwards to the hallway floor as he penetrated the control room door. He lay bleeding from the shoulder in easy range for Nash to finish him off. I waited for a moment more in the hallway as Dan and his deputies burst in to the center of operations. I expected to hear a barrage of gunshots but it was silent. Hahn and I cautiously entered the room through the cloud of blue-gray smoke and the smell of discharged gunpowder, to see Nash facing us with an automatic pistol in his hands threatening anyone else who dared come closer.

"Don't act so holy, Davidson; I only did what a thousand others would if they had the chance." Nash hissed with fetid hatred when he saw me. "What the hell makes you so righteous anyway, your wife is Mallory's heir."

Overwhelmed, but unwilling to surrender, Nash put the gun in his mouth and steeled to pull the trigger. Then unexpectedly, he lurched backwards across his desk as if pushed by an unseen force, the gun jerking from his mouth, dangled in midair until, with the pistol clutched within his beak, Malchizadec materialized beside Nash. We had turned evil back on its self. It was over!

"How in the hell..." Dan started to say, "Oh never mind, I ought to know better than to ask by now."

Stripped of his feigned power and importance, Nash trembled at his own recompense as the deputies straightforwardly cuffed the deposed despot. Malchizadec moved directly into the hall with Dan and Nash behind him, extended his wings over Volley and washed the violet Tempest Light across his body. The bullet lifted out of the wound rolling onto the floor as the flesh closed behind it. Volley sat up smiling wider then a platter full of Betty's flapjacks as he stared in amazement at the great raptor that had healed him.

"Some things, just like Betty's breakfasts, can't be explained." Dan said looking at his bewildered friend almost as if he had read Volley's thoughts.

The atmosphere had changed; where chaos and corruption had ruled, order arose as the officers took charge, calling in assistance from the state po-lice, and corralling the arrestees into one area awaiting vehicles to trans-port them. They would hold Nash separately to avoid any revenge from his soldiers, and to insure that his charges would preclude bail. Oddly, the crowd remaining was only the people who had traveled down in our caravan. Navu was nowhere present but a low-pitched drumbeat sounded from the direction of the wounded mercenaries where I'm sure Malchizadec was performing his healing. How would they respond having never known compassion? Receiving it from a nine-foot tall predatory bird must make it all the more mysterious. The dark shroud that overshadowed us was gone along with the frightening feeling of impending danger beneath the flat starless mantle.

"Remember, there is no enemy, only those who do not yet understand." Malchizadec repeated.

"Sometimes, good does win," I muttered to myself.

"When you rely on it as surely as your own breath, good always wins. There is no equal and opposite reality." Malchizadec interjected abruptly as I stammered to ask a question.

"You're learning," Malchizadec continued in his typically terse tongue. "Because you did not make Nash your enemy, even though he saw you as his, the depravity within him had no outlet. Evil must have something, someone to feed on, or it cannot exist. When evil starves, it devours itself. That is how you have shown real strength!"

Understanding his lesson, his understated approval aside, we had one more patient to visit. I had started towards the stairs when I heard a voice from behind me, "As Mason would say, 'been there, done that.'" Turning around I saw an uncharacteristic grin on his face as Malchizadec extended his wing towards the stairs.

"So you have," I replied, feeling gratified to see Mason coming up the stairs unassisted while the great, feathered phantom once again performed his vanishing act.

Jake enfolded his arms around Mason, and gave his dad an embrace deep enough to stroke the soul. All the rest of us quickly joined the embrace thankful for his recovery and grateful that we had finally stepped from the labyrinth of too many dark tunnels. Dan, Volley, and the deputies, would stay to handle all the legal procedures required in the next hours. Mason, Gabardine, and I would ride home with Jake, Ch'ien Li, and Hahn gratified that our deputy days were over. Finding a cell phone, I called Andrea to share the complete success of our Aeolian Woods assault when we walked out the front door of the Main Lodge. Out onto the portico, to only one person's surprise, the exuberant crowd cheered, oh… how they cheered for Mason who, with all his gruff cynicism, could not dodge their affection.

"I'm glad it's over and you're all safe." Andrea said, wishing she could be there to share the excitement but then sadness came into her voice. "I opened the packet from Remington. Enclosed is a letter to us, it might have been his last correspondence. I'll read it to you."

Andrea and James;

Enclosed is an envelope I obtained as your representative from the unclaimed inheritance records in the State of Virginia while searching for the source of the donated monies. I contacted the law office concerned, which managed the estate of Andrea's Great Grandmother, and as instructed, held the enclosed envelope. I have no further knowledge of what it might contain, but based on how long they kept the envelope, I think this could be the edge of something very important.

Remington

"The envelope inside is addressed, 'To be held for 50 years from this date, and given to the first of my direct descendants who makes contact thereafter: Oct. 19, 1933.'" Andrea continued. "How could I be the only heir to find this out and what would she keep secret so long?" She sighed.

"We'll open it when I get home and begin this next mystery together." I assured, still hearing the melancholy in her voice.

Aeolian Woods had another chapter written in a memo from the edge, years before in Virginia. It was approaching dawn but the sky was still dark, lit only by the stars and a thin wedge of the waxing moon as once again we drove into the night, this time to journey west through the hills. Our journey to the Lower World had been successful; we had retrieved Mason and more. Surely, the information that would come out in Nash's trial would lead to many more secrets held within ORTI, and perhaps Mallory Inc. Wherever it led, it would precipitate change in their operations, and change seemed long overdue. I had seen too many mornings from the backside of night lately but the matters resolved this night would make rest come easier in the nights to come.

With Jake behind the wheel, and Ch'ien Li by his side, we were safe and I could wait to see what unfolded from Remington's memo. Yes, if places could speak of what they've seen, Aeolian Woods had stories most authors couldn't dream up and what had ensued there today, was certainly one of them. If once, she was an aged beauty queen reigning over a kingdom of mice and memories; in her current splendor, she had harbored the vilest of vermin. Perhaps like lost memos from the edge of dark imagination they too would become fading footprints spread across the serene dust of time. I laid back and let myself drift off into sleep remembering Remington's face, and the spirit of the river.

CHAPTER 20
ESTUARIES OF TRANSFORMATION

Change is unpredictable. Sometimes it comes like the tide slowly, relentlessly, exchanging one grain for the next, re-sculpting the timbre of the shores. Occasionally, it's like the sunrise, proclaiming its arrival long before it shows its colors. At times, change comes like a flash flood that sweeps away normality replacing it with something unimaginable to which we must adjust. It sweeps us along until we flow into some great course guided in our change by an unknown river's banks. Most of the time it happens unnoticed, creeping in and rearranging the bastions of our life until one day we awaken amazed that it's become so different and yet so comfortable. We wonder how we came to prefer blue instead of red, or one style of music over another. When we are children, we monitor change excitedly, eager for each new mark of growth scribed on the doorcheek by our mothers hand. Later in life, change scribes its marks upon our cheeks, as our visage portrays the substance of our spirit and change turns inward. During the past months, change had come like a flash flood radically reforming our reality, yet it seemed as if a slow, relentless transformation had been in progress for longer than we knew. Remington's memo about Andrea's heritage was the predawn light that heralded new hues' before the sunrise.

Upon returning from Aeolian Woods, we needed a good rest and to reorient ourselves from courage under crisis to sustaining the work already underway. The intense pace of the past days had drained all of us and life on the farm even felt a bit anticlimactic in its aftermath. Not knowing how the enclosed envelope in Remington's packet may affect our course, Andrea and I put off opening it until we regained a sense of normalcy, as abnormal as that had become. The letter had waited since 1933 for a reader; it would wait a few more days. Feeling restored, Andrea and I sat down at the kitchen table on this morning prepared for whatever news it may hold.

"It's from your Great Grandmother, you should be the one to open it," I said handing the letter-sized envelope to Andrea.

We were both speechless as the reality that something important enough to hold for so many years was waiting for our attention. What was the connection between Luther Mallory and Andrea if any, and what was important enough to hide? Could what Nash said about Andrea be true? Finally, Andrea dumped out a slip of paper that said, "Founders Bank and Trust of Virginia" and a smaller envelope that contained a key for a safe deposit box.

"We can't tell anyone about this until we know what it means," Andrea said heavily. "I don't want people speculating about it. My Great Grand-mother wasn't a wealthy woman. She worked as a secretary in some little office in Washington D.C. all her life. I don't see how she could have had any connection to Luther Mallory. It must be a family heirloom or a Sav-ings Bond but I need to honor her wish and go find out," she concluded slipping the key into her purse.

Before taking off for Virginia, we decided we'd better check in on Bashira and Sorrano. The clinic's long limestone front faced south with many large windows and though the structure was constructed with the most modern technology, the aged stone burrowed into the hillside made it look as if it had peered out from that spot for more than a century. There were several animal pens on the west end of the building even though there was little need for them the way Malchizadec teleported animals to and from the clinic. They served the farm animals and pets brought for treatment by local residents. Similar to the media center, Gabardine had created atri-ums within the structure that opened the otherwise underground rooms to the sky. All we could see as we approached was the barn/clinic's lime-stone wall sweeping out of the hill and three glass pyramids that rested on the grass covered hill above it to shelter the atriums below. Upon entering the Avan's room, we found it interesting to see Lorenzo by the nest with Bashira standing down by Sorrano and Malchizadec engaged in a lively conversation.

"He's been here nearly the entire time you've been gone." Breanne explained, noticing our attention on Lorenzo crouching intently a few feet from Bashira's nest as we entered. "He's sits and stares at the egg for hours," she concluded.

"Don't worry; I'm ready." He communicated to me, his gray strips bristling with anticipation. "I heard noises and it moved a little, there could be a mouse problem in the straw." Lorenzo added, turning his attention back towards the nest ready to pounce ferociously at the slightest sign of a rodent.

"It's time," Sorrano said proudly. "Lorenzo's observations are the young one moving around inside and trying to break the shell, it should break through soon. You are welcome to stay." He concluded eager with parental anxiety.

"The young one's form will likely be different from ours," Malchizadec said aware that the egg was now shaking violently. "It is not the hatchling alone that is having a new experience."

Lorenzo was beside himself with readiness; he couldn't tense his muscles any tighter for an attack to foil the great mouse invasion. Then a piece of the shell began to break loose. The leathery nature of the shell prevented the piece from cracking free, the young one had to keep pushing, pecking, and tearing until the piece finally fell into the nest. Through the small hole in the egg, we could see an eye peering out at us. The eye had Bashira's soft temperament but it appeared as if the young hatchling was tearing at the shell's edge with teeth, good-sized teeth and no beak showing through. Bashira started making cooing noises that encouraged the young one's struggle until the opening was finally large enough to poke through its head. It didn't look like a bird at all; the head was more reptilian. The skin was gray-green, rough, and leathery much like the egg, and its eyes! Its eyes were emerald like Bashira's but with Sorrano's golden undertones that uniquely made them appear rich chartreuse.

An air of anticipation and excitement permeated the room as we waited, watching the little one work the egg until a fissure formed all the way around the shell. Lorenzo wisely decided that this gray-green creature was not a mouse and gave up his readied stance for a more secure hermitage underneath a cabinet. Then with a grunting thrust, the young Avan forced his shoulders through the crack, and two clawed feet pushed the section apart. The hemispheres of the ellipsoid tumbled aside, one part rolling off the nest, shattering as it hit the floor and sending pieces flying towards Lorenzo's fortified observation post which prompted a hasty retreat. There squirming about on the nest, was what looked like several hundred pounds of reptilian hatchling. Though I had never seen one, it looked similar to a pterodactyl.

Upon seeing what emerged from the dissembled egg, Hahn and Ch'ien Li kneeled to the ground, bowing their faces to the floor where they remained prostrate for several minutes until Bashira invited them to rise thanking them for honoring their newborn. The extended tribute mystified Andrea and me as we assumed it was a Chinese tradition.

"The dragon is most auspicious. A fulfillment of ancient prophecy," Hahn exclaimed, looking elatedly around the room to accent his point.

"Ancient Sages told us there would be a long darkening on Earth." Ch'ien Li explained. "It would be a time when men would fly, do great things and believe they were advancing. Their self-involvement would drain every living thing, even the Earth, and all would fall into grave jeopardy. They prophesied that this time would not abate until a Green Dragon was again born on Earth. Then a cycle of change would begin. The Ching Dragon represents the East and the coming of a new era."

"We are blessed. The Earth's children will awaken and begin to heal." Hahn interjected. "I see dragon one moment above crowd in rescue. Fear my eyes trick me. Never dream I see prophecy realized in my lifetime!" He finished ecstatically.

A dragon in Kansas, I thought to myself, was somewhere beyond Pluto with mystification, it was almost as if the jade token pulled from the ashes of Perfect Form had become real before our eyes. Dragons were the stuff of dreams and mythology, but it didn't exist in the far reaches of imagination; it lived, breathed, and had its being. This must be the effect of the morphogenetic fields as Malchizadec explained I thought. I'm sure everyone wondered what the Avans looked like in their natural form on Satoria.

"I and those trusted with this work before me, have come to this planet many times over tens of thousands of years." Malchizadec began, responding to my rumination and obvious questions. "There was a time when dragons roamed the Earth and it was easier to assume the form of a dragon when we materialized. Birds, dinosaurs, and dragons are all similar in their evolutionary development to Avan life. We knew the morphogenetic fields would affect the development of a gestating egg here on Earth.

"However, as your scientists say, 'ontogeny recapitulates phylogeny'," he stated to our blank stares. "That is, during development, an embryo goes through all the stages of evolutionary development experienced by that species. We hoped that Bashira's energetic fields would direct the developmental process more than the residuals fields on the Earth. Unfortunately, when the egg had to be removed from her body because of her injury, it eliminated Bashira's energetic influence. The phylogenic development must have changed at that time. We believe that when the offspring is old enough and travels back to Satoria, it will return to Avan form.... We are neither birds, nor dinosaurs, nor are we dragons. Each is but a shape embedded in the Earth's morphogenetic memory."

"Oh," Sorrano added with a quirky smile, "we don't breathe fire or eat sacrificial virgins either.

"If you're wondering about the darkened sky over the crowd at Aeolian Woods," Malchizadec continued with didactic purpose. "It was Sorrano. He allowed himself to take a larger, more fearful shape. It was a little encouragement for Nash's men to surrender. The Counsel of Elders also projected their presences from around the globe to increase your numbers and were with you in spirit."

"Although we are familiar with the dragon legend," Bashira said, addressing Hahn and Ch'ien Li, "we did not choose this birth form. Through forces beyond our control, or knowing, it may well be the fulfillment of your prophesy."

"Our purpose, these many millennia, has been to mitigate the portended crisis. Malchizadec added. "If this completes an ancient prediction, then it is a blessing to see it in our lifetimes as well. What will you name him?" Malchizadec asked Sorrano and Bashira who were doting tenderly on their newborn.

"His name will be 'Astralys,' because he is the one born by a distant star," Bashira said looking at Sorrano with great affection.

How much like human parents I thought, even to the point of asking Mateo to film all of their activities with the stipulation that he could only show it after they had left Earth. The thought of them leaving hit me with unexpected sadness and like the predawn light, it heralded the hues of another approaching change. Our past and present were interwoven, we were family and I couldn't imagine a future without them in it. I also needed to make plans for our trip to Arlington, Virginia; that was family too. The Founders Bank and Trust of Virginia still existed so I booked reservations for the next morning.

In the evening, we went out to the barn for the newborn's official introduction. Essentially a baby shower, the quandary was what does one give to a dragon? It was fun to watch the reactions of people as they saw Astralys for the first time. Nothing really prepares you to experience a mythical creature, a wispy fantasy of Avalon and ancient dynasties. Seeing Astralys was visceral and somehow evoked our primal nature, the memories of our past as a species. It reminded me that our spirit lives within a human animal, and all wondrous creatures are but fragile beads hung upon the gossamer veil of light. It was good to be together, to honor and welcome a new bead upon that veil.

After informing everyone of our trip, we headed east above the clouds the following morning, it appeared as if our destination would bring more adjustment. Whether we found the link to Luther Mallory or not, this trip would alter our lives. Perhaps there was something in the shape of the billows that foreshadowed a great shift as if the river of change along which we flowed was about to open into an ocean. An ocean of change where time and tides, sea and shoreline, would all be different even from the anomalies we had come to accept. We sailed peacefully for the next few hours listening to the drone of the jets and imagining what may await us on the ground.

Several of the founding fathers of our country had started the Founders Bank and Trust of Virginia in 1776. Unlike the merger mania, which had swept through most of the banking system, much like its founders, this bank clung proudly to its independence and history refurbishing the old building through the years with great attention to preserving its character. Marble columns towered in the lobby to an arched roof with frescos painted to portray the hopes of a young nation. Each step into the edifice was a step back in time to when the ideals of America were untainted by power and excessive profit. Even then, the scourge of slavery infected the raw wish for freedom with a canker that has yet to fully heal. Still, I could almost hear the founders hopes as I walked; hear the words they had inscribed on the wall above us:

"We the people of the United States, in order to form a more perfect union, establish justice, insure domestic tranquility, provide for the common defense, promote the general welfare, and secure the blessings of liberty to ourselves and our posterity...."

The founders were idealists, liberal thinkers with the courage to be visionaries; how well did we live up to their ideals today. What would they think? If we do still believe these values, I questioned why we treat others outside our borders so differently, why we treat other forms of life so cruelly. The values lauded in the founder's words were another expression of the same simple spiritual law, "do unto others as you would have them do unto you."

Seated in front of the old vault, a woman waited for us to present our safe deposit box key and then showed us to a private security room. In a few moments, the vault attendant brought us a very long deposit box and left the room. Andrea opened the box with anticipation to find a rolled up canvas, an envelope, and a sealed packet. She carefully unrolled the canvas; it was a beautiful painting of a utopian landscape done in the style of the 1920s titled, *The Wings of Paradise.*

"That's Satoria," I whispered. "Sorrano projected this image in my mind when we met."

More curious by my recognition, Andrea opened the envelope hoping its contents would provide some explanation. Inside was a handwritten letter from her Great Grandmother, Mallory Gimble. Andrea laid the aged linen parchment, inscribed with pride and penmanship, between us on the heavy maple table. The only sound was the muted hum of the ceiling fan above us stirring the air in the well-appointed vault less quickly than the questions stirred in our minds. Questions we hoped the letter would answer as we both began to read in silent anticipation.

Oct. 19, 1933

To whom it may concern,

Since you are reading my letter, I assume that you are looking for your connection to the affairs of Luther Mallory. I have enclosed a few documents and pictures to verify the story I am about to tell you which, for any person but yourself, would be unbelievable. Please forgive the length of this discourse but it contains matters of import and it is a great relief to share this special, and unexpected, part of my life with my descendant, and to encourage you to pursue wherever this leads you.

The secretarial pool for President Theodore Roosevelt was my first station. One day President Roosevelt summoned me to the office. Alone with the President, he told me that his friend John Muir had taken him to the mountains of California where he had introduced him to a remarkable being. I have enclosed a photograph of the President with Mr. Muir and this being. Because of that encounter, the President created the Office of Long-term Maintenance, a secret project that, beyond my understanding, he assigned me to run. I was to tell no one and answer only to the President.

I had an office in the Whitehouse basement and the mandate to purchase stocks on all the exchanges with the following provisions:

1) I was never to purchase more than 50% of any company, and never to sell any stock.
2) The monies to make these purchases came from an offshore, numbered bank account.
3) All dividends were to return to that account for reinvestment.
4) I made all the purchases in cash in the name Luther Mallory

The name was the President's idea of a joke combining "Luther," my husband's first name, with my own. There was of course, no Luther Mallory. President Roosevelt informed me that the duties with which I was charged would someday change the world and further instructed me to leave this explanation as addressed and preserved. I presume that your awareness of this letter means that the time has come for such changes.

William Howard Taft was Roosevelt's Secretary of War. In 1909, he succeeded Roosevelt as President and I continued my post. President Taft moved my office to the basement of the Federal Reserve Building concurrent to implementing the Federal Income Tax, and the Federal Reserve Bank, in 1913. The funds I was investing were from the War Department and the project was for long-term economic growth with 1% of the tax income secretly going into the investment account through the War Department. The President made the office a part of the permanent Federal Reserve Bank to remove it from political vulnerability but my orders remained intact, responsible only to the President. President Taft had an extremely small device installed as part of my communication with the Oval Office that was never to be removed. The President told me the peculiar apparatus connected with telephone, telegraph, and news service lines thus securing our communications.

President Roosevelt, and President Taft, both gave me one final executive directive. Each of my distinguished superiors gave me a formal letter of introduction verifying that I worked under Presidential authority and which granted me private audience with succeeding Presidents as might become necessary. The proper occasion to do so was at my discretion. They also gave me permission to reveal my life's work to my family no sooner than fifty years after my death. As my health now fails, I am recording this information to my best, honest recollection. I have continued working alone in this office faithfully investing, and diversifying, as mandated until the date of this letter.

Last week I had a strange, beautiful vision in my mind, which bids me that this is the time. I painted the 'Wings of Paradise,' the enclosed illustration that I have bequeathed to you. I will cordially meet with our new President Franklin D. Roosevelt tomorrow under the authority granted me, to deliver the pertinent information about the Long-Term Maintenance office, specifics about Luther Mallory, the whereabouts of all accounts, and end my enduring stewardship.

I wish you success my heir, with whatever your part has become in this prestigious undertaking. I close with the President's words by which I have tried to perform my tasks. Hear them well.

"Be practical as well as generous in your ideals. Keep your eyes on the stars and keep your feet on the ground ..."

Theodore Roosevelt
President of the United States

Respectfully yours,
Mallory Gimble

I looked at the pages of the long letter turned face down before us, relieved of their duty, they had delivered their message after these many years. With a satisfied sigh, Andrea pulled out the packet that - containing the picture mentioned along with three signed letters from Presidents Theodore Roosevelt, William Howard Taft, and Franklin D. Roosevelt - verified Mallory Gimble's notable declaration. We looked at the photograph and there, sitting on the huge stump of a Giant Sequoia, were President Teddy Roosevelt, John Muir, and Malchizadec, connecting our present to the past in sepia toned detail.

"Yes, the giant trees were magnificent; it was pleasant company, and very beautiful that day." A voice said, scaring us half out of our wits in our vaulted privacy. "Until now," Malchizadec continued, having appeared in the room without our notice, "no one other then those mentioned in the letter, and the Counsel of Elders, has known about this plan. As you can see, I have been on Earth before… many times. My task has always been to help restore that interconnectedness between all life which, through our own greed, we helped sever many millennia ago."

Despite Malchizadec's startling arrival, Andrea and I were still stunned that there was no Luther Mallory and trying to digest all that had happened in the belief that there was. Equally astounding were the revelations about Andrea's Great Grandmother but we had yet to understand how it related to us.

"It is now time to reveal everything." Malchizadec resumed. "Humans have the Creator's ability to manifest their imagination with immense beauty and innovation; this gift must flourish. If selfishness and greed are the motivation, the creations envisioned have the potential to destroy all life on the planet. More encouragingly, wondrous things are possible as they bring technology into harmony with nature, and in service of the Creator. Humankind has the right to choose. It is free will. Nonetheless, if humankind fails to find the harmony, it will cause not only their annihilation, but also an irreparable disturbance in the Great Chord and further destruction in worlds far beyond. This hard lesson took us a long time to learn on Satoria. Fortunately, there are signs that the positive choice is beginning."

"No it's not," I interrupted. "Look what this Mallory plan has led to. Nash was right; thousands of others will do anything for their own power and profit. How can technologies that dominate and destroy nature be the solution?"

"True, we haven't reached the solution," he patiently replied. "Technology in itself it is not the problem. Societies will always seek to advance, as it is natural to grow. The problem arises when individuals, or nations, seek to control its use for their individual benefit or put personal profit above the good of the Whole. The Whole is the Earth and ALL of her inhabitants. This has been true throughout your history whether the commodity was spices, tea, opium, cocaine, minerals, or energy. To horde and control, something that is an inherent part of the Whole is the implementation of evil. It is the intention, not the technology that is to blame."

I could never supplant Malchizadec's logic; his premises were irrefutable. I thought how firearms first improved our ability to gather food but then separated us from nature. How what seemed like protection had led to arms dealers instigating dissension between groups to profit from both sides. How nations even profited from weapons, no longer did we hunt for food, now we hunted enemies with mass destruction. No matter what example I thought of from cars to computers, I saw how selfish intention diminished the Whole, and turned wonders into warfare but how do we keep intention form being corrupt?

"There are voices," Malchizadec interjected, "finally many voices within humankind that are asking the right questions. Those questions will lead to solutions if they are encouraged."

"Why have such complex systems? If we have free will, can't we inform people and let them decide?" Andrea asked a little perplexed.

"Knowing is not the same as understanding, and understanding is not wisdom." Malchizadec continued seemingly pleased that we were asking the right questions. "To quote James, 'wisdom is knowledge peened by experience.' Understanding is the practical application of knowledge through trial and error. Wisdom comes as we know when, where, or even if, we should use our understanding. One always has free will but all must bear the consequences.

"Free will comes with accountability. A child without accountability would choose food that diminishes its health, activities that impede its intellectual development, and emotions that might cause harm. On the path to wisdom, one must acquire experience safely, with the help of good parenting. Otherwise, it overwhelms and destroys. You need only look at world affairs to see that many people on Earth have not the wisdom to manage their experiences. Thus, you see wars, poverty, starvation, and addiction. As individuals, and nations, the choice is far more often to indulge power and advantage rather than wisely promote the whole of life. Humanity has reached the age of accountability but has failed to develop sufficient wisdom. Having the ability to intervene, to save life, we have the responsibility to do so. That is why we responded to the Counsel's request for help."

"I agree with Andrea, I'm still lost trying to understand the complexity of Mallory Gimble's tasks. I guess your intervention was to help life here endure its experience and someday achieve wisdom. Is that right?" I asked attempting to accommodate the information overload.

"Like a natural being, simple processes when functioning together, appear complex." Malchizadec patiently continued. "The plan we developed with the Counsel had four stages. Your Great Grandmother and Grandfather, Mallory and Luther Gimble accomplished the first stage by 'bringing the natural being to life.' Their work established a strong economic force that stimulated growth in all areas. The communication device mentioned in Mallory's letter developed the second stage. It was a simple cybernetic device from Satoria programmed to interface with the world's economic development as if the economy were a natural being. I will explain its two levels of programming.

"First, it monitored the communication lines constantly searching for a technology with which it could communicate. It made first contact in the 1940s during the war when the government was developing the earliest forms of computers. Once in communication, the program replicated itself, thus making a backup in the receiving device, much like your current computer viruses but without causing any damage. Eventually, it used the communication systems of the entire globe, with all its devices as redundant backup and co-processing units. The device demonstrated that it had successfully accomplished this task when we monitored the program code embedded within the signal sent out by the SETI radio telescope.

"The second level of its function was to continue the functions of Luther and Mallory Gimble with some additions. It was to reinvest the earnings in the same region of the world until the economy in that region had increased by 1000%. Once realized, it then changed the region of investment to stimulate other economies. Thus, each region advanced more evenly, gaining experience as it evolved. It will repeat this process as it has since its inception until the entire globe prospers. Importantly, the investments were never to take complete control of any company; that is why it never purchased more than 50% of any company's publicly traded stock, and it did not vote in stockholder meetings. We did not want to create a benevolent dictatorship if you will. The program was designed to grow, but with safeguards in stage three.

"We knew that prosperity would first breed opulence and greed." He continued. "However, the people of the world must experience the betrayals of greed to believe it. A shepherd who has never felt the stare of the wolf cannot understand how to protect his flock. Stage three is to strengthen society's "shepherds," those who shield the Creator's flock here on Earth.

Franklin D. Roosevelt in 1937 embodied the principle of stage three by saying, 'The test of our progress is not whether we add more to the abundance of those who have much; it is whether we provide enough for those who have little.' Following the same regional strategy, the device began to distribute a portion of the dividends to service organizations that represent, and actuate the self-healing consciousness of the Whole, hence, the answer to your mysterious donation to JOE.

"Those with burgeoning wisdom will check the greed and bring it into balance. The shepherds, when given the resources, will shield the flock from the stare of the wolf. Like a living system, the plan uses the vital energy of the economic organism to heal itself. Even the rampant greed of recent times will only hasten its own demise. Now the system is strong and it is time to move to stage four. That will be your job."

Our job! That got my attention. I sat in the quiescent vault once again aware of the hum of the overhead fan and trying to steel myself for what his statement was going to mean. Wondering how we could be more than a shepherd trying to care for our growing flock. Malchizadec shapeshifted into his human form, bending over to pick up the packet, he handed the remaining envelop to us which bore a wax seal impressed with the official seal of President Theodore Roosevelt.

"It would be easy for many to think of us as rescuers," Malchizadec continued, "to see us as saviors from another place come to bring in a utopian 'Kingdom of Heaven or, at the very least, to save you from yourselves. Many have waited on mountaintops for aliens and Avatars, or upon sandy shores for needed cargo, the appearances of which would bring salvation to their current impasse. That is not our purpose. Nor are we the return of one of your great spiritual beings. The Creator has given humankind the abilities needed to solve its problem. 'For whomsoever much is given, of him shall be much required' as St. Luke wrote. Our intervention is to encourage you to use those abilities.

"The spiritual gauntlet you have endured prepared you for the tasks ahead. It peened your knowledge into understanding, and by understanding, you are acquiring wisdom. It was necessary for the Counsel, and you, to know your courage, the depth of your commitment, and the colors in your heart. Use what you know, learn all you can, and the rest has been provided. Creation appears like the breath of Spirit on the window of consciousness. Lay down your dogma, it separates you. Pick up your faith and bring all life together." Malchizadec concluded.

Leaving us mysteriously as he had appeared, Andrea clutched the remaining envelope in her hand. Inside we unfolded a document assigning us the irrevocable executive power of attorney for all the holdings of Luther Mallory, Inc. Though not the heir apparent to the invisible man, we were the unwitting heir to very visible power.

The trip home was as deliberative as the flight to Virginia had been, but the feeling of looming responsibility had replaced the sense of impending change. To help repair the world was why we started, it was now within our reach. Our rag-tag band of idealists had control over unimaginable holdings and the authority to influence transformation. Once we mused about what we would do if we could change the world. Now we pondered our actions because anything we did would change the world! As Malchizadec said, "Money can be as much a problem as it is a solution." Change, real change on a global scale meant shifting people's mindset to interconnectedness rather than personal importance, showing them how to entrain to a community rhythm rather than an individual drummer. A paradigm shift that fostered a world where all life was sacred wouldn't be easy. I would use what I knew, but I didn't know enough so I would learn all I could, but I couldn't learn enough. I could only trust my heart and have faith that the rest would be provided.

As we drove in the drive, Lorenzo sauntered up to the car to greet us. Beside him was a fluffy black cat with white paws, a milk moustache, and a bushy tail she carried upright like a sail pushing the furry feline through the wind.

"Who's this?" I asked, stepping out of the car to greet his new friend.

"The mice are playing too loudly." Lorenzo promptly replied, "Don't worry, I've hired help." With that, Lorenzo and his still nameless "employee" scampered off towards the barn. Life was multiplying on the farm but this time the mice might not appreciate it.

"What did you find out?" Mason and Janell asked in unison as they sat together on the porch swing.

"We have met the enemy and he is us." I said, not knowing where to begin. "I believe that's the phrase. There is no Luther Mallory. For now, know that this is bigger than we ever imagined."

"Much bigger," Andrea added, "and we'll all need time to accept it." Constant change had been the measure of our time; some changes that swept us away, while others passed without notice. Through them all, the inner and outer landscapes of our lives had altered beyond recognition. The new vistas were broader than before, the dreams more lucid. The river of change had carried us to undiscovered lands where the anomalous had become the everyday and the corporeal "Sultan of Wall Street" was but an illusion. The transitions began when I slipped from the safe shores of quiet acceptance and listened to the silent symphony within, the inter-acting nodes upon nodes of resonance that exists where body, mind, and spirit merge without distinction. Where form and fancy reside as one in the sacred union of resonant being. We had come to where the current lost direction and blended with a greater ebb and flow, the place where change comes from all directions and heads in none. Faith, commitment to Spirit without question, had protected us this far; it would guide us through this estuary of transformation.

CHAPTER 21
THE NEXUS

Heisenberg's *uncertainty principle* says that we cannot know both the position of a subatomic particle and its momentum (velocity and direction) at the same time with certainty. Werner Heisenberg, a founder of quantum physics, states that if we carefully measure a particle's position, we change its momentum. On the other hand, if we track its direction and velocity, we can know little of its position. At the nexus, where position and momentum exist, the more we know about one, the less we know about the other. At this infinitesimal level, we can't observe without causing change.

A *spiritual uncertainty principle* also seems true. We can know what direction we are going (momentum) but can never tell for sure where we are in our development. Conversely, if we spend too much time noticing how developed we are (position), we arrest or alter the course of spiritual growth. Pride often results. At the nexus where the position and momentum of our spiritual selves exist, the best we can do is act knowing Spirit ultimately steers our course and pay little attention to quantifying our development.

Several months had passed since our return from Virginia. Shades of chartreuse and gold lined the trees meaning fall would soon turn to winter. Work at JOE, both old and new, continued to grow. We had named something and crossed the last frontiers of denial; our organization was an entity unto itself that had taken root on terra firma and grown from infancy to a young adult. Every entity, whether incarnate or organizational, has a Body, Mind, and Spirit. We were the body of JOE, rooted in the corporeal, while Malchizadec and the Counsel were its higher mind. Spirit, like some rarefied, infinitesimal substance, infused and connected us beyond our observation that we could only sense through the glass darkly. On such a course, Spirit divulged neither our position nor velocity, but our direction was clear. Whatever the ultimate result, we were committed to its unfolding.

The forth stage of the plan revealed that JOE was the steering committee for Luther Mallory, Inc. and would cast LMI's vote in all shareholder meetings. Not as benevolent dictators, we were to be shepherds, the conscience of the corporations in which LMI held stock, with a board of advisors from every nation where there were holdings. Our focus was not only to encourage the companies to operate in an Earth friendly way, but also to initiate Franklin Roosevelt's principle "providing enough for those who have little." We had enough stock, in enough companies, in enough countries to stage a peaceful revolution. The same strategy of investment and donation continued as the simple program had replicated in millions of computers around the globe, each one standing ready to take over if another fails. It is unstoppable. As we did business, we treated Mother Earth as if she was our own.

It would be easy for many to think of us as rescuers too, as Malchizadec had said and even more dangerous, if we began to see ourselves as bringing in a utopian 'Kingdom of Heaven'. That was not the Avan's purpose nor would it be ours. Humankind had the answers to its problem. Our job was to ask the right questions, our interventions only to encourage alternatives that would let humans "play softly" in the Great Chord and lessen the strain we put on the life of the planet. With the infrastructure already available from dozens of major technology and energy companies, it was easy to assemble the finest minds to take on the deepest questions. All they needed was the will; the way would follow. If we were the physical body of JOE with a conscience, Ingmar and Breanne were like our immune system, reviewing every research idea to insure its development was Earth friendly and not just a new way to cause the old problems. We had a long way to Eden, but we were nudging changes in the right direction. Required only, was the commitment to make it right, rather than make a profit.

Unscrupulous corporations once could locate environmentally unsound operations in far off lands where people, thankful for any income, were unaware of the danger to themselves and their land. We could sway the operations of the Mallory companies, but other corporations were not so willing. Our media group could bring the immediate focus of world opinion on companies that operated without concern for people or their environment. When millions of people speak up, companies listen. You have to act as if you care and you have to say you care to everyone who doesn't. There are no enemies; there are only people who don't understand. Make them understand. That was our mission.

It had been a season of good growth in the vineyard. The young vines flourished and the older plantings had a bountiful crop. With the grapes crushed, we made our first premium wines, it was very satisfying to see full bottles, and casks result from the years of labor. When I had planted the orchard and vineyard, they were an Elysian field, a sanctuary where the solitude of the soil gave me a respite. Watching them grow provided a visible reward for my work that was far different from the abstract, or even invisible, returns I experienced as a musician and writer. The connection with the Earth gave me a chance to heal, and led me far beyond anywhere my writer's imagination had ever conceived. In a way, these vines had grown me and the vineyard symbolized the transformation.

Malchizadec had continued his healing sessions and each of us had learned how to use the Tempest Light as it found expression through our particular soul's ray or quality. Confirming what Navu had told me, the light shown in different hues, like the rainbow, as each one of us emanated our innermost qualities. The meditation Malchizadec had taught us helped us integrate our personal abilities with the higher purposes of our indwelling soul; the results showed in the color of the Tempest Light and in how we chose to serve.

Being a First Ray soul, Mason used his humor with great effectiveness to awaken the minds of people, often tearing down old notions with his wry wit and causing them to consider new ideas for the first time. Hahn's Second Ray qualities of love and wisdom helped him absorb English and become a magnetic personality who used his Tai Chi class to train students in that martial art and about humanity's place in bringing balance to all beings. Jake added to this with his Fourth Ray sensitivity, always harmonizing the old paradigm with the new one and synthesizing ideas in such a way that the transition did not falter. Ch'ien Li, being a scientifically oriented Fifth Ray soul, along with Breanne had begun a clinical study of the healing work connecting it to the body of knowledge science already understood about subtle energy and energy medicine, a necessary step if it were ever to be accepted. The Seventh Ray, at the core of Janell's being, showed in her organizational ability since she arrived, but after her healing conversation with Malchizadec, she had steadily integrated the esoteric traditions of her past into her contributions to JOE.

Andrea's Sixth Ray idealism found several avenues of service, after she learned the ego could never be perfect, and that the soul always was. She adapted the light work in her fitness programs. Client's minds, bodies, and spirits, were shaping-up in ways they had never envisioned because she was able to inspire people's desire for the undeniable beauty within themselves and in their communities. In a different venue, Andrea was able to express her ray's finest qualities when she addressed shareholder meetings and corporate boards, inspiring ideal policies and practices that brought their industries into balance. Like the grapevines and me, Andrea was a transplant, but having put down deep roots in Kansas, she was all the stronger for it.

Most of Andrea's life she had sought perfection inside and out trying to overcome her injuries. In so many ways, our life now seemed ideal and it had happened through no plan of our own by the most unbelievable set of circumstances. We had love, we had power, we had money, and it was almost too perfect. Weighty responsibility tempered the situation. We could never do our part flawlessly; we were human. Striving for perfection was the work of the ego and could only prove our imperfection. Ideals are the gentle encouragement of the soul, held internally, one cannot impose them on others nor do they need outside approval to bring reward. We could aspire towards our ideals and inspire others to do the same without having to judge whether we or anyone else was perfect.

Malchizadec had begun to teach me how to work with the light body.

First, I learned to transport the animals to and from the barn, and then reliably travel myself. More importantly, he taught me how to listen to the Great Chord and to recognize all the different notes. Interpreting the chord was the key to knowing how to direct the healing work to the most critical need. I was learning to perform triage on a spiritual level. I was a Third Ray soul; it was my task to find ways to communicate this new view understandably to intelligent men and women through writing and speaking. The point that connected space, time, and dimensions, was the last challenge and I would have to learn for sometime to master the use of the Nexus.

Drumming was my tool. As it had since my first exposure in that small temple in Brazil, it connected me with the morphic field that Shamans have accessed throughout history. Similar to the fields affecting the Avans form, this field was part of the Earth's memory like a library that when I entrained to it, knowledge transferred. Through drumming, I came to remember my spirit as a Shaman; it was something I was born to do. A Shaman accesses alternate states of consciousness at will, fulfills the needs of their community that are otherwise unmet, and mediates between the sacred and the profane. Like the connection at the grove, I was a nexus. My place wasn't to dress in animal skins and wear antlers on my head. The "Old Ones" used what was available to them in their time to accomplish their work. I used the tools available today for the same purpose and, since our society didn't understand alternative healing, I would work without drawing attention to myself. I would remain an invisible Shaman with nature as my guide.

On the wings I had first used with Malchizadec, I soared alone today to the edge of the heavens, turning to look back and as I had done many times now, I glided along a pathway through sunshine and shade. Remembering the first time I had traveled this way coming back from the Before Time, I recalled Owl and Coyoté, Rabbit and Beaver, Squirrel and Stone, but most of all Little Oak, the Coyoté Oak. Each among them had been my first teachers that the boundaries between one life and another were only an illusion. I had come to know the interconnectedness, the impalpable lace woven with cavity and cord, where I had seen the nodes of life like beaded jewels in which every other jewel reflects. Spun of light, all life in every way interconnects and it is stunning beyond description. Below was Earth, my beautiful home, enfolded in the now familiar tempest glow; a vibrant living being, and I was part of her.

The blue-silver ribbon of light draped across the Earth's shoulders marking the boundary between yesterday and tomorrow. I soared back towards the Earth, riding the edge of light and shadow. I recollected Owl's words, "Watch this day, learn, and remember," when he spoke from high atop his tree in my vision. With those words, I realized what I watched that day, what I was to learn and remember. Sprouted in barren soil, I too had moved from place to place. The torrents of life had gnawed me to the ground repeatedly and my kind had rejected me before I found a place to flourish. It was the story of my transformation; I was the work in progress that had adapted, changed, and survived without malice. Like Little Oak, not knowing what I couldn't do, I had done a lot. One person does matter. With my love for the Creator, and creation, I knew the colors of the sunrise painted my heart. I was the little seedling; I had become the Coyoté Oak.

Swoosh! The exuberance of flight sounded behind me as Sorrano swooped into formation beneath me with his great wings outstretched as they were when I first flew, riding on his back above the farm.

"Now that you've remembered, be careful not to rise above it all," his voice projected. "Along with remembering your transformation, don't forget the scars, reminders of wounds still healing. When Spirit's wonders appear, evil's response is to dazzle you with the light, to offer an escape into what seems like the higher realms so you will assume those old wounds no longer matter."

"Doesn't the Tempest Light indicate that Spirit is healings those wounds?" I questioned.

"Yes James, it is a clever seduction but Spirit must build its house on the foundation of a healthy personality," he responded. "You must remain vigilant that the flaws of the old personality don't usurp the work of Spirit. Your 'spiritual uncertainty principle,' demonstrates the point, a 'flight into light' to compensate for the past can cause one to focus only on where they are going and forget to live in the present. Conversely, they may get stuck in piety, their perception of their own importance and lose direction completely. Either way, spiritual development fails. Today is more than the sum of the days that have come before it; it is the groundwork for all that follows. To remain the Coyoté Oak, you must preserve all the colors of your heart."

"So I should watch every day, learn, and remember," I quipped, understanding his point as he glided off.

Soaring down over the plains, renewed verve lifted my wings, eastward I flew, over the Flint Hills rising and falling with the folds of the terrain. I mounted eddies jetting upward from the slopes and plummeted down again accelerating across the valleys, following the creeks as they merged into streams and streams into rivers. I drifted on the wind over the Missouri river by Aeolian Woods. The weather had changed; the air was cooler and a fog rose from her waters but neither the river nor I had forgotten my promise. From this vista, I could see the scarred land along her tributaries. Replanting trees and ground cover in broader bands along her banks, we could protect the waters and give wildlife back its home. We only needed to grant them respect. My time complete, I banked my wings westward feeling the cool crosswind from the north as I headed homeward. Retracing my flight across hill and dell until, at last high above the prairie that I loved, I made a final sweep around the farm.

The season of growth was evident everywhere. I flew by the innovative buildings Gabardine had completed that were operational now, all save one. The old barn, the repository of the farms history, was still being reborn. Gabardine found old cottonwood lumber and, using photographs as her guide, was erecting a replica to stand in the same location. I hovered above its gambrel roof noticing the progress. My hunger for the clouds satisfied, I fluttered through the upstairs hay door into the loft and perched on one of the rafters. Sunlight filtered through the spaces between the boards of the cottonwood siding filling the room with dancing bands of light. A dramatic stained glass window depicted the Avans in amazing detail, right down to their unique coloring and the Tempest Light surrounding them, which displayed Jake's ability as a stained glass artist. As the sun danced through its colored panes, the portrait would bring their presence and wisdom into the conference room for JOE and constantly remind us of the source of our actions. Mallory Gimble's painting will hang at the other end of the room right below the hay door. Restoring the barn felt as if we had retrieved the soul of the farm and found new life.

It was a good flight but the shift from aerodynamic feathered form to an upright human shape always felt strange as the center of gravity and balance reoriented to standing on two legs. Walking out of the barn, I joined Andrea as she left the gym at the end of her day. Slowing our step, we walked hand in hand around the pond past a fountain we had created in memory of Remington. Though we still felt the loss, we had come to terms with the tragedy and accepted that his passing was his commitment to a higher purpose. Still, Remington's presence remained strong and I often felt as if he continued to offer wise counsel from wherever the spirit goes once it's free of this life. As if to confirm my inklings, when we stopped to look at the fountain, we saw seven pennies arranged in a circle at its base.

Briskly making our way across the rearranged farmyard, we stepped onto our familiar porch and entered the kitchen, which was abuzz with lively energetic conversations. The women were huddled together on one side of the table around Ch'ien Li who was holding out her hand displaying an elegant engagement ring. Love had also grown this season; Jake had asked Ch'ien Li to marry him. She had accepted which delighted both Mason and Hahn and further deepened their friendship. Andrea quickly joined the gaggle of gab and delight. Together, the women started planning a spring wedding on the hilltop that was likely to remain a subject of conversation all the way to spring. From the shy girl that crawled out of the haystack, Ch'ien had flowered into a clear, perceptive, young woman with a beautiful naïve curiosity.

An oil lamp burned in the corner of the kitchen and, as I watched its mellow glow, it seemed a perfect metaphor for my relationship with Andrea; like the lamp, ours was an old-fashioned love in full flourish. With a warm steady light to the surroundings, passion flickered and flared, adapting to the moment, but the winds of change could not extinguish the love between us. We shared closeness that seldom required words and always seemed to know what each other thought, felt, or needed, responding without hesitation. Our experiences over many years had seasoned our affection the way time tints old lace by deepening and enriching its patina.

Astralys became the topic of discussion for the men; his growth was astounding. In the few months since his arrival, he had advanced rapidly from the wriggling hatchling to a rambunctious youngster able to move fluidly, think on his own, and was nearly as big as Bashira. Sorrano and Bashira were good parents, teaching Astralys constantly and often transferred the information directly into his mind, as they had with me, giving complete knowledge that didn't require a learning process, or test to verify. Consequently, he developed much faster than a human child and it seemed there was urgency in his learning.

"I think I'll ask him." Mason proposed. "I'll stump that feathered wizard tonight. I want to know the answer to the age old question; which came first, the dragon or the egg?"

"That's easy," Hahn replied, countering Mason's wry shenanigan. "Old Chinese proverb say: 'The Yellow Emperor knows the journey of a thousand miles begins with one egg and always ends with a chicken crossing the road.'" Hahn enigmatically smiled and concluded, "Care for an omelet?"

Mason gawped at Hahn speechlessly trying to understand if he was serious or not. He always came under the radar with something unexpected but he wasn't used to someone flying below his screen.

"You should have seen his face." Dan said sticking his head in the kitchen doorway. "Oh, I don't mean Mason's," he added acknowledging Mason's perplexed look, "you should have seen Nash at his preliminary hearing when he found out there was no Luther Mallory. I guess he completely lost it when he found out ORTI wouldn't pay for his legal expenses. Nash thought HE was the company but he won't be so arrogant in Federal Prison."

It was good to laugh together; it was good to be together, better still to have that experience behind us and with the evening shadows growing long, we left the house trekking towards the grove. The usual solemnity came over us as we traversed the vineyard feeling the shift from the mundane to the magical approaching the trees. Though I had experienced it many times, I was still awestruck each time the humble trees dawned their stately eminence around the stone circle. Inside the grove, Malchizadec and Navu were waiting for us around the fire pit with Sorrano, Bashira, and Astralys. Malchizadec directed us around the circle as always. The second circle moved in behind us but felt incomplete without Remington. Then Malchizadec moved to the North of the circle, Navu to the South. Bashira stood on the East and Sorrano on the West. The Circle of Seven completed in spirit within the four directions.

"Tonight we enter a new era of learning." Malchizadec announced. "Before we do however, it is wise to review. Each of you found your way to this group, to this moment, along a path guided by your own Soul, that part of Spirit that individualized to seek wisdom through experience here on Earth. Through these stones, I helped you each identify your Soul's qualities, but you learned its purpose, and now impart its service from the observer inside you. You awakened to your Soul's purpose through many crises and you did not falter. You resisted anger, the first seduction of evil, and overcame fear, its second trick. On your own, you discovered the third seduction, helplessness, the feeling that nothing will change and that no one can make a difference. Now you must resist becoming so enamored by the light that you focus on you own piety and lose your direction. Individually, and as a group, you have made a difference. To continue, you must remain vigilant against the feelings of anger, fear, helplessness, and self-importance. Always be certain that actions taken to meet a personal need are not the rudiments of greed. Be in service that advances the good of the whole; that is your protection.

"Tonight we will activate the Nexus, the point where time, space, and dimension connect, so you will see it in use. It is neither Yin, nor Yang; it is the membrane where one exchanges itself into the other. It exists nowhere yet connects to everywhere for it is where order unfolds from unbounded potential. Your Einstein postulated, 'There are an infinite number of universes, some existing in the same time in different spaces while others occupy the same space in different times.' Thus, to move through a point with infinite connections requires great precision if one wishes to reach their destination, or hopes ever to return."

Curiosity saturated the crisp fall evening air. The humble fire pit had been the locus of so many wonders it was impossible to envision the potency of the portal Malchizadec described. Even though he had been teaching me about it for some time, I was still mystified how it could exist between the pairs of opposites at the base of all physical form. Then, transforming into his tall human-like form, his feathers melding into a long, gloriously colored, iridescent cape much like the *temiak* I'd seen in the jungle, Malchizadec bent his lofty figure to the ground and reverently picked up a drum made from the rich golden orange heartwood of Coyoté Oak covered with a luminous skin.

"First we must align ourselves in Body, Mind, and Spirit." He began. "Once individually aligned, we extend Spirits to each other. When the group aligns as one, we can join with all those who have drummed before us, all those who have reached the plane of wisdom and left markers for us to follow in our hour of need." Then he turned to Navu and nodded.

Navu sat beside a large ceremonial drum that stood about three feet high and was almost four feet in diameter. Carved from a great hollow trunk, a water buffalo hide stretched across the top. Around its girth were inscribed the seven markings found on each of the circle stones. Navu lifted his arm and with one mighty swing, thrust the striker down to the rawhide. A thunderous resonance leapt from the drum passing through my body with enough force that it felt as if it were rearranging every molecule. I could hear a snap in the trees, the rocks, and every blade of grass, as the sonic wave moved out across the landscape. Then Navu struck again. This time the sound was slightly different and felt as if it resonated mostly in my head. The final beat on the drum shot like an arrow into my heart, and there the sound did not fade. The lingering sonorescence began to build, discharging from my heart and the hearts of the entire group.

"The voice of the Body and thoughts of the Mind have joined in concert with the song of Spirit. Let it begin." Malchizadec intoned softly.

He started to beat his drum slowly and directing us to pick-up the drums laying beside each of us, he indicated for us to join him. When we came to a common rhythm, he slowly increased the cadence giving us time to synchronize until we were striking our drums at about four beats per second. The rhythm continued for several minutes, my arms were getting tired and starting to ache. Then about ten minutes into the drumming, the pain begin to ease, striking the instrument no longer required effort but seemed to continue on its own power as if all the drummers throughout time supplemented their energy for our own. Over the next few minutes, I felt a shift come over the group as if we became one, entrained with each other and all those who had come before. The shell of illusion that allowed us to believe we were separate from one another cracked open and we stood together in common spirit. The trees and rocks, earth and air, setting sun and rising moon, all stood humbly with us, united in the endless moment of the Creator's grace. We could hear ancient voices echoing chants in a thousand tongues, choirs in angelic praise rang through the grove's arched cathedral boughs, and one by one nature's hidden lives joined the chorale. The Counsel of Elders with all the people we had seen at Aeolian Woods encircled us, ring upon ring. There too, was an invisible presence, the Soul of the Earth joyfully sounding her Great Chord.

The sun had set and only a small streak of deep violet shown in the clouds above when Malchizadec stepped towards the circle and put his drum down to his side. Time seemed to stand still in the celebration but we had played together for an hour or more, judging from the sky. When the drums quieted, Malchizadec began to speak.

"Watch this day, learn, and remember," he said. Words I knew well.

With out stretched arms Malchizadec struck the beater against the stone upon which Mason was sitting causing it to sound its familiar tone. Struck a second time, the tone expanded downward by octaves and with a third strike, sound extended upwards until a ladder of octaves reverberated far beyond our normal hearing.

"We Will Open!" A primordial voice boomed through the cascading resonance.

Holding his two hands together palm to palm over the resonating stone, Malchizadec began to separate his hands as if he were pushing through and dividing some invisible field before him. The tones coming from the stone began to widen, sliding in pitch, until the tones of the two adjacent stones added to the ladder of octaves merging and dividing their harmonics in cadence.

The sounds progressed around the circle of stones in both directions at once, one ascending the scale, the other descending until they came full circle back to the original tone. Increasing in speed, they followed one after another with such rapidity that they blended into a pulsating white noise. Within the pulse, a glimmer swelled from the center of the fire pit into a golden white column of light that streamed upward out of the earth while simultaneously a silvery white beam descended from beyond our sight to encompass the first. Both beacons seemed in constant flux flowing equally in either direction. Then within the merging beams of light, I saw a room or compartment. It was like a hologram, three-dimensional yet translucent, and resplendent. From our seats upon the stones, we could see the beam upwards and down into the fire pit without dimension, or end. Inside the light were an infinite number of similar rooms, each enfolded into all the others and yet a thing unto itself. Observing the many mansions, we could see ourselves enfolded in the other rooms, not as in a mirror, but existing in another space, time, and dimension. We were everywhere.

"The Nexus allows us to step through the interconnectedness of all things." Malchizadec began to explain. "As you can see, you are already omnipresent. Every room contains the elements of every other wrapped in it and since it is infinite, the finite mind can never learn its course. Therefore, we must rely on our infinite Spirit to find our way. It is in learning through your heart to hear, and trust, the Spirit's voice that you will learn to use the Nexus. I can only show you the door; your Spirit must remember the rest.

"Our time here has come to an end." Malchizadec said to Andrea and me with words we never wanted to hear. "My faith in you both has been proven correct. James and Andrea, you have learned a great deal, but there is much to heal and you are here to help repair the world. Navu will continue teaching you where we must conclude. He must teach you more before you can use the Nexus, but through this point, we will always be together and at your aid. Our task for this visit is complete and with your help tonight, we will return home through the Nexus," he continued this time turning to the entire group. "The events of the past months have been fulfilled and you are not together by coincidence; each of you brings a unique talent that will serve well in the tasks ahead, and many tasks remain. I leave you with my blessing, and entrust you to the Creator's grace. Remember, there is no enemy, only those who do not yet understand. You are not to rule, or wield a gentle hand that merely replaces an iron fist. Help them understand, really understand."

There were tears in my eyes, and I felt a swelling emptiness, a hollowness for which there would never be a substitute. As they enfolded us in their great wings for the last time, the emptiness filled with unconditional love. What they had given us, the thing of real value, was a deep appreciation and understanding of the interconnectedness of all life, of all creation. We would protect that and give that gift to others. Malchizadec motioned Bashira and Astralys to step into the beam of swirling light. Sorrano, my first friend among them, gave me a knowing look one last time and followed. Many teaching say that when the student is ready, the teacher will appear. Malchizadec, the most powerful teacher I could have imagined, appeared when like the Little Oak, I had just opened my eyes to the beauty of existence and he mentored me to become the Coyoté Oak. Then passing the luminous drum to me, he shifted back into the giant raptor with which I scouted the heavens. I saw a mix of emotions in his eyes, the deep affection he felt for all of us, the sadness he felt leaving us behind, and his hopeful anticipation of returning home.

"Walk with me," I heard projected in my mind as I tucked the colorful instrument beneath my arm. Side by side, as he had flown with me, we advanced to the pulsating vortex of illumination until my sagacious guide stepped into the light. Nothing seemed to occur, and then all of them were gone. To our astonishment, in the beam we could see our enduring friends standing beside the Nexus looking back at us. Behind them, we saw the landscape of Satoria exactly as Mallory Gimble painted it, the way we would envision it for the rest of our lives.

Navu spread his arms out wide and stepped up beside to the Nexus, slowly he brought his hands together until they rested palm to palm. The pulsating arpeggio of tones stopped, the beams of light retreated into the fire pit and the heavens above. Silence, lonely silence remained.

"It is closed for now," Navu said. Then he picked up a smaller drum and walked around us all beating it lightly, acknowledging the Counsel for their presence and thanking all the spirits that had joined us. Then they too faded into the twilight.

We had lived a season of growth, a season of transformations that would not wither. Once, this Earth was a land of promise, an Eden bounded only by the Creator's imagination and in which there was no enemy. Enmity was our creation, sown in the dust of lost hope, fear, anger, and position. That Promised Land remains, waiting simply for the sunrise in us to blanch the stain of malice from its soil; the connecting point, the nexus through which we travel from malice to munificence is in our hearts. The Nexus exists where Heaven and Earth join, and where the Creator's love flows outward through us without measure. Here on the Central Plains, the Nexus existed in this special place, but it was more than a place, much more. A blue-silver ribbon of light drapes across the horizon in my heart but there is no boundary between yesterday and tomorrow; it is infinite beginning. The little sapling, the Coyoté Oak, I had found my place in the most fertile ground, where wisdom burgeons and there are no boundaries. I had grown to understand the peace found in the endless moment of the Creator's grace.

Creation appears
like the breath of Spirit
on the window of consciousness.
Be flawless with your intention
and ask the right questions.
In the end,
it's just Our Earth.

WANT TO TALK ABOUT IT?

The author is available for seminars, presentations and lectures. Would your book club enjoy discussing this book with the author? Personal and telephone appearances can be arranged by email to <u>author@vantagequest.org</u> or by contacting Reality Press.

NEW TECHNOLOGY
FOR THE ANCIENT ART OF TRANCE

Gateway to the Universe in You

The Vantage Quest© System is a series of audio CDs designed to help you stop the mindless brain chatter long enough to synchronize with Higher Mind and explore the deep reaches of our inner universe. Like Doorways in Consciousness, the 12 CD set precisely entrains both brain hemispheres using its Harmonic Matrices® to open different areas of brain wave activity and perception. Like a shaman's drumbeat this scientific, laboratory-tested, recording is a metronome for the Soul that allows you to lock-on to the life-promoting information that permeates the Void, the not so empty space around and within us. Called by many "the most powerful brain wave entrainment tool on the planet," Vantage Quest is an exceptionally easy to use and potent means to enhance your intuitive - creative ability, complement your healing and growth processes or, find the deep relaxation you've been needing.

Dr. John Jay Harper, author of Tranceformers: Shamans of the 21st Century says, "This is the tool then that opens your third eye and puts you in touch with the wisdom of your Higher Self in the zero-point field of the fifth dimension."

"Over the millennia, sound has been one of the powerful tools used to alter consciousness, and to transform moods and feelings. Vantage Quest follows in this venerable tradition, utilizing cutting edge technologies to provide deep, intense experiences for its users that they can use for enhancing personal enjoyment, evoking mental imagery, identifying bodily energies, and intensifying sensations and perceptions. The number of effects is diverse and potentially beneficial. People who utilize Vantage Quest will find that it challenges their creative potential in a variety of ways." Stanley Krippner, PhD, author of The Spiritual Dimensions of Healing and Personal Mythology

So are you ready to co-create a whole new you? Take an adventure you can sync your mind into.

Used by thousands of people around the globe, Vantage Quest VI, the first CD in the series, is available now. The remaining Harmonic Matrices® will be released soon. For more information or to order, see www.vantagequest.org, listen to a sample recording, read testimonials, and learn the technical specifications of this product.

Let me repeat: Observe a particle as a wave, and it is a wave. Observe it as matter, and it is matter.... Thus, it is our point of view, the way we look at reality that makes reality the way it is.

Nada Brahma: The World is Sound

ABOUT THE AUTHOR

Creating always makes me tick. Whether it was the first song that I wrote when I was about four, building straw forts in a hayloft, or getting a poem in the paper in grade school, somewhere along the line I got hooked. Later, as I started to take it seriously, I made my way onto the stage, first as an actor, and then performing the songs I wrote. I was lucky, no matter if I made a big splash or had to learn to swim out of dangerous waters, I was paid to do what so many people wanted to do and I had fun at it. I jumped in with both feet writing songs all day and playing music all night. I was always surprised when people thought I should get a "real job." I've had plenty of those but the most "Real" thing I know is the connection I feel when I'm creating something. When we shut-up and listen, it's where we cooperate with the Divine. It's really the only thing happening here on this little blue marble and like G.I. Gurdjieff, I've had many meetings with remarkable men (and women). Along the way I studied music and drama at Univ. of So. Cal and earned a B.S. in biology from Kansas Wesleyan Univ. Then,

Carlisle Bergquist

when my first album was ready for release, the worst happened – Disco – and overnight I was a country-rock dinosaur. During my readjustment to "real" life, I started creating landscape environments – still fun – and reading a lot. I had been studying psychology, metaphysics, and esoteric texts for years to understand a number of unusual experiences so…I decided to take that seriously and went back to graduate school. I received an M.A. from John F. Kennedy Univ. in Transpersonal Counseling Psychology and I continue Doctoral studies at Saybrook Institute. Then the best happened! Music, psychology, mysticism, and academia all came together when I created Vantage Quest. Now I am a practicing therapist privileged to help others re-create their lives as well as an author, and producer of some very unique CDs. Through it all, I'm still creating.

Printed in the United States
91660LV00003B/70-90/A